MARKET SHOCK

MARKET SHOCK

9 ECONOMIC AND SOCIAL UPHEAVALS THAT WILL SHAKE YOUR FINANCIAL FUTURE—AND WHAT TO DO ABOUT THEM

TODD G. BUCHHOLZ

HarperBusiness
A Division of HarperCollinsPublishers

HarperCollins books may be purchased for educational, business, or sales promotional use. For information please write: Special Markets Department, HarperCollins Publishers, Inc., 10 East 53rd Street, New York, NY 10022.

FIRST EDITION
Designed by Joseph Rutt

Library of Congress Cataloging-in-Publication Data
Buchholz, Todd G.
       Market shock: nine economic and social upheavals that will shake
your financial future—and what to do about them
             p.   cm.
       Includes index
       ISBN 0-88730-949-6
       1. Business forcasting.   2. Stock exchange.   3. Financial crisis.
4. Economic history—1990– I. Title.
HD30.27.b83   1999
332.6—dc21   99-17576

99 00 01 02 03 ❖/RRD 10 9 8 7 6 5 4 3 2 1

To my daughter Victoria,
who sneaked snacks to my office and
delivered hugs when we ran out of cookies

Contents

PREFACE

When friends asked how long it took to write my prior books, I usually stuttered, and tried to explain that they emerged from a sporadic combination of late nights and long weekends, not a disciplined schedule. This book, however, has taken my whole life – meaning that it is speckled with experiences I had as a boy, as a White House adviser, as an investment director, and as a father. It is no autobiography (I haven't been involved in enough scandals to justify that) and yet it has offered an opportunity to share some stories I have heard from my grandparents and parents, about their lives in the twentieth century.

This book reaches across the spectrum from the finances of families, to the history of China, to the physics of cyberspace, to the philosophy of criminal punishment. In tackling so many issues, I have surely made some mistakes. But even the Renaissance men tripped up. Michelangelo's sculpture of Moses, after all, shows the patriarch with horns on his head, a mistranslation of the Old Testament. Still, the statue deserves more than a glance. In a garish clash with modern technology, I recently discovered that Rome's church of San Pietro in Vincoli placed a coin-operated spotlight in front of Moses in order to cash in on Michelangelo's masterpiece. After depositing a coin, I had about three minutes to marvel at the peep show.

I doubt that you will marvel at this book. But I hope you take more than three minutes, and I hope you find it provocative and illuminating. In the end, the book itself does not deserve the spotlight — but the critical policy and personal finance issues of the twenty-first century certainly do.

Rather than thanking Moses, Michelangelo and other luminaries such as Alan Greenspan, I will simply thank my wonderful wife Debby and darling daughter Victoria. When I explained to my five year old daughter that I was writing a book and would therefore miss out on some weekend fun, she immediately started dictating a dedication. She wanted you readers to know how patient she is and that she likes to perform in musical shows. She is, and she does. And she doesn't mind sharing this paragraph with Michelangelo.

INTRODUCTION

Here today, gone today. Doctors in the nineteenth century warned that if people tried to travel faster than 60 miles per hour, their bodies would crumble. Now, automobile advertisements promise 0 to 60 in just five seconds, and we grumble when transatlantic jets pull into the gate five minutes late. The hands on our clocks seem to be spinning ahead of us. At the turn of the next century, it's not just that the times they are a changin', but that they are a changin' dangerously fast. And the changes will etch new chapters in human history.

The Berlin Wall crashes down, flooding the free market with millions of new workers. A scientist in Scotland clones a sheep, supercharging the imaginations of biotechnicians across the world. Daimler Benz and Chrysler, two companies that manufactured battling armored vehicles in World War II, stun the financial markets by merging. The Dow Jones average doubles in less than three years, a pace that recalls the high-flying, loud-crashing 1920s.

Doctors may be diagnosing millions of people with attention deficit disorder, but that's not a problem when nothing stands still for more than ten minutes anyway.

Woven together by wires, fibers and satellite waves, the world's financial markets act instantaneously to any news or rumor. The chairman of the Federal Reserve Board turns on his microphone to deliver a speech, and bond yields get ready to soar or plummet. The French president, visiting an obscure fishing village, whispers to some fisherman that he is suspicious of Italy's budget, and Italian bond prices fall off a cliff. A twenty-four-year-old kid, still fighting acne, spreads a rumor that the treasury secretary looks pale, and blue chip stocks lose their color, too.

Slapped around by political, technological, and demographic waves, should we sit back bemused, sit up nervously, or try to ride them? With the Internet, twenty-four-hour news networks, pagers, and wireless telephones, we don't lack for information. Technology has permitted us to create what I call the "scissors economy," where we can cut out the middleman—from the retail clerk to the stockbroker to the travel agent—from nearly every transaction. As consumers and investors, we do not lack power. We lack guidance. So far, it has not mattered much to investors. What a swell party it's been! The U.S. stock markets have rolled over the skeptics and the alarmists, despite some frightening episodes. Even the politicians can brag: A roaring U.S. economy squashed the jobless rate to near-record lows, and that haunting U.S. budget deficit suddenly vanished. Even cab drivers started recommending stocks.

The blissful news has tempted millions of people to turn over their portfolios to an automatic pilot that forever steers their money into stocks. Sounds great—at first. But how would an automatic pilot land a plane if the terrain kept changing? Is the automatic pilot prepared for the "eco-quakes" that will shake the financial markets in the next few years? Japan's new plans to buy up technology firms and build what I call the "jelly doughnut economy"? The surge in criminal violence that will reverse the recent good news on the crime rate? The graying of America? The threat to farmers from global warming? Neither the automatic pilot, nor your neighborhood stockbroker, has a black box or secret file that holds the answers. Because the changing world continually buffets the markets, we cannot blindly throw money into stocks, into mutual funds, or into a bank account. It is simply *not* true that "everything we need to know about investing we learned in kindergarten," or B-school, or some other place. Protecting and growing our money means being vigilant. If "eternal vigilance is the price of liberty," it's also the price of a nice nest egg.

Investors were certainly right during the 1990s to "go with the flow," since it turned out to be a steady stream of prosperity. In fact, my 1995 book *From Here to Economy*, urged readers to plow their funds into stocks, particularly the index funds that simply track the broad market. But as we race into the twenty-first century, the flow is shifting. Individuals and families who want to protect and grow their wealth should not blindly jump on the bandwagon. The markets will, no doubt, react to the explosive changes in the world, some good, some bad. This book is aimed to show people how to get off the dangerous bandwagon and start looking after themselves in the treacherous financial markets. George Soros, Julian Robertson, and Warren Buffett didn't get rich merely following the crowd. They waved to the crowd in their rearview mirrors. When others dismissed Coca-Cola as merely an American soft drink, Buffett looked ahead and envisaged Coke as a worldwide superstar with as loyal a following in China as in the United States. Indeed, Coke was a forerunner of Michael Jackson, Michael Jordan, and Madonna. George Soros, "the man who broke the Bank of England," foresaw the jobless crisis in Europe while most European analysts were still arrogantly deriding the "folly" of Ronald Reagan's deregulatory policies. Julian Robertson understood the bankruptcy of Japanese banks years before the Japanese government unveiled a teeming reservoir of red ink.

By focusing on the big changes ahead, investors can drive to the forefront of the market and avoid being left to clean up after the parade. What kind of stocks will thrive if the political environment turns suddenly dangerous? After all, when the Cold War thawed, it helped spark the raging market of the 1990s. Today's frothing young traders on Wall Street do not remember Leonid Brezhnev or the frightening power of OPEC in the 1970s. Can they handle the new China or an angry Japan that has felt both bullied and abandoned by the United States during its excruciating seven-year recession? Not all of the shifts are crises. The aging of America is surely a good thing, since it simply means that Americans are living longer. "How does it feel to turn sixty-five?" "Better than the alternative," goes a common joke. Nonetheless, savvy investors must tackle the issue and plan ahead, both in their personal lives and in their portfolios, for example, buying stocks that will take advantage of the baby boomers' retirement and the rise of Generation X. Abercrombie & Fitch, an old name in clothing and sporting goods, is best known by two distinct groups that are growing fast: (1) older people who remember its pre–World War II retail reign and (2) young people in their teens and early twenties. No surprise, then, that middle-aged Wall Street analysts missed out on this firm's explosive tripling in stock price from January 1997 to December 1998. Many years ago, my grandfather bought sports shirts at Abercrombie & Fitch. In 1963, Rock Hudson portrayed their expert outdoorsman in an amusing, old-fashioned movie, *Man's Favorite Sport*. The company would not have survived without the demographic shifts and talented management. (I cite Abercrombie & Fitch as an example, not as a stock recommendation. Throughout this book I refer to specific corporations because they illustrate a trend, a potential beneficiary, or a possible loser. I may even have owned shares in some of those companies when I drafted this book.)

While facing the dramatic scenarios portrayed in the chapters ahead, readers should remember a key point: To justify putting your money into an investment, you do not have to believe that the scenarios outlined here will definitely come true. You simply must believe that the market underestimates the actual odds. An example may help. Chapter 9 warns of global warming, which would flood the coastal regions, while enriching farmers in northern climes. If the stock market completely ignores the threat, and you think the odds are 60 percent, the market is offering you a bargain. As investors, we must search for where the market looks ignorant, lazy, or misguided. The overwhelming majority of the time, the market is none of those. But now and then you can swoop down and win big.

Do you have to be a genius? I don't think so. Any dope can have a high IQ, and Nobel Prize–winning economists can go broke. I once delivered a lecture at the White House library titled "Honesty, Modesty, and Clarity in Economics." For those serving in the White House, the recession of 1991 certainly taught harsh lessons in modesty. In my years teaching at Harvard, advising at the White House, and serving as a managing director of the eminent Tiger hedge fund, I have finally learned to stop looking for Mozarts. They hardly ever come around, and they die before you can figure out who they are. Van Gogh died broke and with only one ear; now his flowers fetch $82 million at Sotheby's. So forget Mozart. Most successful people are more like his mortal rival Salieri: trying to pluck out a decent ditty, trying to pay their bills, and trying to retire like the modest millionaire next door. You don't have to be a savant, and you shouldn't listen too much to the chattering Wall Street "experts" who pretend that they can discern the market's trends based on reams of charts. Many of them are halfway toward being idiot savants.

As you follow the chapters ahead, I would also suggest you try to bring some of your own insights into your portfolio, as Peter Lynch has often suggested. That means that you must lead a life not 100 percent devoted to following the stock market. Do not think that you can beat Wall Street by living and breathing CNBC, the *Wall Street Journal*, and *Barron's*—though they are all important tools. As Yogi Berra said, you can see a lot just by looking. Go shopping, take a vacation, talk to friends. Lead your life, then ask yourself whether you have learned anything that could give you some investment insight. Nor should you feel obligated to always be investing. If you are having trouble sleeping or eating because of your investments, learn to take a break. Idle hands may be the workshop of the devil, but hands too busy and itchy will land you in bankruptcy court (a place just as steamy).

Demons aside, this is serious business. Will your mutual fund blow up? Will Europe's single currency collapse, taking your savings with it? Will the demographic headstand force the United States to repeal child labor laws? I assure you that as alarming as these issues sound, Chapter 2's rhapsody on technology will keep you from calling Dr. Kervorkian. In fact, even the most alarming situations hold some promise for readers. Mutual funds will explode precisely because individuals will demand—and ultimately receive—cheeper fees and better service. If we suffer from global warming, your house in Minnesota will rise in value.

Most of us are trying to save for college, a home, or for our "golden years" in a world of shifting sands—or is it quicksand or a sand bar? Planning our finances is no day at the beach. And yet, if we stay vigilant but keep our sense of humor, we may be able to afford palmy and balmy days ahead.

MARKET SHOCK

1

GOING GRAY

How America's Aging Can Shake Your Portfolio and Bankrupt the Government

HARRISBURG, PENNSYLVANIA

Hannah Barker picked up the knife and plunged it so deep into the turkey that her husband thought he'd have to phone 911. Ted was truly frightened of her whenever those stress lines showed up on her face looking like the off-ramps of the Pennsylvania Turnpike. He did what any normal, red-blooded American would do on Thanksgiving Day faced with a wife on a rampage: He ducked into the TV room to fill the pretzel bowl while his father-in-law watched the Detroit Lions play.

"Ted," she called from the kitchen, "would you please open the can of cranberry sauce! I can't do everything." And she certainly felt helpless today. Her bony, fifty-year-old arms shook as she carved the turkey.

Her husband cautiously reentered the kitchen.

"Ted, I can't let them do it. I just can't. If my parents move to Florida, they'll expect me to hop on the plane every week, just to take them to the podiatrist to get their toenails clipped. They think they're making it easier on me by moving," she said, while pulling the string bean casserole out of the oven, "but it's impossible. Besides, who's going to pay for all of my trips to St. Petersburg? We can't afford it, not with Becky in college."

"Can't they pay for the trips?" he asked.

"With what? Old green stamps? That's about the only thing they saved up over the years."

1

"Hannah, you better talk to them tonight, before they sign the apart-ment lease."

"Fine, and what'll you be doing when I tell my seventy-two-year-old parents that I'm going to treat them like irresponsible children?" she said while wiping her eyes with her apron.

"Me? Oh, I'll be hiding the carving knife."

Newsflash

The President today warned that IRS agents, along with Alcohol, Tobacco & Firearms agents would be storming the headquarters of the "Just Say No Brigade," a taxpayer rights group that has sparked a nationwide strike against paying taxes. In a spoof of the Boston Tea Party, the "Just Say No" leaders, cheered by Nancy Reagan, threw tax forms off the roof of the John Hancock building in downtown Boston.

"We're mad as hell, and we're not going to take it any-more!" shouted Hal Phillips, a thirty-five-year-old accountant, who declared that Congress should have cut Medicare and Social Security payments to old people, rather than confiscate the incomes of the young.

The White House is in a state of siege, surrounded by angry college students, a situation not seen since Lyndon Johnson became a captive of Vietnam War protests. . . .

If you are like me, you have attended too many weddings and funerals where the preacher quoted Ecclesiastes, reminding us that there is always a season, a time to be born and a time to die. If the preacher did not say it, then the wedding disc jockey played The Byrds singing it instead. But it is not so simple as the homily makes it sound. Unlike the summer season, which blankets a whole town in the same sunshine and warmth, the time to be born and the time to die is different for each of us and can even pit one generation against another. The United States, which always prided itself as a youthful republic, is getting old fast. Our national priorities are switching from the schoolhouse to the nursing home. For the first time in history, we will have more old people than children. It is September, and the crinkled orange and gold leaves are falling, in a country that has only known spring.

The turn of seasons does not mean that we are going out of business, or that depressing books like Paul Kennedy's *The Rise and Fall of Great Powers* are proving right. I am an optimist. We must, though, reinvent our economic policies as a nation. As individuals, we must reinvent our investment portfolios to protect against disaster while taking advantage of the change ahead. Retiring baby boomers will remake the market for retail goods and the service industry, just as generations X (born between 1965-75), Y (born 1976–90), and Z (born after 1991) are putting their stamp on the economy. Ecclesiastes reminds us that there is a "time to get, and a time to lose." With due deference to the Bible, there is no time to lose in preparing your portfolio against losses and setting it up for gains.

The Problem: The "Me" generation of baby boomers will be retiring in massive numbers over the next twenty years. But the country cannot afford it. Unlike their parents, who sacrificed in the Great Depression and World War II, the boomers have been raised on "having it all." Can the "Me" generation learn to live with less? Will they give up the absurdly generous promises of Social Security, Medicare, and the traditions of job seniority? Or will their children have to wrest it from their soon-to-be-wrinkled hands?

Today's anxious class of twenty-something workers would have to give up most of their future earnings just to meet the government's obligations to their parents and grandparents. That would leave virtually nothing after paying for shelter and food. Forget about paying back school loans! Generations XYZ will "just say no" to these burdens, and granny could find herself scraping by on the paltry savings that she has socked away. Unfortunately, the average family today has just over $10,000 in savings.

This threatening scenario should force you to take a crucial first step: Figure out how risky your financial predicament is. How much savings do you have? What is your net worth? I suggest you take a piece of paper and add up the value of your bank accounts, brokerage accounts, retirement savings, home, car, and valuable household possessions. Now subtract any mortgages, loans, and credit card debt. What's left? Are you the "millionaire next door" or the pauper who must hang on to every buck? Too often it is the pauper who recklessly tosses away money. As Thomas Stanley and William Danko pointed out, millionaires tend to clip coupons, live modestly, and save big portions of their income. A rule of thumb suggests that retirees need about 75 percent of their working income in order to keep up their preretirement lifestyle. They spend less on work clothes, commuting costs, and college for their children, but spend more on vacations and home expenses.

Even if young people start saving early, though, generations XYZ could find themselves in the unprecedented and excruciating position of supporting four generations, not just the traditional three. Imagine the year 2021: Our hypothetical Hannah and Ted from Harrisburg are now seventy-two-year-old baby boomers and starting to need some medical attention. They have programmed their telephones to speed dial their internist, cardiologist, and chiropractor. Their daughter Becky has hit her forty-second birthday. Becky's children are teenagers, and totally depend on her for food, shelter, and clothing. This doesn't sound unusual by today's standards. But remember, Becky's grandparents are living into their mid-nineties, in failing health, but hanging on long enough to require intensive nursing care. Three generations are pushing down on Becky's shoulders, all the while the government saps more dollars from her paycheck. At the family Thanksgiving dinner, Becky realizes that of the four generations eating, only she and her husband are footing the bill. She had read of the "sandwich generation," but somehow an extra layer has been piled on top.

This is not just an American problem. In fact, most other industrialized countries will face even nastier generational warfare. The ratio of young people to old people in Europe is rapidly approaching two to one. That means, for every codger on the golf course there are just two young, low-wage, tip-dependent caddies sweating so that they can keep up with the retiree's pension, Social Security, health benefits, etc. In Japan, which is aging faster than sushi, the ratio may come close to one to one. Today, future retirees are already facing the wrath of young Japanese who cannot find jobs amid Japan's deepest recession since World War II. A society sewn together by the Confucian respect for seniority is ripping itself apart. The old story about Eskimos sending their elders out of the igloos and off to die with dignity doesn't seem so far-fetched, after all.

When the U.S. Congress invented Social Security, the young to old ratio was about ten to one. Soon after World War II, the suburbs teemed with babies, new schools, and a seemingly endless supply of future workers to pay for their elders. No more. In fact, the boomers themselves helped create the problem. Remember the 1960s mantra about the "population explosion," which discouraged some parents from having kids? Between 1970 and 1980, the number of school kids actually dropped by 14 percent. By lowering the birthrate in the 1960s and 1970s, boomers shoveled more economic responsibilities on those children who actually were born. Here's the irony: By having fewer kids and yet promising themselves more benefits, the boomers created the population time bomb—but it's not their children, the boomers are the bomb!

THREE NAUTICAL MILES NORTHEAST OF ANTIGUA, BRITISH WEST INDIES

"Lift 'em up high!" Steven Pert screamed in a hoarse voice to a group of sixty-five-year-olds. *"C'mon now touch your toes!* You old goats," he muttered to himself, while staring at his straining aerobics students. God must have set the sun on bake today. It was at least 100 degrees on the deck of the cruise ship MS *Dazzle*. The twenty-year-old pinched the top of his red T-shirt and pulled it away from his heaving chest, noticing that the sweat has turned the shade from scarlet to burgundy. He grabbed his shirt by the bottom, lifted it over his head, and twirled it around like a stripper. He tensed his abdominal muscles just to make the old men jealous. Many of them hadn't seen their feet in thirty years, much less a rippling six-pack. A wrinkled lady with leather skin in the front row put her fingers in her mouth to whistle, but once her fingers got in, she decided instead to adjust her dentures. Steven threw his wet

shirt overboard, knowing full well that someone in the crowd would report him to the captain for fouling the environment. The EPA could fine the owners of the MS *Dazzle* for waste mismanagement. No kidding. A tuna could get caught in that smelly shirt and die.

Steven wasn't so cynical when he boarded the ship two months ago. Not until he got his first paycheck. Unlike most cruise lines, the owners of the *Dazzle* actually deducted U.S. taxes. But surely the accountant made a mistake. How could his take-home pay be just a third of the gross? And what's the point of doing jumping jacks on the steamy teak deck of a ship in the Caribbean if Uncle Sam wipes away most of the money? Steven showed his paycheck to one of the vacationers, a pale accountant from Chicago.

"Does this make sense to you?" Steven asked.

"Sure does, my boy. It's the new surtax Congress passed last year. See all these people sipping piña coladas and margaritas? You're paying for their retirement and health care. Now work hard, and make us proud!"

Over the next few decades, the happy, "Wonder Years" vision of America's suburban schools and rambunctious playgrounds will be replaced by the sight of countless nursing homes with their struggling inhabitants, taking staggering steps within the chain-linked yards.

This depressing scene is not the whole story, though. Any economic story will have winners and losers. This chapter will spell out the troubling trends, but also point the reader to investments that will ride these waves. As we will discuss later in the chapter, before the baby boomers check into nursing homes, they will be creating jobs (and investment opportunities) in the vacation industry, the recreational vehicle industry, and even some parts of the housing sector. Nor is it all downhill for younger workers. At the same time as the baby boomers burden the young, the world economy will highly prize the labor and ideas of the youngest members. A shortage of labor pushes up wages for the fit. Businesses will more than ever look to smart, literate, internationally net-worked young people to solve problems. As individuals, talented young workers may very well command extremely high pay and privileges. But as a group they will have to give up much of their future gains to the government.

A FINANCIAL HANDSTAND

The American family is about to perform a collective head-stand. It is not a trick that we have performed before, and the degree of difficulty is treacherously high. Our fastest growing group is our slowest moving, the over-eighty-five-year-olds, a pop-ulation that will double to 8 million by 2030 and more than double again to 18 million in 2050, making up 5 percent of the population. By 2050, one in five Americans will be retirees. The coming clash between young and old is not just history repeating itself. The his-tory of every civilization going back to ancient Egypt is sprinkled with clichés about old people resenting loud, boisterous children, and children in return resenting stodgy authority figures. A gray-bearded Moses really did hurl down the tablets on a carousing crowd, didn't he? In Chapter 8 of this book we'll see that even Amish teenagers get rambunctious.

This time, though, the generational dynamic *really* is different. How so? First, until the late twentieth century, the United States had always had many more young people than old people. In 1870, for example, there were almost ten times as many youngsters five to fourteen years old as there were people over sixty-five. In 1920 schoolkids outnumbered those sixty-five and older by five to one. And even in 1970 schoolkids still clung to a two to one advantage. No more. In fact, by 2050, senior citizens will turn the tables and outnumber schoolkids by two to one. The second reason "it's dif-ferent this time" is that old people no longer think of themselves as old. Although they may retire earlier than ever before, they keep spending as they never have. They are big consumers of vacation travel and social activities. Go on a cruise to Alaska and watch the thousands of liver-spotted hands waving at the whales.

Third, historically, when young people outnumbered old people, they were able to support generous retirement benefits. A retiree born in 1915 would have paid in about $50,000 over the course of his lifetime, but takes out about $90,000 (all in 1993 dollars). A pyramid plan, or a Ponzi scheme, works only when the base of the pyramid keeps growing. When it stops, the blocks tumble. We are nearing that historic moment. Here we may find the central contradiction of the welfare states: Generous government programs encourage workers to save less, retire early, and perhaps have fewer children. But those results undermine the financial viability of the programs. Karl Marx talked up "dialectical materialism." We are witnessing "dialectical welfarism."

A CULTURAL HEADSTAND

Along with our population statistics, our cultural norms are flipping over on their heads too. For most of human history, and even during the first few decades of this century, adults viewed children as income producers for the family. More hands on the farm meant more bushels of corn to sell. Sure, their parents loved them and cuddled them (depending on the family), but children were expected to give something more than love in return. Phillipe Aries's classic *Centuries of Childhood* described how adults generally treated children like miniature adults. The only difference between a midget and an eight-year-old was that P. T. Barnum could turn the former into an international spectacle. Instead of traveling in a circus, eight-year-olds routinely started working in a trade or in the agricultural fields. Only the upper classes could afford to cuddle and coddle much past infancy. We now find child labor offensive and the idea of viewing children as income-producing assets as backward if not downright repulsive. But could baby boomers end up turning the clock back on this ethic?

The "Me" generation of baby boomers raised in the 1960s certainly did not feel an obligation to produce income for their parents at an early age. While their Depression-era parents may have been raised in a spirit of frugality and sacrifice, the post–World War II suburbs raised an indulged generation. Off the farm and into a postwar consumer explosion, baby boomers were reared more like luxury goods or fancy pets to be cherished, rather than as financial assets. The suburbs emphasized schools, and the rate of college attendance skyrocketed, with higher property taxes paying the way. In the 1950s and 1960s the entire Western world seemed to worship the teenager, and Gidget, Frankie Avalon, and the Beach Boys brought the concept of a beach party weekend to landlocked counties in Nebraska. Even in the rebuilt rubble of post–World War II Berlin, the pulse of American youth rocked and echoed off the Wall. Humorist Dave Barry has written that the baby-boom generation is "defined, technically, as people who, when you say 'Shirley, Shirley, bo-berly,' instantly respond 'Bonana fanna fo-ferley.'" Young Americans cheered when John F. Kennedy implored them to "ask not what your country can do for you," but they asked anyway.

The baby boomers clearly intended to pass along the indulged childhood to their offspring. More so than ever, today's parents see a child as a precious financial *drain*, not as an income-producing asset. One of the fastest growing medical technologies involves *in vitro* fertilization of embryos, an extremely expensive procedure that can be justified only by a couple's desire to parent, not by their desire for a return on investment. How many articles have you read on the cost that families bear for college, music lessons, preschool, tennis camp, Nike sneakers, etc.? And these are aimed not just at the upper classes. Madonna's 1980 "Material Girl" echoed through Benetton stores throughout the world and across income cohorts. Depression-era babies raised on Yip Harburg's "Brother, Can You Spare a Dime?" find this astounding when recalling their own childhoods.

Now, though, as we look at the generational handstand, we must wonder whether the only way to care for aging baby boomers is to yank back the privileges of their grandchildren. Which raises a good question: Have today's youth been raised with the cultural values that will steer them toward extraordinary generosity? I have my doubts. The kids of boomers have learned that in the job market they must make their own way, forgetting old-fashioned norms like lifetime employment and guaranteed benefits. Teamwork sounds great on the surface, but self-reliance and entrepreneurship now look like the keys to success, rather than a gray flannel suit or corporate button-down white shirt. Offices are dressing down for casual Friday, but the pressure on individuals to perform or be "downsized" is more intense than ever. What are the cultural icons and slogans that shaped this generation, and what do they suggest about the Xers' and Yers' willingness to coddle their elders? Try as they might, all the platitudes of William Bennett and Barney the purple dinosaur cannot overcome the legacy of Nike's "Just Do It," Wendy's "Where's the Beef!" and Jerry Maguire's "Show Me the Money!"

And yet their elders will ask for beef and money. In order to make the arithmetic add up, we may push our youth into the labor market at an earlier age than their parents or their grandparents. This seems at first a bitter, brutal step backward. But remember, labor in the next century will not be performed in filthy coal mines that infect young bodies with black lung disease or in humid fields without lavatories.

DUBLIN, IRELAND

Fiona Flanigan kissed her mother, wiped her forehead with the back of her hand, and straightened her blouse before walking into the board meeting at the Bank of Dublin. Her mother would wait in the car, as nervous as a getaway driver for Bonnie and Clyde. Fiona had been on the Internet all night with her partner in Bombay, preparing for the presentation. Sunil generated a whole new set of profit projections and created a 3-D graph that would knock the old socks off the old boys. The bankers were still a crusty group, mostly men, mostly over fifty, some of them looking a lot like her Uncle Bob, who couldn't understand why women would want to leave the kitchen for the workplace. Of course, he never really worked. Mostly sat around a foreman's shed, while the union workers mowed lawns.

She shook hands and jumped right into her sales pitch, turning out the lights and closing the shades in the piney conference room. Dark was good light for her. That way they wouldn't keep staring at her smooth, fifteen-year-old skin.

They had never seen such stunning graphics; it was like a laser show bouncing off their overhead projectors. It had to be good. How else to con-

*vince them that her new consortium of Irish and Indian computer pro-
grammers could steal market share from Microsoft?*

*"Congratulations, Ms. Flanigan," the chairman said. "I'm sold. How
much do you need?"*

Soon, we could see fourteen- and fifteen-year-olds getting homework assignments from computer software companies—homework that pays in learning and in cold cash. Our fictitious Fiona
would not mind. Perhaps labor laws will force firms to direct the
wages into college trust funds. So be it. Here will stand, though,
the unique irony of the twenty-first century: The most indulged
grandparents in history will end up taking from their grandchildren not just money, but youth itself.

LONGER LIVES, EARLIER RETIREMENT

The treacherous financial headstand is not chiefly the result of
greed or government mismanagement. On the contrary, we should
rejoice that people are living longer. Individuals and the government spent much less on hospital care in 1900 when most people
died before the age of fifty and barbers performed dental surgery,
extracting impacted molars in between haircuts. Fifty years ago,
most Americans died before they could retire. Medical technology
and better diets have lifted life expectancy toward eighty (from
about sixty in 1940), and the average seventy-five-year-old today is
likely to be active, self-sufficient, and probably still driving (with
some level of proficiency). Nonetheless, about half of those senior
citizens will eventually require some extended nursing care. The
more successful we are at extending longevity, the more dollars it
will cost us.

A healthier living standard for seniors does not come free.
Investors will find enticing ways to take advantage of this, through
"miracle drugs" and "nutraceuticals," as we will discuss at the end
of the chapter. Since the goal is to "die young as late as possible,"
people over sixty-five spend about 3.5 times as much on health

care as working-age adults. Flip open a copy of *San Diego* or *Los Angeles* magazine and you will see plastic surgeons advertising their face-lifting services even to the elderly. Of course, there are regional differences in personal vanity and the desire for health care. Still, even after adjusting for inflation, Americans on average spend about eleven times what they spent on health care prior to World War II. That multiple will not fall from here, as baby boomers who grew up in the "Wonder Years" enter the "Parts Break Down Years."

One might surmise that longer, healthier lives would persuade people to stay in the workplace a few more years, especially since fewer and fewer workers perform physically demanding tasks in the factories and mines. Nonetheless, over the course of the last one hundred years, people have retired earlier, not later. In 1880, 75 percent of Americans older than sixty-four continued working. By 1950, the figure fell to under 50 percent, and then steadily dropped to about 20 percent (though the strong job market in the past few years may have pulled the figure up slightly). Many Americans who retire in their mid–sixties are healthy enough to close their office door, turn in their keys, and then jog home for a retirement party. Europe, too, has enjoyed the same trend. While in the early 1960s, about 70 percent of French men aged sixty to sixty-four worked, by 1995, the ratio fell well below 20 percent, and to under 10 percent for those who are sixty-five. Again, I do not quote these numbers in dismay or disappointment. How wonderful that the twentieth century generated so much wealth that the average person could retire and live a healthier and wealthier life than the average king of the nineteenth century! No wonder that public polls show some envy of old people. Fifty-five percent of those under sixty-five think that their financial security and their enjoyment of life will improve after hitting sixty-five (only 13 percent thought that finances would worsen; only 4 percent thought enjoyment of life would worsen). A staggering 79 percent thought that their sex life would either stay the same or improve!

I quote the numbers on early retirement and longevity not to complain, then, but to question the sustainability of the government programs that support so many retirees. We cannot ignore the fact that about two-thirds of them do depend chiefly on Social Security income to pay their bills. The U.S. government has encouraged people to retire sooner, ever since the Union Army started mailing out Civil War pensions. In the 1940s and 1950s, Old Age Assistance, which targeted money to lower-income Americans, dwarfed Social Security and contributed to the wave of early retirement. Not only does Social Security encourage people to retire earlier, but it probably discourages poorer people from saving more on their own. A poor family that receives Medicaid, Supplemental Security Income, and AFDC (Aid to Families with Dependent Children) faces a "means-test" that dissuades them from accumulating financial assets. If they somehow save more than $3,000 in a bank account, for example, they jeopardize their eligibility for aid. This operates like a steep tax, and helps explain why most households with less than $1,000 in assets still have less than $1,000 five years later.

HOW THE CURRENT SYSTEM BANKRUPTS US

Herb Stein, a droll economist of the Nixon and Ford White Houses, proclaimed Stein's law: "If a trend is unsustainable, it will stop." By that logic the Social Security and Medicare system will stop. They do not know when or how, but generations X and Y know that it will. A provocative public opinion poll showed that more young people believed in UFOs than believed in Social Security's survival. And when asked which will live longer, they chose the soap opera *General Hospital* over the government's Medicare program. Both the soap opera about medical caregivers and the government medical program started in the mid-1960s, but only one will survive the next twenty years intact.

Social Security and Medicare

President Franklin Roosevelt heard a screaming cry from America's old people in the 1930s. Many were too feeble to find work during the Great Depression, and so they were almost three times more likely to be poor than the average American. Today they are no more likely to be poor than anyone else. In fact, they are more satisfied with their financial situation than any other age group, with only 12 percent dissatisfied, compared to about 30 percent for the rest of the working-age population. Dependable Social Security payments have made a big difference in supporting their retirement as well as their peace of mind. The system has also been a good business deal for them. In 1937, for example, Social Security taxes (Old Age Survivors Insurance) took just 2 percent of their wages, with a maximum annual tax of $60. Even by 1951, the tax rate was just 3 percent, with a maximum of just $108. Today workers pay 10.7 percent, with a maximum of about $7,300.

These low historical rates explain another financial headstand. Elderly retirees have gotten back almost *twice* as much from Social Security as they paid in. In direct contrast, today's young workers will receive only about 50 cents for every dollar they contribute over their careers. For example, over his lifetime a thirty-five-year-old man earning an average income will pay in about $135,000 more than he will receive in benefits! If he is lucky enough to earn twice the average income, he will fork over about $274,000 beyond his benefits. This huge drain from the wallets of young workers makes it almost impossible for them to save money apart from Social Security. Imagine: An average worker needs to squirrel away an extra $135,000 just to stay even. "Squirrel" is the right metaphor since the scenario conjures the image of a rodent on a treadmill getting nowhere.

Once again, the demographic headstand forces the system to the brink. In 1965, more than eight workers paid for each retiree. That number has fallen to 3.3, and will head toward only two in the next thirty years. In 1983, President Reagan appointed Alan Greenspan to head a commission that would put Social Security on firmer footing. Among other reforms, the Greenspan Commission raised the retirement age from sixty-five to sixty-seven—but that will not kick in until 2027. Considering the treacherous politics of the 1980s, when Social Security was regularly called "the third rail of American politics" and anyone mentioning serious reform would get electrocuted by voters, the Greenspan age adjustment was considered a bold move. Accompanied by benefit cuts for early retirees, the Greenspan reforms actually saved the government over $1 trillion in future payments (offsetting much of the debt buildup during the Reagan years). Far, far more must be done in the next decade, though.

Believe it or not, the Social Security system looks solid compared to Medicare. Both suffer from the demographic headstand, but Medicare suffers from an added burden: the continuing climb in medical costs. Medicare spending has averaged an annual 10 percent jump for the past fifteen years. To pay the benefits, the Medicare tax has leaped from just 0.7 percent in the 1960s to 2.9 percent today. Moreover, that tax used to be levied on only the first $6,600 of wages; now the tax takes a chip out of every dollar earned. Even with these high taxes, though, the Medicare system will slide into bankruptcy in a matter of years. With two-thirds of elderly health spending tied to Medicare (and Medicaid covering poor people), this is a crisis. In fact, our entire health-care system will be at risk unless we reverse the perverse incentives built into the system.

The prime problem is that most medical patients are using someone else's money to pay for their treatment. They are not stealing the money (they get it legitimately from Medicare or from their insurance company), but they are using more of it than they would if they absorbed the cost themselves. This is what economists call the "moral hazard" problem of insurance. People tend to care less about other people's money or property. We tend to treat rental cars less gingerly than our own, daring to parallel park in the tightest spots and slamming down on the accelerator to launch ourselves up the freeway entry ramp. Likewise, if Medicare is paying 80 percent of your bills, you may not pause before dropping by the podiatrist's office for a pedicure. Instead of buying a heating pad for your back, you might first spend $250 on a doctor's visit. Again, these dynamics are not just found in Medicare. The U.S. government's subsidy of employer-paid health insurance creates similar incentives for working people.

Careful empirical studies have shown that people will shop more carefully if more of the cost comes directly from their own wallets. A researcher at Columbia University calculated that raising out-of-pocket costs by 10 percent would cut medical spending by 6.2 percent. The Rand Corporation conducted a landmark study that found when people were total free riders on someone else's health plan, they racked up 45 percent more in medical bills. More striking—they did not end up any healthier! Nor did intensive-care patients in Miami, who spent twice as much as those in Minneapolis. Greater medical spending does not seem to guarantee better health, any more than more expensive, higher octane gas guarantees better fuel mileage in cars. Though, over time, medical advances such as antibiotics and new techniques make tremendous contributions, lifestyle and genes better explain differences in mortality and morbidity levels within the United States (at any one time). In the 1960s, for example, Nevada's infant and adult mortality rates were far higher than Utah's (with only a little of the difference due to bullets flying out of Las Vegas casinos). Nonetheless, residents of those states had similar incomes, environmental conditions, and medical-care access. Prudent spending and clean living probably made a difference.

A PERSONAL PLAN—START NOW

Though the next section examines possible government reforms, you probably should not wait for Uncle Sam to save you. After taking a sober look at your personal finances, you might want to have a stiff drink. More useful, though, would be devising a game plan to cut your costs and raise your savings rate. During the 1980s and 1990s, those corporations that sliced their wasteful divisions and devoted their future to productive investments survived in the competitive marketplace. You must do the same. Saving more means spending less. Here are some nuggets of advice that may not be gold, but may, in the end, prove more valuable:

1. Pay off credit card balances each month, and use credit cards that throw in some extra goodie, whether rebates or credit toward a major purchase. The credit card companies will be disappointed in you, but they'll probably find some other pigeon to take your place. Learn how to pay cash again. It

hurts to pull those dollars from your wallet or purse. Somehow, those credit cards easily slide out.

2. Shop more carefully. The Internet puts amazing technology in the hands of consumers, empowering you to comparison shop on everything from contact lenses to cars.

3. Try to raise your deductibles on automobile and health insurance, which will lower monthly premiums. Urge your employer to offer Medical Savings Accounts, which allow you to save money tax-free, if you do not spend it on doctors' visits.

4. Learn to broil a trout. Learn how to cook quickly, so that eating at home is not a burden. Broiling a trout takes about ten minutes. Going to a fish restaurant takes almost two hours and costs you much more.

5. Contribute as much as you can to 401(k) plans, IRAs, and other retirement vehicles. Because employer-sponsored plans let you save in pre-tax dollars, the federal government effectively pays for 28 percent of the contribution (if you're in the 28 percent tax bracket).

6. Write down how much you spend. If you're on a diet, you can write it in the same book that you write down your calorie intake. Losing weight and gaining wealth will make you happier than will an overpriced cookie from Nieman Marcus (urban myths aside).

If you are closing in on retirement and far short of your financial needs, consider two more radical solutions: First, do not completely retire. Find a hobby or vocation that can pay you. I know retirees in Los Angeles who act as Hollywood extras, earning some money and getting the same free lunch that movie stars get—often a Cobb salad. You might be discovered and find your name in lights. At worst, you'll watch some egotistical stars complain about proper lighting and makeup. Second, move to a cheaper part of the country. Low tax rates, housing costs, and mild weather pull senior

citizens toward Florida. Other states in the south offer similar benefits, as do states like Utah and Idaho, if you do not mind wearing
mittens in the winter.

GOVERNMENT SOLUTIONS—HURRY UP!

That clock is ticking loudly. The longer we wait to fix bankrupt
programs, the bigger the fix. Entitlement programs are a train
rolling too fast for the tracks, carrying too many passengers, and
hurtling forward without even a headlight. A twenty-year delay in
fixing Social Security might mean it will require twice as much
money to repair, as assets dwindle and liabilities multiply.
Twiddling our thumbs on Medicare would devastate the lives of
young workers. Seminal work by Laurence Kotlikoff on the concept of "generational accounting" has calculated that our descen-
dants may face tax rates 70 percent higher than our own, if we do
not act quickly and forcefully. Even a five-year wait for Medicare
could require an 80 percent cut in benefits!

A major political event took place in 1998, though, that shone a
sliver of hope. Senator Daniel Patrick Moynihan of New York, an
architect of many social welfare programs and a historical defender
of Social Security, delivered a speech at Harvard promoting a radical overhaul of the retirement program. The current system takes
12.4 percent from workers and dumps it into low-yielding but safe
U.S. Treasuries. Moynihan recognized that over the course of the
twentieth century, stocks have widely outperformed bonds, deliv-
ering an average 7 percent annual return. He proposed giving
employees the power to funnel a portion of their Social Security
payroll taxes into the equity market. Such a proposal would have
launched impeachment hearings if President Reagan had proposed
it during the 1980s. But Moynihan's move effectively turned off the
electricity on the third rail of American politics. With Moynihan's
blessing, politicians could openly discuss privatization, without
skulking into the back alleys or whispering the way people do when
telling an off-color joke. For years conservative think tanks had
floated such plans, but most populist politicians felt that they were
not suitable for decent dinner table conversation. If Moynihan's

conversion leads to a national movement, the bow-tied, ruddy-faced ex-professor may end up saving young people a few trillion dollars. Not a bad return on his salary as a senator.

To some, Moynihan's proposal was a timid baby step (even left-leaning Sweden already allows its citizens to direct some of their retirement taxes to stocks), to others a dangerous precedent for total privatization. Even the most avid privatizers agree, though, that Social Security cannot cut off payments to those already retired or even those baby boomers nearing retirement. The debate is about the future. Certainly, the shift in private pension plans from "defined benefit" ("We'll tell you how much you'll get in retirement") to "defined contribution" ("Here's what we're putting aside for you. Invest it wisely, and it will pay off") has made individuals more comfortable with taking responsibility for their own retirement investments. Privatizing Social Security offers many advantages, including a higher return for the average worker and the ability to pass on investment earnings to heirs. Why not adopt a policy that gives young people a stake in the retirement savings of older people, rather than the current system, which looks more like a zero-sum game? Former Reagan chief economist Martin Feldstein has developed a proposal called "Personal Retirement Accounts" (PRAs) that would permit employees to choose a mix of investments, including bonds and stocks, depending on the individual's appetite for risk. President Clinton's 1999 State of the Union address unveiled a plan to toss some of the federal budget surplus into the United States stock market. Federal Reserve Chairman Alan Greenspan immediately attacked the plan, warning that future politicians would be tempted to direct the funds toward their favorite companies and industries.

Regardless of which plan Congress finally agrees upon, two points appear clear: First, we should not simply bridge the financial gap in Social Security by raising payroll taxes—this drives up the costs of hiring human beings, in comparison to machines. Second, we should not foolishly believe that we can support old people at a level utterly disconnected with the state of the general economy. In other words, everyone retains a stake in the economy, no matter how wrinkled their faces or gray their hair. A weak, collapsing economy cannot afford to pay the bills of pensioners. And so, if ridiculously high pension bills will push the economy over a cliff, the pensioners should have a strong interest in making some sacrifices—sooner rather than later.

The Medicare implosion begs for a similar solution that permits private financial markets to be a friend of the system. In addition, health-care reform must address the problem of "other people's money," that is, moral hazard. A two-pronged attack would work well. First, strongly encourage (or require) young workers to start contributing toward a private health insurance policy that would pay benefits when they retire. This would cost them far less than Medicare's 2.9 percent bite (even if the U.S. equity market achieved a real rate of return far below its 7 percent annual average). Second, encourage young workers to establish tax-free Medical Savings Accounts (MSAs) to cover their current health costs. Under MSAs, an employer buys a catastrophic policy (which costs much less than a low-deductible one), while contributing the savings into a tax-free account that the employee controls. The employee can dip into the MSA to pay for routine doctor bills. However, the amount that the employee leaves in the account grows tax-free into a nice retirement nest egg, much like an IRA. Here's the key point: MSAs give individuals a reason to think twice before spending money willy-nilly on medicine and doctors, because the money does come out of that person's pocket (even if the employer originally placed it there). Thus, MSAs work to dismantle that pesky moral hazard. Though Congress has authorized a pilot program for MSAs, vocal opponents in Washington have put a chill on the idea. Too bad. Of course, even these two reforms would still leave the system burdened with the baby boomers who are already too old to plan for their own health-care coverage in retirement. The generational warfare cannot be entirely avoided, then. We are headed, unalterably, toward some benefit cutbacks, higher deductibles, and a bigger squeeze on doctors and hospitals.

DO WE CARE ABOUT OTHERS?

The sacrifices that generations XYZ will make for their parents and grandparents raises a good question: How much will they give up? Already, we see that one-quarter of American families are caring for at least one elderly family member, with 40 percent of them simultaneously supporting their own children. In the overwhelming number of cases, it is a woman who feels the generational vise squeezing her. But caring for your own flesh and blood comes far more easily than paying for strangers, as Blanche Dubois acknowledged. Adam Smith surmised in his *Theory of Moral Sentiments* that "Every man feels his own pleasures and his own pains more sensibly than those of other people . . . more strongly directed towards his children than towards his parents . . . [and the] children of cousins, being still less connected, are of still less importance to one another; and the affection gradually diminishes as the relation grows more and more remote." Biologist William Hamilton developed a cost-benefit formula, implying that a parent/child or two siblings will sacrifice when the benefit to the other will be worth twice the burden. In other words, a child might pay an extra $50 per month, if it bought her mother $100 of health-care coverage. According to this "coefficient of relationships," half-siblings or a grandparent/grandchild combination will sacrifice only when the benefit is worth four times the burden. First cousins face a steeper cost-benefit ratio of eight to one. Evolutionary biologists have tried to validate the Hamilton rule by following birds, while economists follow heiresses.

For stranger-to-stranger sacrifices, the Hamilton ratio tilts awfully high. We all know that in extreme circumstances, a man may throw down his life for a stranger, for an ideal, or for a dollar. *Saving Private Ryan* seared the minds of moviegoers with its bloody story of duty, honor, and strangers. In the course of normal events, though, we hear "I gave at the office" more often than a noble "I'll bear any burden, pay any price." I am afraid that by 2020, generations XYZ will feel as if they gave more than enough at the office and in their homes to their own needy, leaving little emotional and financial resources to share with strangers. It will take a leader with Theodore Roosevelt's vigor, Franklin Roosevelt's soothing charisma, and Ronald Reagan's confident conviction to energize young workers and motivate them toward bringing the scarlet red generational accounts back into the black.

If you are a boomer or a retiree who does care about your grandchildren—you can help now, rather than wait for them to read your will at the funeral home. Trusts and estate lawyers, as well as qualified financial planners can dazzle you with all sorts of tricky but legal structures to funnel your wealth and even boost your ego. Feeling imperial? How about a "Dynasty Trust"? Since the Internal Revenue Service now nabs 37 percent of estates beyond an initial $650,000 exemption, your children and grandchildren would surely appreciate some advance planning. Though Congress passed legislation in 1997 that will push that exemption up to $1 million in 2006, larger estates face tax rates as high as 55 percent. Here are some straightforward tips for helping your kids maneuver around the demographic headstand:

1. Give them money! You can give up to $10,000 a year to anyone without triggering the IRS. The $10,000 limit should not intimidate you, if you can only afford $100.

2. Give fewer "trinket" presents and more stock on their behalf. Rather than take them to McDonald's four times for a Happy Meal, take them once, but buy them a few shares of McDonald's stock. In the long run, Ronald McDonald will help pay for their education, and you will probably spare your arteries some cholesterol buildup.

3. Give them "zero coupon" bonds, which cost "little," though their value blossoms over time. (Unlike typical bonds, zeroes do not pay out interest until the end of the term, when the beneficiary will need it) for $10,000 now, you can give a baby a bond that will mature into about $30,000, just in time for college expenses. You could even combine this gift with a requirement that they maintain a certain grade point average!

4. Contribute money to an "Education IRA" for a child, where funds can build up tax-free and then be used for tuition. If the child does not go to college, the money can be turned over to a different family member. Many states have enacted "Qualified State Tuition Programs," where family members can prepay a child's tuition, room and board expenses, while deferring taxes.

5. Give your time. As the adage goes, grandparents and grandchildren get along so well, because they have a common enemy!

A SLIPPERY WORLD ECONOMY OFFERS NO SOLID GROUND

Many of the problems highlighted so far could be handled financially and psychologically by generations XYZ, if the world economy were welcoming them with the same open arms and open wallets that the baby boomers found in the 1960s. During that decade, the U.S. economy galloped along at 3.5 percent growth, and wages climbed along with the Dow Jones average.

Nowadays, though, the Federal Reserve Board has pulled down expectations, suggesting that growth above 2.5 percent could eventually bring inflation and must be restrained. (The Federal Reserve Board believes that the unusually low U.S. inflation rate of 1997 and 1998 resulted from the recession in Europe and Asia, which pushed down world prices, despite strong U.S. growth.) During the 1990s, wages shrank compared to corporate profits, and workers competed with not just technology but also with foreigners willing to work for less. In the global workers' "food chain" there's always a country where laborers will sweat for less. Take electronics. In the 1970s, Americans found themselves losing jobs to the Japanese. In the early 1980s, the Japanese lost those jobs to the Koreans. And in the 1990s the Koreans lost those jobs to the Chinese. All the while, the Latin Americans have tried to squeeze into the act, never sure whom to undercut, and never successful enough to push their incomes into the upper tiers.

In this environment, individuals no longer find themselves coddled by stable corporations. Instead, they must look out for their own pensions. Each year firms cover fewer and fewer workers with pensions and health-care plans, and those existing pensions have switched from "defined benefit" to "defined contribution." While in 1982, over 70 percent of pension plans were "defined benefit," that number has been sliding toward 40 percent and lower. While "defined contribution" plans may be more efficient, they certainly heap new responsibility on the shoulders of unsophisticated laborers.

Since generations XYZ find themselves working in a high-flying world with no carefully knitted net, they are less inclined to guarantee a luxurious safety net for their elders.

LITTLE STAKE FOR MINORITIES

While few young people will be able to escape the financial squeeze, there's little doubt that minorities will suffer most. For one thing, blacks and Hispanics are underrepresented among boomers and overrepresented among youngsters. Consider, fewer than 18 percent of the boomers are black or Hispanic, but 33 percent of the kids are. Black males can expect to die 7.5 years earlier than whites. Even worse, their life expectancy rates are actually falling.

The problem is compounded by the deteriorating stature of the black family over time. The last black generation dominated by a stable family is dying off. Among black males fifty-five to sixty-five years old, 63 percent live with a spouse. Each successive age group has found marriage less and less attractive, with only 35 percent of the twenty-five- to thirty-four-year-olds married (compared with 54 percent for whites). As we have all read, the black illegitimacy rate now stands over 60 percent. Again, compare that to an illegitimacy rate of just 36 percent in 1970.

These sad statistics should warn us that the black generations XYZ have even less reason than white young people to pay taxes to fund the retirement of their elders. The irony is that the nation's finances need young minority workers more than ever. But it looks like a raw deal. While it's a cliché for "angry white males" to claim that blacks are a drain on society's finances, believe it or not, a

Rand Corporation study found that Social Security forces blacks to make a transfer of between $2,000 and $21,000 to whites. All this, while black families have an average net asset value of zero. How could this be? The answer: Blacks are typically poorer than whites, and poor people tend to start work earlier in life, and die sooner, collecting fewer benefits.

Finally, our brave and brutal new global economy places ill-educated minorities in direct competition with low-wage foreign laborers. While lower-income blacks and Hispanics have not protested international trade in a particularly vocal way, it is only a matter of time.

INTERNATIONAL RIPPLES

Compared to its industrialized allies, the United States will still be the "new world." Despite our debt overhang and financial headstands, Europe and Japan will suffer even more. Our future public pension payments add up to 25 percent of our GDP; Germany, France, and Japan have each promised over 100 percent of GDP to future pensioners. Nor have Europe and Japan escaped rising health-care costs. Even Canada, with its nationalized system, watched health-care costs rise at a similar pace as the United States from the 1960s to the 1990s.

The Japanese used to have the world's fastest growing economy. Now they can only boast of the world's fasting *aging* economy. Between now and 2020, the proportion of senior citizens will more than double, and then triple by 2050. The median marriage age for females has crept up to twenty-seven (from twenty-three in 1972) and those wives are giving birth to fewer than 1.5 babies (from about two in 1972). Despite the warning sound of demographic gongs, Japan's fractured political system and anti-entrepreneurial spirit seem paralyzed in the face of the challenge. A widespread racist attitude generally forbids solving the problem by permitting younger immigrants into the country. The Japanese have an awful record of discrimination even against Koreans, much less Latins, Africans, or Indians, who could conceivably come as guest workers. These problems help explain why Japan has rapidly built up manufacturing plants in China. Japan will try to solve its labor shortage by exporting potential jobs. While that may help the bottom line of Japan's corporations, it has crippled the public's perception of the economy and the society.

The Japanese problems are not, alas, confined to their islands. Their crisis endangers all of us. For the past twenty years—because the Japanese have a high savings rate—they have been creditors to the rest of the world, especially the United States. By providing about one-third of the world's savings, they have kept down worldwide interest rates. As the Japanese age, they may begin drawing down their massive savings and collecting on their debts from everyone else. The United States will feel higher interest rates and suffer slower growth. Profits will be squeezed and, again, the stock market pinched, unless Japan's savers make extremely prudent investments around the world that can yield high dividends (see Chapter 5).

Europe is in denial and, like an addict, needs a twelve-step program to recover. Unfortunately, so far the steps are mostly backward. After a bitter strike, the French government capitulated to truckers and now allows them to retire at fifty. Renault is closing a highly efficient Belgian auto plant to "save jobs" at an inefficient French-based operation. And German labor unions have urged that firms cut back the number of working hours per employee in a futile effort to increase the number of workers. Former chancellor Helmut Kohl faced a revolt when he proposed cutting back the government's guaranteed promise of an annual day at a health spa. With these heavy social and financial burdens weighing on employers, it is no surprise that while the United States increased its jobs by 27 million between 1982 and 1997, continental Europe had, on balance, not created one new job. Unlike Japan, which undoubtedly will struggle toward consensus and a bureaucratic solution, Europe also faces the threat of nationalistic, xenophobic tirades. The French right-wing radical Jean-Marie LePen finds his support growing, while frustrated Germans stew amid high unemployment. All in all, a combustible setting.

Within Europe, only the United Kingdom has disciplined its public pension debts and defused the demographic time bomb.

Margaret Thatcher's controversial reforms partially privatized social security, leaving the United Kingdom with future public pension payments equal to just 5 percent of GDP, compared to over 100 percent for her continental neighbors. Meanwhile, the United Kingdom has grown a huge nest egg, as Brits have stashed away more money into private pension funds than all of the rest of the European Union combined.

In the race to get older, the developing world is far behind the large industrialized countries—and, in this case, lagging behind is a good thing. Countries like Mexico and India are still too poor to be dominated by pensioners. Instead, they can help provide new workers for the world economy. While the average age among the G7 is in the mid-thirties, the average age in Latin American, Africa, and Asia is in the twenties.

WILL THE STOCK MARKET CRASH AS BOOMERS HEAD FOR THE GATES?

"Die Broke!" screamed the cover story of *Worth* magazine a few years ago. The article argued that retirees should happily, guilt-lessly spend all their money, leaving nothing for the kids. If the baby boomers take that advice and "die broke," their kids and grandkids will "live broke."

At a breathless pace, panic-struck boomers spent the mid-1990s dumping money into the U.S. stock market, doubling the Dow Jones average between 1994 and 1998. Mostly, they dumped those dollars into mutual funds, which now control over $4 trillion in assets. Quite prudently, people looked at their bank accounts and realized that they had not saved nearly enough to retire on. At the same time, they learned the history of stocks and bonds in the twentieth century: Equities are better in the long run, despite 1929 crashes and 1987 scares. So far, so good.

But what happens when the boomers need to withdraw their money to pay bills in retirement? Perhaps you have seen the bumper stickers that announce, "I am spending my kids' inheri-tance!" The great Victorian economist Alfred Marshall once boasted that he could teach a parrot to be an economist: Just teach it to squawk "supply and demand." That goes for the stock market as well as the price of tea. The stock market will have a tough time keeping its footing around the same time that Medicare looks most shaky. Remember, this is a global event. A gray, wrinkled Japan will no longer be able to supply a third of the world's savings.

Of course, corporate treasurers will come to realize that stockholders need more cash. You can bet then that stocks that can afford to pay higher dividends will be bid up in the market, at the expense of smaller, more adventurous stocks. That could mean less R&D in our economy. The extraordinary twentieth-century high-tech drive from breakthrough to breakthrough may take a nap as the boomers start taking naps in retirement.

When should we worry? Is it time yet to run for the hills, collect canned goods, and stuff dollar bills into our mattresses? The first baby boomers will hit sixty-five around 2010, while the last ones cross the retirement finish line in 2030. One investment bank warns that it is already too late; we have passed the "fail-safe" point in the stock market. Their analysts calculate that the stock market has lagged the baby boomers by about ten years. Therefore, the market is already beginning to feel the sag of the 2010 retirement benchmark. Other researchers urge more patience, including John Shoven of Stanford, who agrees that we will suffer a big fall in stock prices, but probably not until the baby boomers are well into retirement.

Can anything save us from a stock market meltdown? Here are four possible saviors:

1:   *Social Security to the rescue.* If we re-create Social Security so that individuals (or even the government) begin directing payroll deductions into the equity market, instead of just into Treasury bonds, that could provide a whole new source of buying for stocks. Even if older people begin withdrawing their personal equity investments, new inflows from working Americans could offset much of the selling. Not everyone in the country will be old, remember, and the baby boomers will not live forever. By about 2030, the proportion of Americans in retirement will peak and point downward. The Social Security rescue does have a hitch, however. If the program shifts away from buying Treasury bonds and leans toward buying stocks, interest rates could rise, since borrowers would have to offer higher yields in order to get people to buy their bonds. And since the stock market tends to like low interest rates, that could reverse some of the positive impact on equities. There is no free lunch for stocks, then, even when the Social Security Administration is picking up the tab.

2: *The Taxman Cometh.* The current tax system does favor bonds over stocks. When corporations sell bonds, they can deduct the interest payments from corporate taxes, for example. When individuals buy municipal bonds, they do not pay federal taxes on the interest payments. When individuals buy U.S. Treasuries, they do not pay state taxes on the interest payments. Yet the taxman takes a big chunk out of stock dividends and capital gains on equities. If the baby boomers are a big threat to the U.S. stock market because they need cash to pay for housing, vacations, and orthopedic shoes, Congress could overhaul the tax code and at least create a balance between debt and equity, rather than the current tilt toward bonds. Cutting taxes on dividends—or even eliminating the tax on long-term capital gains for stocks purchased after, say, 2010— would allow retirees to stay invested rather than to shove them toward the selling window.

3: *Foreigners Can Buy.* In the 1970s and 1980s a number of books came out denouncing foreign investment in the U.S. economy. First, the Arab oil barons bought up hotels, then the Japanese manufacturing giants gobbled up high-tech firms and golf courses. "America is selling off its crown jewels!" the Cassandras cried. Then, after the 1987 stock market crash and the 1990 recession, everyone wondered when the foreign buyers would return to help bail us out. As baby boomers look to sell their equity shares over the next twenty years, we should hope that young developing countries have created enough wealth to purchase some of those shares. The youthful populations in Latin America and Southeast Asia have suffered in recent years, but have enough time to rebuild their wealth so that they can be partial owners of U.S. companies.

4:   *The Grim Reaper Does Not Make Appointments.* I doubt that baby boomers will want to die broke. How could they plan for it? In Ingmar Bergman's harrowing *The Seventh Seal*, a disillusioned knight returning from the Crusades delays Death by inviting the grim reaper to play chess. But when will the game end? Boomers have lived during a century when doctors and diet have nearly doubled the average life expectancy; when biotech researchers have cured fatal diseases, and when cosmetic surgeons have cut enough extra skin from Hollywood starlets to populate Kansas. *The fear of living too long has replaced the fear of dying too soon.* Therefore, retirees cannot sell off their assets and quickly spend them down. Who knows how much money they will need from age sixty-five to eighty-five, or ninety-five, or one hundred? In 1938 when Kurt Weill and Maxwell Anderson wrote that the "days grow short when you reach September," they did not realize that the fall could last so long. We are a risk-averse people. We would rather die with a few extra dollars rather than break even. Moreover, we do care about our children and take pride in passing along an inheritance to our heirs. About half of the wealth of American families comes from a combination of inherited assets and gifts from one living person to another. Die broke? Neither noble nor likely.

INVESTING IN THE DEMOGRAPHIC HEADSTAND

America already has more golf courses than McDonald's. There are more boomer duffers in goofy, tacky trousers driving golf balls than teenagers in goofy, tacky smocks dunking french fries in boiling oil. Just a few years ago, McDonald's attempted to capture grownup customers by promoting a "grownup" hamburger served with Dijon dressing. Few bit at the opportunity, and McDonald's pulled the ad campaign. Still, almost every firm in the country is trying to figure out how to appeal to a mature audience, after years of neglect. The CBS television network regained momentum in the past few years by targeting more mature audiences with homey programs like "Touched By an Angel." But it would be a mistake to think of grandparents in the traditional Normal Rockwell image— passive, "retiring" grannies in rocking chairs, who get up only to bake bread from scratch. Now she grabs her latte at Starbucks like her younger neighbors. The only difference is she has the luxury of waiting till after the rush hour. The baby boomers will set new standards for energetic retirement.

Grandparents already spend more on toys and playground equipment than young parents aged twenty-four to forty-four. The next generation of grandparents will spend even more. They have grown used to eating in restaurants and flying to resorts. The baby boomers turned restaurant going into a recreational event. Nina and Tim Zagat (born just before the baby boom) started their eponymous restaurant and hotel guide in 1979, around the time that urban boomers inspired the word "yuppie." Before Zagat's, there were authoritative guides written by professional reviewers. But Zagat's shunned professionals in favor of the thousands of New Yorkers who hopped from one bistro to another in the 1980s. Now, each year restaurant fans look for Zagat's annual rankings just as Yankee fans look for last night's box score in the morning newspaper.

Boomers have turned general shopping into a recreational sport. Walk through factory outlet stores or warehouse "clubs" and you will find as many upper-middle-class shoppers as lower-income shoppers, piling their carts high with forty-eight-roll packs of toilet paper. One of Virginia's biggest tourist attractions, rivaling Williamsburg and Arlington Cemetery, is Potomac Mills, a factory outlet with over two hundred stores laid out in nine different but connected "neighborhoods." Busloads of shoppers roll down Interstate 95 from as far away as Canada to spend the weekend at this mecca, filling their suitcases with stuff.

Oldsmobile once ran a catchy advertising campaign with the slogan, "This is not your father's Oldsmobile." Your father is not your father's father. But how can investors take advantage of this?

RETAILING: SERVICE VERSUS PRICE

Electronic and catalog shopping have been galloping for the past decade, with annual revenues probably surpassing $70 billion. That's great for the Internet business, but explains why the retail sector has created virtually no new jobs even in a growing economy. Remember the 1970s, when full-service suburban malls swamped town centers, bringing anchor stores like Macy's throughout the country? They have lost ground both to the technologically proficient catalogs, and the lean, almost staffless Costco Clubs. Not only that, but the product mismatch of those baby-booming 1970s shopping malls looks astounding. A typical regional mall might contain as many as twenty-five shoe sellers, including ten dedicated shoe stores, and four anchor department stores. While such heated competition and overcapacity hold down prices, they also hold down profits. No wonder the ratio of sales revenue/square foot has plummeted from $200 in the 1970s to under $160 today. The overbuilt retail sector will look even worse in the years ahead. After all, retirees are more likely to be "do-it-yourself" shoppers than any other group.

Not all the boomers, though, want to spend their days picking through pallets at warehouses. I suspect that we will see growth in some premium-service retailers. Surely, Nordstrom's has provided a benchmark for department stores. While Borders Books does not offer the quaint and dusty atmosphere that neighborhood bookstores did, they sure provide a classier service and wider selection than the small, understocked chain bookstores that dominated shopping malls in the 1970s and 1980s. Plus they provide some cushy chairs. By stopping at Starbucks, consumers have shown they are willing to make an extra pitstop to fill up, rather than expecting a big warehouse to provide everything. They stop at Starbucks for a personal cup of coffee. What other goods could be personalized and worth a premium price and an extra stop? Bakeries? Gourmet take-out restaurants? A chain of high-class dry cleaners with a tie-in to American Airlines' frequent flyer miles? When I was a young boy, we still had a neighborhood milk truck, diaper truck, and even potato chip delivery service. The tripling of oil prices in 1973, combined with housewives moving into the workforce, killed off those neighborhood services. With remarkably low fuel prices, they could return to serve the retired boomers.

HEALTH CARE

You do not have to be a member of Mensa to figure out that older Americans will require more health care. Investors should focus on *home* health care, though, rather than just throw investment dollars into nursing homes. First of all, sick people naturally prefer to stay in their own environment. Second, the Medicare and Medicaid systems will not be able to sustain rapidly expanding nursing-home care. Today, many middle-class, elderly people give away their assets to family members in order to qualify for Medicaid. This maneuver forces the government to pay the huge monthly bills for nursing homes. Over the next ten years, the federal government's debt explosion will tighten regulations and squeeze the reimbursements to nursing homes. Instead the government will encourage more home-based care, for example, visiting nurses and portable monitoring systems. Eventually, every elderly person will own a computer in order to hook their body up for diagnostic tests, where heart, blood, and urine tests can be conducted at home and diagnosed by lab technicians via the Internet. Investors should stay alert for home-based opportunities, including drug delivery systems such as inhalers to replace injections.

Another factor will spur home-based health care: the rising longevity of men. Because more men will reach elderly status (rather than dying at forty-seven, as did those born early in the century), more married couples will share their retirement years (rather than most women spending their retirement years as widows). When spouses are both alive, they are better able to take care of each other at home. Widows, in contrast, generally find themselves unable to care for themselves when serious illnesses or handicaps strike. The upshot: "There's no place like home" for baby boomers when they are sick; there's no place like a restaurant for boomers when they are healthy.

Investors must pay attention to "miracle drugs" and nutritional supplements (see Chapter 2). For weeks before Pfizer's impotency drug Viagra received FDA approval in 1998, stories about the drug circulated in popular magazines and newspapers. But financial analysts on Wall Street did not anticipate that it would become the biggest sales blockbuster in the history of the drug industry. During the same year Merck introduced an anti-baldness drug and Eli Lilly brought forward a drug that fights thinning bones (osteoporosis) in older women. In each case, the Generation X analysts at investment banks probably underestimated the important of these drugs to boomers. When professionals misjudge something, it is a tremendous opportunity for amateur investors.

When Mark McGwire smacked seventy home runs in 1998, detractors pointed to his routine of taking Creatine, an amino-acid powder, and Androstenidione, a testosterone-producing steroid. Babe Ruth never took such wonder drugs—the only nutritional supplements he would have swallowed were trace elements that mistakenly drifted down onto a head of beer. One of his teammates recalls that Ruth actually cooked a squirrel pie for him! We would not consider eating squirrel today, but Ruth would probably balk at eating yogurts with "active culture" and "added bacteria" to help the immune system. The line between nutritional food and drugs is getting as blurry as yogurt. Orange juice comes with added vitamins and calcium. Celestial Seasonings offers Echinacea herb tea to help ward off colds, as well as "Tension Tamer" tea. And, of course, oat bran has been poured into boxes of cereal in order to reduce the risk of colon cancer. Quite a bit of progress has been made since my mother told me to eat fish because it was "brain food." Even more since the 1800s when Sylvester Graham urged people to try his new-fangled cracker. Retiring boomers like the idea of linking nutritional supplements with their daily diet. Why? First, they have been inundated with studies (sometimes contradictory) over the past twenty years linking diet to longevity. Common sense reinforces this. There are few truly fat people in retirement villages, for example. They either die too soon or are forced to lose weight. Second, boomers have also seen how drugs have frequently replaced the surgeon's scalpel during recent years, whether for cardiac conditions or certain cancers. Surgeons no longer command super-premium salaries (compared to other specialists, for example), as they did twenty years ago. Third, boomers, like just about every kind of person, do not like pain; nutritional foods/supplements give us a "gain without pain."

Many firms are pursuing "nutriceuticals," including Nestle SA, ConAgra, and Kellogg. There will be failures, of course. Campbell Soup abandoned its "Intelligent Quisine" project in 1997 after test marketing nutritional frozen food dinners in Ohio. Testers got healthier, but also got bored of the limited selection. "Best raisin bran I ate in my life," said one participant. Unfortunately, other items also tasted like bran.

I cannot forecast which company will best exploit the fervent desire for tasty treats that also make boomers healthier (perhaps if I'd eaten more fish I could). Who would have guessed that 113 years ago an Atlanta pharmacist would have splashed some coca extract in a soda and called it "Coca-Cola," the "ideal brain tonic." By 1906 this beverage, which originally had traces of cocaine, was known as the "Great National Temperance Drink." Now Coca-Cola knows no national borders. The point of investing is not to guess the future, but to act on new information before the whole world pounces on the idea.

HOUSING

The 1987 stock market crash and the 1990 recession devastated and demoralized the U.S. real estate sector. Homeowners feared that they would be stuck in their homes forever, as home buyers refused to cough up enough money to allow owners to break even. There seemed to be a standoff in which the buyers thought it was the 1930s but the sellers thought it was the 1980s. Around that time two prominent economists, N. Gregory Mankiw (who went on to sign a million-dollar contract to write a textbook) and David N. Weil forecast that as the baby boomers neared retirement, they would bust the housing market for the next twenty-five years by selling their family homes. At the White House we received blistering letters and angry telephone calls from real estate developers, protesting the 1990 recession. In response President Bush proposed a "first-time home buyers" tax credit. But nothing seemed to help until interest rates began to plummet in the mid–1990s, bringing mortgage rates down to the lowest levels since the Kennedy administration. By 1997 and 1998 the housing industry was enjoying a powerful surge, as the unemployment rate fell, incomes rose, and credit looked easy. What happened to the forecast boomer bust?

In the midst of the 1990s housing boom, it is hard to remember the Mankiw-Weil forecast. But there it stands, a warning to anyone who buys a home over the next fifteen years. I take the warning seriously, but think that there are more subtle ways to play the real estate market than just buying a family home in the suburbs. Family homes built in the 1960s through the early 1980s will suffer most, for they do not have the modern features that buyers look for, including large kitchens and bathrooms. Many still suffer from what Realtors call "paneling disease." Nor do they have the electrical systems to support the high-tech equipment that continues to roll out of computer catalogs. As the boomers dump these homes on the market, buyers will not rush in to pick them up. Of course, these homes have already lagged the general market. The only reason to buy a suburban family home these days is because you like a particular house and want to live in it. That ought to be a good enough reason. If you find such a place, hang a sign that says "home sweet home" and forget about a capital gain. That would be a pleasant fortuitous outcome.

Where to make money? I would ignore the middle of the real estate sector and instead follow the top end and the low end, meaning vacation homes and manufactured housing. A large segment of baby boomers will have enough wealth to afford vacation homes. Historically, people aged fifty-five to sixty-five are more likely to buy vacation homes than any other age group. The oldest baby boomers will shift into that age group in just a few years. Vacation businesses would also profit, including companies like Carnival Cruise Lines. At the lower end of the market, makers of manufactured and prefabricated homes look enticing. These homes are between 30–50 percent cheaper than conventional ones (in comparable sizes) and do not induce snickering in the fastest growing geographic regions, the south and the west. While upper-income people associate such homes with the Weather Channel's footage of twisters blowing through Texas trailer parks, manufactured housing has some proven appeal among the less well-off elderly and younger families. I am not suggesting you move in, but you might want to own some stock from a distance. You don't have to like oatmeal to own stock in Quaker.

The recreational vehicle industry has been revved up, too, on the basis of cheap oil prices, low interest rates, and the demographics of the baby boomers. Television shows from MTV's "Road Rules" to Nickelodeon's "Rugrats" have made RVing cool even in the eyes of moody teenagers.

CONCLUSION

We have a confused view of aging. We sometimes find old people wise, other times just wizened. More traditional cultures tend to revere older people. In Israeli buses, over the front seats, are signs "rise for the elderly." In our society, few will admit to being old enough to require a front seat. My grandmother would not tell her neighbors about her sixtieth wedding anniversary because they might deduce that she could not still be sixty-five years old. We cannot yet tell how the baby boomers will act in old age, nor how their children will act toward them. The boomers are the college kids of the 1960s, whom Jerry Rubin told, "Don't trust anyone over thirty-five." (After becoming a yuppie investor, Rubin switched his mantra to "Don't trust anyone under thirty-five.")

The generation that shouted "Hell No! We won't go!" is now repeating the refrain, but this time, aided by drugs and plastic surgeons, they mean they won't *leave*. Nonetheless, as the twenty-first century wears on, their gait will slow, and they will find their address books filled with crossed-out names. They will eventually be the old fogies they derided in their youth. Their aging will be among the most exciting and risky demographic events of the twenty-first century. Will they go on a spending spree and pile up even more debt for their grandchildren? Will they care more about their health or resign themselves to an existential fatalism? Investors, indeed the world, will have to watch to find out. George Burns bragged "I smoke ten to fifteen cigars a day." He seemed to be defying longevity. Then he explained why he smoked, "At my age I have to hold on to something." What will the baby boomers hold to?

2

THE LEANING TOWER OF TECHNOBABBLE

How to Invest in the Internet and Bioscience Revolutions

___

LOS ANGELES, CALIFORNIA

He didn't mind the blood. Of course, if it squirts out, that's another matter. After all, you can't mop your face with slippery rubber gloves. So you call for help.

"Nurse! My forehead, please," barked Dr. Jack Winter, his arms hovering about seven inches above his patient's chest, like a magician's over a rabbit. Hell, he was a magician. He could turn the dying into the reborn, with a slice of a scalpel and a stitch of a vein. He could turn the old into the young, with a nip and a tuck behind the ears. And if you'd ever operated on a heart, you'd know that sawing a lady in half isn't just for Houdinis.

After thirty years under the glaring lights of the operating room, he hadn't lost his touch, his nerves, or his surgeon's license. "Sharp as his scalpel," they said about Jack, first in his class at Cornell. A tall, wavy-haired, blue-eyed god of the OR.

But now he was broke. He had the hands of a master surgeon but the financial finesse of a clod. He ran with a fast crowd, real fast. The Porsche Club of Bel Air. Which meant he had to live in Bel Air. Back in the 1970s, a surgeon could afford Bel Air. That was before TV screenwriters got $1 million retainers for shows that would last two weeks. That was before HMOs stomped on surgeons' fees like a horde of Riverdance freaks. That was before pharmaceutical companies figured out how to save livers, lungs, and kidneys with drugs. He'd get $2,000 for this three-hour surgery, but net only $125 after paying taxes, his nurses, and his alimony. That would have been enough for a week's worth of gas for the Porsche, if he'd been able to keep up with the payments.

As Winter aimed his scalpel for the X on the patient's chest, a buzzer sounded and the lights blinked.

"What the hell?"

"Jack. Sew her back up," said Miles Franklin, the twenty-eight-year-old chief of surgery.

"Why?"

"She didn't sign the disclosure form. And her husband wants her to try drug therapy instead of surgery. Sorry Jack. Maybe she'll be back."

"Not with me, Miles. I hold a grudge."

Newsflash

Tonight, across the world we will see two historic events take place simultaneously, linking high finance with high-flying medicine. They're calling it "pay-per-view medicine." A group of molecular biologists in Sydney, Australia, will unveil over the Internet the human retinas that they have grown in a petri dish, which could be used to cure blindness. For a fee, their investment bankers will allow viewers to access the proprietary formulas which enabled the researchers to grow the retinas. Then the bankers will solicit bids from pharmaceutical companies for the patent rights for the procedure. Louis Pasteur, meet J. P. Morgan . . .

At the time that Hamlet declared about man, "How infinite in faculty! . . . in apprehension how like a god!" mutton-fat soap was considered a bold invention. Eight hundred years later, we get the automatic flushing toilet. How godly we are! Since the 1960s, NASA has spent $200 billion on the space program, and the astronauts come back with Tang, an orange breakfast drink. The Pentagon spends $45 million on a stealth fighter, and the same technology gives us microwavable popcorn. I do not cite these examples to mock scientific progress. I enjoy microwaved popcorn and appreciate toilets, whether they flush automatically or not. I appreciate that stealth fighters help keep us safe, and that penicillin helps keeps us healthy. As investors, though, we should remember that often the most flashy scientific discoveries create profits for those who develop the most mundane uses. Popcorn king Orville Reddenbacker may have earned more profits from the stealth program than the Lockheed Corporation (whose future was teetering until merging with Martin Marietta in 1995). Investors must also remember that new technology often creates financial victims. Where is the Jiffy Pop popcorn that I knew as a child, the kind that you shook over a stove until the kernels popped up the aluminum foil bag to look like a chef's hat? When Frigidaire came along in 1918, men who delivered ice blocks really started shivering.

In this chapter, we will take a close look at two stunning areas of innovation, biotechnology and information technology. Newspapers seem to declare breathtaking discoveries every week, from cloning sheep to ordering New Zealand lamb chops direct from Auckland via the Internet. We will also try to understand the new economic forces at work that push scientists out of the laboratory and onto Wall Street within minutes of their latest discoveries. Investment ideas instantly jump out from new innovations. But are they good or bad ideas? This chapter will spell out rules for investing in bio- and information technologies. In addition, I will suggest the most promising areas for new innovations. Investors must approach technology from both an offensive ("Which stocks should I buy?") and from a defensive posture ("Which of my stocks are vulnerable?"). Too often investors tend to forget that some companies in their stock portfolio will suffer when new technologies come along. (You don't see too many typewriter companies racking up profits these days!)

KING CONSUMER IN THE
SCISSORS ECONOMY

Technology writers feel compelled to refer to Aldous Huxley's 1932 book, *Brave New World*. So here is my reference: Huxley got it wrong. Huxley portrayed a dehumanized utopia, where people no longer suffer from disease, pain, or guilt because modern drugs and psychotherapies rob them of human passion. They feel contentment, but never joy. They sigh, but never wince in agony. While Huxley's supporters might claim victory today by pointing to Prozac, I see the amazing scientific progress mostly liberating individuals and families from both natural and bureaucratic restraints. Until very recently, if "nature" gave a family an autistic child, little could be done. Now, drug and behavioral therapy can open up the world to such a child. Until recently, if your child's school could not afford a good encyclopedia, she would fall behind her peers in the next county. Now, we can choose between a telephone modem that can download the entire *Encyclopedia Britannica* in one hour and a cable modem that can do so in five minutes.

Following Huxley, the economist John Kenneth Galbraith assured the world that consumers no longer had much say in the economy, that they were reduced to mere cogs in the wheels of corporate commerce. Throw away Adam Smith, he suggested, and pick up the GM corporate manual: Buyers must accept what the oligopolists offer, at the price they set. In *The New Industrial State*, Galbraith wrote that a mature corporation has "readily at hand the means for controlling the prices at which it sells as well as those at which it buys." The designs of General Motors "do not reflect the current mode, but are the current mode. The proper shape of an automobile, for most people, will be what the automobile majors decree the current shape to be." To Galbraith, Adam Smith's fantasy of consumer choice belongs with Tinkerbell and Peter Pan.

Galbraith, too, was wrong. Technology has liberated shoppers everywhere. In the late 1980s, airlines lost billions of dollars when computer reservation systems allowed people to compare prices. The Internet allows me to compare the prices of everything from those New Zealand lamb chops to a chateau in Chamonix. People who stroll into automobile showrooms today clutch in their hands the (formerly) secret data, telling them how much the dealer paid for his cars. Hundreds of websites now offer auctions on everything from a 1936 Olympics to vintage Barbie dolls from the 1960s (by January 1999, online auctioneer eBay had eight times the market value of the venerable Sotheby's). The Internet has driven down the cost of buying and selling shares of stock to the price of a coffee and doughnut. And you can get coffee direct from Costa Rica via overnight mail. Marx said, "Workers of the world, unite!" We have quite a different message today: "Shoppers of the world, fragment yourselves!" Consumers now hold the joystick, and it is exceptionally hard for oligopolists to hang on to power. Investors must seek out those firms empowering consumers most.

In Chapter 3 on mutual funds, I will further spell out my view of the "scissors economy," where consumers can clip the middle-man out of almost every transaction. Who needs a travel agent? A stockbroker? An insurance agent? A bookstore? A few years ago, Barnes and Noble sued Amazon.com for false advertising because Amazon claimed to be the "earth's biggest bookstore." But it owned no books and no stores. This is quite a revolution and permits firms to do business with each other at a far lower cost.

Back in 1937 Ronald Coase (later a Nobel Laureate) explained that firms grow bigger and bring more functions in-house because it is expensive to farm out work to others. By the time a firm searches for a subcontractor, negotiates with it, and devotes resources to policing its activity, the firm might as well do the work for itself. But if technology wipes out (or severely cuts) those transaction costs, companies do not need to conglomerate or vertically integrate. For example, Compaq, the world's biggest seller of computers, doesn't manufacture its own computers. This trend has inspired what some call the "*Law of Diminishing Firms*: As transaction costs in the open market approach zero, so does the size of the firm." I wouldn't call the trend a law, but it does strongly suggest less vertical integration. In the old Bell Telephone system, the bureaucracy piled bodies so high that corporate directors were known as "fifth levels" and were discouraged from communicating with those who clung to lower rungs.

The scissors economy not only implies vulnerable middlemen, but also a quick and sweeping pace of change. Old systems depart in a snap, or a snip. Remember how quickly the Berlin Wall tumbled as East Germany realized it couldn't hold back its people from the free information flow that sped across computers and fax machines. To the raucous beat of unstoppable American rock and roll music, Berliners took picks and hammers to the Wall. In the United States, new technologies now chip away at the encrusted monopolies that federal and state governments supported, including telephone and electric utility firms. A company called Starpower recently invaded Washington, D.C., promising low-cost Internet, telephone, and video service, using telephone, cable, and even electrical lines. Their advertising mascot, hung on the sides of city buses, was riveting: A grim Lenin, hovering over the slogan, "No Empire Lasts Forever." Indeed.

WE'VE SEEN IT BEFORE

As impressive as today's technologies are, though, we should remember that the first half of the twentieth century also saw rapid and spectacular gains. When motion pictures first arrived from Edison's studios, one observer commented that it was like watching God write with lightning. Paul Krugman, who retains a healthy skepticism toward the "new economy," points out that the progress between 1917 and 1957 far surpasses the developments between 1957 and 1997. Americans in 1957 managed with black and white televisions, gas ranges with pilot lights, and non-self-cleaning ovens. But Americans in 1917 suffered with iceboxes, without radio, and frequently without running water or electricity. (Krugman does admit his nostalgia for the 1950s might be related to his never-remodeled 1950s-era kitchen.) I might add that I am still waiting for the slick videophone that AT&T promised us at the 1964 World's Fair in New York.

Nonetheless, it makes little sense to waste time comparing two innovative eras. I am happy to applaud both halves of the twentieth century. In medicine the last hundred years have leaped over the prior millennia, allowing researchers and doctors to exploit X-rays,

DNA, CAT-scans, and the tools that allow them to grow living cells outside the body, a necessary condition for developing modern vaccines. For decades after the invention of anesthesia in 1846, almost half of surgery patients died from microbes introduced into patients by surgeons. Doctors had not yet learned about germ theory and handwashing from Louis Pasteur and Joseph Lister. Harvard economic historian David Landes sums things up with a simple anecdote. Nathan Mayer Rothschild, the richest man of his time, died in 1836 of a an infected boil on his back that a nurse today could cure in minutes with a $10 shot of antibiotics. "A horse! A horse! my kingdom for a horse!" Richard III pleads. Forget the horse—my kingdom for a tablet of penicillin . . . amoxicillin . . . Viagra.

ECONOMY LITE

Biology and information technology have lightened the U.S. economy, and we must learn the rules for investing in it. The massive fortunes made by entrepreneurs in the late nineteenth and early twentieth centuries were made from *weighty stuff*: Vanderbilt's heaving locomotives moved Mellon's gleaming steel and Rockefeller's teeming tanks of oil. Bushy-browed labor leader John L. Lewis led his troops out of the coal mines and into the picket lines. Leading Dow Jones stocks including such plodding cyclicals as Bethelem Steel, American Smelting and Refining Co., and National Lead. The names sound as sweaty and muscular as the workers were. Picture the Arm and Hammer logo, with a bulging bicep, gripping a blunt tool.

Now picture Bill Gates and Stephen Spielberg. The word "bicep" doesn't come to mind. But the word "wealth" does. You do not need biceps to flip a Windows CD into your shirt pocket, and yet the program is worth billions of dollars, as is Spielberg's *Jurassic Park* and James Cameron's *Titanic*. More and more, our economy is powered by the very lightest materials. A bottle of Viagra weighs only a few ounces, but packs a wallop for its users, and for the stock of Pfizer. People don't seem to complain that the pills do not weigh much. Nor do users of Merck's baldness drug, Propecia. Patented ideas are worth more than the stuff we used to dig out of the ground. Intellectuals count for more because intellectual property counts for more. In 1964, health, finance, and technology firms together made up less than 8 percent of the S&P 500's market value. Today their value exceeds 40 percent. Even if our GDP weighs less than it did thirty-five (or seventy-five) years ago, it is worth a whole lot more.

Finally, the lighter economy tends to produce less waste. Smokestacks give way to computer-graphic design centers, and e-mails may waste our time, but not our trees, as does regular mail. Until recent decades, most American products were "cooked": smelted, boiled, or vulcanized.

THE SCIENTIFIC MIND

Scientific researchers have developed new technologies by challenging conventional physics and biology. Niels Bohr pointed out that anyone who was not shocked by quantum theory must not have understood it (the theory implies that an electron can act as a wave or as a "hard" object, or that two of them can communicate with each other). So, too, for cloning, DNA research, and in vitro fertilization. Scientists have opened up the "boundaries of both inner and outer space," George Gilder writes, "within the microcosm of the atom, it turned out, and beyond the macrocosm of the galaxies, Newtonian axioms do not apply. Rather than 'solid' matter, the atom turns out to be a quantum kaleidoscope." Twirling prominently in the kaleidoscope today are the Human Genome Project, in which researchers are mapping the eighty thousand human genes within our DNA, and the Internet, in which electrons fly across the sky and through wires, instantaneously bringing us visual, audio, and text data.

Though the heroes of modern science have redefined physics and our physical limits, they themselves are not known to be physically imposing. The 1984 movie *Revenge of the Nerds* depicted high school science and math students as sexless, limp-wristed intellectuals. Around the same time, Arnold Schwarzenegger's *Terminator* and Sylvester Stallone's *Rambo* films attracted young moviegoers.

"Look into the mind of the average high school student," psychologist Abraham Maslow reported, and the "girls will often shudder at the thought of marrying a scientist, as if he were some sort of respectable monster." It seems, though, that almost as soon as *Revenge of the Nerds* was released, techies began taking over the world, with the Apple MacIntosh debuting in 1986 and Bill Gates's Microsoft unveiling its Windows program in 1985. By the 1990s, Stallone and Schwarzenegger characters were keeping on their shirts and even donning spectacles.

While most people cannot understand high technology, Thomas Edison's comment about perspiration accounting for 99 percent of the success formula still seems right. In a recent book called *Medicine's 10 Greatest Discoveries*, two Yale researchers concluded that while they admired the minds of the great discovers, they were "not amazed . . . primarily because we can follow the working of their fine minds. Indeed, we almost believe that were we in their situation, we might have arrived at their discoveries. None of us, though, has any illusion that we could equal the genius of Mozart's music, Shakespeare's dramas, or Newton's laws of physics." No doubt, top scientists have top minds (with the average Ph.D. physicist having an IQ in the 140 range), but hard work is almost always necessary. Of course, some sciences require more laboratory work and empirical study than others. The physicist Leo Szilard reported that after switching to biology he could no longer take a comfortable bath: As a physicist he could lie in the bath and cogitate for hours, but as a biologist he always had to jump out to look up a proven fact. Even high school biology students could empathize.

While good luck also helps, Louis Pasteur argued that chance favors a prepared mind. He launched the study of bacteriology while trying to resolve practical fermentation problems for the French wine industry. Crawford Long, who developed ether as an anesthesia, stumbled upon the idea at a party after injuring himself while tipsy. The chancy aspect of science helps explain why many of the most esteemed scholars have frequently wagered on their beliefs, bringing a machismo dare to science. The renowned physicist Richard Feynman lost a bet that physics in a mirror world would be unchanged. Cosmologist Stephen Hawking lost a bet regarding black holes—the victor won a subscription to *Penthouse*. "Many bottles of the finest champagnes and malt whiskies . . . rest in abeyance while observers struggle to count rare photons from remote galaxies," reported two prominent scientists. It turns out that techies are not, as high school kids thought, driven solely by brainpower, but have their own brand of macho swagger.

INVESTING IN BIOTECHNOLOGY AND MEDICINE

Six years after James Watson and Francis Crick's 1953 discovery of DNA, biologists began contributing to a new periodical, the *Journal of Molecular Biology*. Over the next decades, its pages would contain some of the most startling discoveries and innovations, pointing medical science to new directions. Instead of dwelling on the symptoms of diseases, modern science allows researchers to uncover the root causes, often genetic. As investors, we are often told to invest in the future. But who knows where? If even Richard Feynman and Stephen Hawking lose scientific bets, how can we possibly pick the winners in the biotechnology market?

First of all, remember that, with a diversified portfolio, you do not have to win each bet. In fact, you do not have to win *most* of your biotechnology bets, so long as some of your stocks are big winners. Venture capital firms, for example, assume that the majority of their high-tech investments will strike out, but that some home runs will more than offset the many small failures. In any event, biotechnology should not dominate your total portfolio of holdings.

Here are my rules for increasing your odds of finding those winners:

1. Focus on technologies that will aid *large groups* of people.

2. Stick to research areas where discoveries may come in a *reasonable time frame*, rather than totally speculative bets.

3. Invest only in projects that will be able to patent their processes or inventions, make it *proprietary*, and keep innovating.

4. Don't overlook *replacements* for old medicines and technologies that are losing their potency or market share.

5. Try to anticipate which firms will suffer when new technologies come on line.

By following these rules, you will at least avoid stupid investments, though the search for "wise" investments will remain challenging. The sections ahead will set forth some of the more promising areas, and explain how they fit into the rules.

PUTTING THE RULES TOGETHER

Albinism is a rare condition that can cause great suffering. Nonetheless, because so few people suffer from it, the inventor of a "cure" might achieve great fame, but not great fortune. In contrast, preliminary reports that zinc lozenges could cure the common cold sent hordes of sufferers hurtling into their pharmacies, enriching the owners of Cold-Eeze. The lowest common denominator may not be the way to choose your favorite restaurant or movie, but it is a respectable way to choose your pharmaceutical investments.

AGING

Since everyone ages—and today's baby boomers are fretting about their wrinkles—drugs that ease the fears of older people are promising investments. Based on the booming business of plastic surgeons and anti-aging cosmetics, baby boomers seem intent on stopping the aging process. Yale surgeon Sherwin B. Nuland, author of *How We Die*, has pointed out that it "is one thing to enhance life with a new drug that can prevent osteoporosis, quite another to pursue the erections and hair of yesteryear." Despite his reservations, the search goes on. The cosmetics industry often leads the way, since it faces less onerous government regulation than the pharmaceutical industry. Before a drug can pass from the petri dish to the public, it goes through a process of clinical trials and Food and Drug Administration hearings, a process that usually costs about $500 million and can take up to fifteen years. But flip through a copy of *New Woman* magazine and you will find advertisements for such products as Oil of Olay's "Age Defying Series: Proven to Give You Younger Looking Skin" and Neutrogena's "Anti-Wrinkle Cream" with Retinol (vitamin A). (The magazine title, *New Woman*, recalls me of Joan Rivers's old joke that she had so many facelifts that the doctors made a whole new woman out of her extra skin.) These compounds work better at masking shallow wrinkles than filling in the footprints of deep crows' feet. Nonetheless, cosmetic products have high profit margins and a huge potential audience.

Deeper anti-aging products require deeper science, though. For example, the female hormone estrogen, combined with progesterone, has been used in "hormone replacement therapy" (HRT) to offset menopause symptoms, especially bone loss. HRT also seems to reduce the risk of heart disease, colon cancer, and possibly delay Alzheimer's. Like many potions, the results are not completely positive, and researchers have linked estrogen to breast cancer, for instance.

Beyond fighting menopause symptoms and skin wrinkling, researchers are trying to figure out how to actually stop the aging process. The latest target are "telomeres," the biological counters that tell cells when they should stop dividing. Back in 1961 a biologist named Leonard Hayflick discovered that cell division seems to turn itself off after about fifty divisions (the so-called "Hayflick limit"). With an enzyme called telomerase, researchers have figured out how to turn cell division on and off, opening up the possibility of extending organ life, or even shutting off cancer cells. Cancer activates telomerase so that cancer cells divide without limit, a process called "immortalization." A company called Geron Corp. has patented some telomere processes, though the research is still a lot more speculative than opening up a jar and smearing on an anti-wrinkle cream. We are years away from practical telomere manipulation, even under the best-case scenario. Since anti-aging discoveries would help just about everyone and are patentable, investing in such companies conforms with Rules Number 1 and 3. However, their speculative nature is contrary to Rule Number 2. How to resolve the conflict? Invest only a very modest proportion of your capital in such projects.

Alzheimer's costs the United States about $100 billion per year. President Ronald Reagan's poignant "ride into the sunset" farewell letter in 1994 reminded people how this devastating disease could strike even the heartiest physical specimens. It is worth noting though, that we are seeing Alzheimer's more often than in the past precisely because people are living longer. In 1900, when most people died before reaching sixty, few lived long enough to develop Alzheimer's. Now that more people are headed toward Alzheimer's, a race for the cure is underway. Researchers are fairly optimistic, and so investors should be, too. Alzheimer's triggers in the brain certain proteins and filaments that riddle the brain cell activities. Since cell biologists have identified the genes associated with Alzheimer's, they have a head start in developing new drugs to at least delay the process.

As the effects of aging strike more people, we can expect governments to devote more resources to research and development. This, too, should aid those biotechnology and pharmaceutical firms pursuing cures for diseases such as Alzheimer's. The federal budget for health research and development more than doubled from about $5 billion in 1986 to $12 billion in 1996. Studies have shown that pharmaceutical innovations have both expanded our life spans and raised our lifetime incomes. According to one report, drug innovation not only saves millions of lives, but boosts our lifetime incomes by 0.75–1.0 percent each year. It is no wonder that a man like Jonas Salk became a folk hero after developing the polio vaccine. Just as we associate polio with Franklin Roosevelt, its most famous victim, and with Jonas Salk, we will someday associate Alzheimer's with Ronald Reagan and a Nobel Laureate to be named later. Let's hope sooner.

Is there a risk in too much success in fighting the aging process? The Bible tells us that Methuselah lived nine hundred years, but Gershwin and DuBose Heyward reminded us "it ain't necessarily so." If it became so, immortality would not leave much room—or much need—for heirs. Like a population of Dorian Grays, a nearly immortal race could turn selfish and exploitative, selling our souls for vanity. With smooth skin and a quick gait, only our photos in the attic would tell our age. "How sad it is! I shall grow old and horrible, and dreadful. But this picture will remain always young. If it were only the other way! Yes, there is nothing in the whole world I would not give! I would give my soul for that!," says Dorian, suggesting the Faustian bargain. I suppose the answer is to swallow futuristic anti-aging pills with a grain of salt and to adhere to a strict diet of continuing moral education.

THE BODY SHOP: GROWING ORGANS

Jack tossed magic seeds out of his window and woke up to find a giant beanstalk. His mother was angry. After all, he had traded in the family cow for those seeds. What could a poor, hungry family do with a beanstalk? Suppose, though, that Jack could direct the seeds to grow into any living thing: a cow, a cabbage, a rutabaga. Now *that* would be magic! Welcome to the world of "stem cell" research, in which scientists at Johns Hopkins and the University of Wisconsin have isolated embryo cells that have the capacity to grow into any bodily organ. Usually, these cells commit themselves to a particular organ within days of their "birth"—they become brain, heart, or liver tissue, for example. But researchers have not only figured out how to extend their "limbo" period, but have specifically directed them to form into muscle, neural, and bone cells. Front-page newspaper reports in November 1998 suggested that stem cells could eventually patch up damaged hearts, repair spinal cords, and restore kidney functions. The reports certainly excited the fifty thousand Americans awaiting organ transplants, though their situations are too urgent to wait for new science.

Stem cell researchers have already experimented with transplanting fetal brain cells into victims of Parkinson's disease, which metamorphosed into dopamine-producing neurons, sometimes restoring physical abilities. "We've opened a door, but it's not yet clear you can drive a truck through it," says Dr. Ronald McKay, of the National Institute of Neurological Disorders and Stroke, who led the study. Despite the usual doubts and caveats, a Rhode Island company called CytoTherapeutics is planning similar trials for this exciting technology. As in the case of telomeres, Geron Corp. is funding some of the leading research.

Another fast-growing science is "angiogenesis," which targets blood vessels. By triggering new blood vessel growth around the heart, cardiologists try to stimulate circulation by bypassing clogged arteries. Neurologists are conducting similar experiments for stroke victims. Meanwhile, oncologists are injecting anti-angiogenesis compounds into tumors in order to slow down their proliferation. Over one hundred drug companies are hot on the trail of angiogenesis. The trail is sometimes treacherous, though, for small biotech firms. The stock price of a Maryland company named EntreMed dropped about 50 percent on February 10, 1999, when Bristol-Myers Squibb discontinued joint research on an anticancer, angiogenesis drug. One day later the stock price doubled when the National Cancer Institute announced promising laboratory test results.

In addition to implanting stem cells and manipulating blood vessels, researchers have learned how to grow living skin and cartilage tissue. Doctors long ago began performing skin-grafting operations on burn victims. In the fifth century A.D., Hindu doctors performed rhinoplasty and skin grafts to treat adulterers whose noses were sliced off as punishment. Modern science does much more than cut and sew. In the late 1970s MIT researchers figured out how to grow new skin in a laboratory. Now those researchers have patented a product, under the name Integra, that sounds much more appealing than conventional grafting procedures, which included harvesting skin from pigs and from cadavers. Research is more than skin deep, though, as other scientists have learned how to grow cartilage. Now doctors can form a polymer mold and deposit cartilage cells into them. The cells will multiply until they fill up the mold, at which time the mold gradually dissolves. These techniques offer great promise to burn victims, accident victims, and newborn babies with structural defects.

Is there a downside to these heroic innovations? Not really. I suppose that books about disfigured villains, like the *Phantom of the*

Opera, won't make much sense to future generations. On the other hand, movies like Woody Allen's 1973 *Sleeper* will. In that film, Allen plays the proprietor of the Happy Carrot health food store, who is cryogenically frozen and then defrosted two hundred years later. Disguised as doctors, Allen and Diane Keaton get ready to kidnap all that is left of the Leader—his nose. They sneak into the operating room where a new Leader will be cloned from cells of the nose. Allen nervously bites Keaton's fingernails while urging her to stay calm. Allen then taps the guard on the chest and proclaims with authority: "We're here to see the nose. I understand it's running."

But not running as fast as the biotechnology industry today.

GENOMICS

Just like the bar code on a bag of potato chips, we each will someday have a bar code either under the skin or (for the squeamish) in our wallets that will tell which diseases we are most vulnerable to and which drug treatments would work best on us. With just a few drops of blood, laboratories will be able to lay out our genetic profiles. The swirling, complex double-helix shape of our DNA occasionally gives way to "typographical errors" that suggest a predisposition toward cystic fibrosis, for example. A firm called Affymetrix is developing a "gene chip" system for recording such data. By identifying the root defects, doctors will be able to target the repairs, by turning off, for example, a hypertension gene with a specific drug.

Cell biologists are now using the terms "smart bombs" and "suicide" genes to describe targeted treatments. A drug called Herceptin (developed by San Francisco–based Genetech) gives hope to breast cancer victims who suffer from a faulty gene (specifically called the HER2 gene) and acts like a smart bomb, interrupting only the cancer growth, without the vicious side effects of chemotherapy. A new treatment for brain tumors attaches a "suicide" gene from the herpes virus to cancer cells so that the tumor can be attacked with anti-herpes medicine. These same techniques may someday help counter the AIDS epidemic.

REPLACEMENTS FOR FAILING MEDICINES AND TECHNIQUES

As investors, it is tempting to jump on top of the flashiest biotech breakthrough screaming across the news wires. But there are old battles to be fought, too. In fact, as researchers push forward to reclaim lives from rapacious diseases, some of those microbes are fighting back. Killer microbes that spawn pneumonia, tuberculosis, and gonorrhea have mutated in forms that we cannot kill with old antibiotics. Microbes learn new tricks, apparently communicating with each other, even exchanging genes, according to the Nobel Prize–winning research of Joshua Lederberg. Our doctors may carry smart bombs and smart drugs, but drugs are engaged in hand-to-hand combat with smart bugs. Within a few years of deploying penicillin, almost 15 percent of staphylococcus strains in a London hospital had built up a resistance to the "once and for all" miracle drug, penicillin. By 1950, the frequency jumped to 59 percent in the same hospital. After a series of pharmacological successes in the 1970s, drug companies paid less attention to the pesky but nasty microbes in the 1980s, leaving people more vulnerable in the twenty-first century. And we are especially vulnerable when we stay in hospitals. According to the Center for Disease Control and Prevention, hospital-spawned infections jumped 36 percent between 1980 and 1995, killing about ninety thousand patients each year. Many infection strains seem to laugh in the face of weapons such as amoxicillin, erythromycin, and tetracycline. As people rushed to swallow these medications in the 1970s and 1980s, it gave microbes a better opportunity to assess their makeup and mutate against them. Now we are less well-armed. *Rule Number 4: Those pharmaceutical companies that jump back into the fray to fight the "supermicrobes" will be richly rewarded by the marketplace, and relieved patients.*

WHO WILL LOSE FROM NEW TECHNOLOGIES?

New cardiology drugs have wiped out our fictitious surgeon, Jack Winter. U.S. doctors still perform about 360,000 coronary bypasses. Someday doctors will look back at today's surgical technique as a barbarous relic. To access the heart, surgeons saw open the breastbone and then force open the rib cage with steel tools. The advent of new drugs, angioplasty techniques, and stents (tiny mesh springs that keep arteries open), are providing alternatives to open-heart surgery. In Europe, high-tech companies are experimenting with "closed heart" surgeries using robots that operate with far slimmer tools than a surgeon's comparatively beefy hands. Instead of forcing their arms into the chest cavity, the surgeons manipulate a computer keyboard, turning the patient into a video game where a mis-click of a mouse could be fatal. Ironically, the computer-robot wears rubber gloves, while the surgeon need not.

LOUISVILLE, KENTUCKY

Trouble was coming. When the veterinarian walked down the corridor, Hank Fripps quickly threw a bright red blanket over the back of his sweaty filly, Grove. When the doctor jammed a needle into her buttock, Hank yelped. When he saw the blood start to fill up the big vial, he held tightly to Grove's neck, not so much to comfort her but to prevent himself from fainting. Her huge brown eyes looked at him, not sympathetically but with annoyance. She was ready to run, not to stand around like a lamppost for her squeamish trainer to lean on.

An hour later, Grove burst out of the gate, just behind her toughest competitor, Starry Eyes. Hank watched with one hand on his binoculars, another clutching a small pen in his pocket. Grove kept up with Starry Eyes, and then pulled ahead by a body length. Just before the homestretch, Starry Eyes pulled even and a nose ahead. Then a body length. The others were five yards behind. Hank put down the binoculars and brought out the pen. Aiming it at the horses, he clicked on the top. No one could see what happened next; they only saw the result. Grove's back legs kicked hard and she jumped ahead like a rocket booster had just ignited behind her. She dashed across the finish line, with Starry Eyes and the others sniffing the fog of dust. Hank was proud. The Derby veterinarians would never find the tiny microchip embedded next to her heart, which sent a surge of adrenaline, an electric shock, and a burst of oxygen into her cardiopulmonary system. He was light years ahead of his competitors, and his horse would be a furlong beyond hers.

* * *

In medicine, the tools are often as important as the drugs. The marriage between computers and medicine will last a long time. Though the story of Grove sounds more like a James Bond than Johns Hopkins, we have gotten used to the idea of pacemakers rather quickly. Someday surgeons will leave computer chips in the bodies of patients to monitor the healing process. More daring researchers have actually implanted computer chips into their bodies. A professor at Reading University in England had a surgeon burrow a hole near the muscle of his left bicep and implant a silicon chip that communicated with laboratory computers: "We programmed the building to say 'Hello' when I came in and to tell me how many e-mails I had." Doors opened and closed, and lights turned off and on as he walked around. Though it sounds farfetched and silly, the professor suggested some practical uses, for example, implanting chips in pedophiles, which would warn school officials of their presence. The professor did not say whether he planned to run in the Kentucky Derby.

Rule Number 5: Investors should try to keep track of new drug delivery systems. Because children and adults shudder at the idea of shots, firms like Dura pharmaceuticals and Inhale Therapeutics are developing inhalers to replace needle injections of insulin and other critical agents. Almost 16 million Americans suffer from some form of diabetes. The FDA is now assessing an inhalable flu vaccine called FluMist, and the agency recently approved a narcotic lollipop called Actiq, which cancer patients can lick, in order to ingest a painkiller even more powerful than morphine. Skin patches can transmit hormones like testosterone. Finally, researchers are figuring out how to inject, not people, but fruits with antiviral vaccines. Instead of taking a flu shot, you might be able to munch on an apple or banana. Since bananas can be grown in many of the poorer countries of the developing world, the banana could be a lifesaver. If nothing else, it could justify the fat content of a banana split.

Not only must investors look for the leading companies, they must make sure that the companies keep their lead. In 1996 Johnson & Johnson, for example, held almost 90 percent of the market for coronary stents, which prop open arteries when they are clogged with fat. Two years later, their market share plunged to just 10 percent, as competitors like Guidant Corp. and Boston Scientific unveiled more flexible stents. Health Maintenance Organizations have inadvertently pushed pharmaceutical firms toward investing in new blockbuster drugs, and away from "me-too" medications that merely mimicked the results of existing drugs. By only paying for the cheapest versions of similar drugs, HMOs took the profit out of lazy me-tooism. Instead the drug companies have plowed far more into original research, upping their R&D investments to $21 billion in 1998, from $8.4 billion in 1990.

A BIOTECH FRENZY?

While the laboratory activity is frenzied, investors have been cautious about biotech companies in the past few years. Internet stocks looked more revolutionary and glamorous. Still, there is little doubt that biotech will almost literally remake our lives in the next century. Some of the more highly touted therapies will fail, of course. Quacks will keep quacking, as honest scientists pursue their dreams. If you visit Minneapolis, you might want to visit the Museum of Questionable Medical Devices. There you will find everything from a 1925 "Radium Ore Revigator," which unleashes radioactive ore in your drinking water, to a 1918 prostate gland warmer, advertised to increase virility. Just plug one end into a socket, the other into ... Let's just say that science has moved pretty far along since 1918.

INFORMATION TECHNOLOGY:
YOU GOTTA HAVE A GIMMICK

The titans of yesteryear, Rockefeller, Vanderbilt, and Gould gave their companies no-nonsense names like Standard Oil. Simply named companies selling valuable, useful products: "Buy our oil to run your heater." What would they make of "Yahoo!"? Or "Excite"? They sound like down-market bordellos, not stock market giants that could multiply their stock prices eightfold between 1997 and 1998. As I suggested earlier, the computer/information revolution permits the lightest firms to be the financial heavyweights. They do not move dirt by harnessing horses or tractors, but instead they harness the human mind and spark the interests of consumers. Some call it the "experience" economy, where people buy products because of how it makes them feel, not necessarily about what it does for them. Leisure industries have been exploiting the "experience" concept for a long time. The executives at Vail Resorts no longer talk about skiing, but about the "Vail Experience," which conveys hot cocoa, good music, and shopping as much as it does the slopes. Consider the beverage industry: Surveys have shown that most wine drinkers cannot judge an expensive wine from a cheap one, and blindfolded beer drinkers are as happy with Old Stale Bubbles, as they are with the more popular brands.

When we consider the "experience" aspect of products, we blend the information aspect of a product with its real, practical use. Take the simple T-shirt. During the 1950s, after Marlon Brando's performance in *A Streetcar Named Desire*, wearing a ripped T-shirt gave a man the sense of machismo and daring. In the 1980s, a T-shirt with a horse and polo player gave a man a taste of the upper crust (brought to you by a designer whose original name was Ralph Lifshitz). Is the T-shirt a simple woven dry good, or is it an information product? Rip off the logo and the price drops by 90 percent. That polo player is carrying a lot more than a mallet. Because we often identify ourselves by what we consume and by how we respond to such visual codes, historian Daniel Boorstin coined the term "consumption communities." Instead of saying to a new acquaintance, "I'm also an Eastern Orthodox Virginian," we might say, "I also drive a Volvo and watch 'Good Morning America.'"

Because the economy rests more on intellectual property, there is more room for market value to come from "softer" sources. Doctors refer to newer, more expensive antibiotics as "designer drugs"—particularly when the doctors doubt their efficacy. The key is for new products and new companies to distinguish themselves from their competitors and from commodities. Wall Street rewards those firms that have a proprietary product whose price is not at the mercy of a volatile and vicious market. Sometimes they prove their uniqueness by the performance of their product, sometimes just through gimmicks and advertising. Take the semiconductor chip business. During the mid-1990s, the price of standard DRAM memory chips used in everything from VCR's to personal computers slid like they were skiing at Vail, actually falling by about 90 percent in 1996. Since DRAM chips seemed interchangeable, South Korean manufacturers were hammered and their stock prices plummeted. At the same time, though, Intel, continued to upgrade its unique microprocessing chip, the Pentium. To reinforce the message of uniqueness, computer companies slapped stickers on their video screens saying "Intel inside," further emphasizing that the chips were not a commodity. Intel's stock price more than doubled in 1996, while the South Korean DRAM firms suffered.

BUT YOU NEED MORE THAN A GIMMICK

Just because the sales gimmicks and advertising slogans help revenues, does not mean the products are vaporware, or as useless as the Radium Ore Revigator. Indeed, the computer revolution has been staggering, enabling engineers to build new lifesaving medical equipment and vastly more efficient and safer automobiles. Moore's law, named in 1965 after Intel cofounder Gordon Moore, has correctly forecast that computing power would double every eighteen months. You may have already heard the clichés that the new VW Beetle has more computing power in it than the Apollo rocket that brought Neil Armstrong to the moon; or that computers today are 100,000 times more powerful than those of the late 1950s; or that if automakers had progressed as swiftly as computermakers, a Cadillac would be the size of a matchbox and cost just a few dollars. The latter story has launched a parody defending Detroit by suggesting that if Microsoft ran General Motors, every few weeks you would have to re-install the engine, and every time they repainted the lines on the road, you would have to buy a new car!

Though it is fun to compose parodies and deflate the more starry-eyed techno-hypers who wander around Silicon Valley, we cannot deny that there is an authentic, powerful revolution, especially affecting communications. And it touches all of us outside the Valley. Every time some motorist gets stuck at night on a dark street but with a wireless telephone in the glovebox, that individual bows down to some technology engineer in Schaumburg, Illinois, or Helsinki, Finland (home offices of Motorola and Nokia, respectively). In comparison to the cheap and easy wireless telephone, even the 1980s seem backward, recalling the television show "Green Acres," wherein Eddie Albert had shimmy up to the top of a telephone poll in order to place a call.

New innovations do not come free, though. In fact, many corporations probably lost money in the 1970s and 1980s by switching to computers, or upgrading to new models, too quickly. With word processors, for example, lawyers can rewrite memoranda forever, whereas with typewriters, their secretaries would glare their bosses into submission if they made too many changes. Excessive editing slows down the legal process and costs the clients more. And now that the Internet requires any reputable firm to develop and maintain a website, a paid "webmaster" has been added to the payroll. Because of these initial costs, economists joke that the computer revolution is found everywhere but in the productivity statistics. Federal Reserve Board Chairman Alan Greenspan has surmised that the payoff from technology does not come until ten to twenty years after firms start deploying it. With firms devoting between 25–30 percent of their investment dollars to technology, this is a big gamble.

RULES FOR INVESTORS IN INFORMATION TECHNOLOGY

Once again, we must be modest. Imagine: Even Bill Gates underestimated the Internet in his 1995 book, *The Road Ahead*. If a man with $60 billion and the most powerful software company in the world missed a turn in the road, we better tread carefully. Nonetheless, by understanding some of the economics behind the information economy, we can figure out some pretty helpful investment guidelines. They may not get us that estate in Silicon Valley, but they'll keep us from losing our car to the repo man.

1. Invest only in companies that can charge a premium for their service. It's okay for a firm to distribute its product for free, at first, but eventually it must prove that it is selling something worth a price.

2. Find companies that can tailor their service or product to individual users, but also maintain a wider audience.

3. Look for existing, low-tech firms that can ride the Internet wave without paying huge costs.

FOLLOW COMPANIES THAT CAN DIVIDE AND CONQUER THE CONSUMER

"Every man has his price," goes the expression. As consumers, each of us has a different price we are willing to pay for a product or service. When I am in Russia, I would not pay a single ruble for the Russian language version of *Izvestia*. Cyrillic letters look pretty, but tell me nothing. The English version might entice me to pay 100 rubles. A Russian might feel differently. Companies that can appeal to many different people, but can charge different prices deserve your attention, and maybe your investment dollar. Economists call it "segmenting the market" or taking the "consumer surplus under the demand curve." I watch the financial markets using a product called the Bloomberg, named after founder Michael Bloomberg. You can access Bloomberg's news service on the Internet for free and find out where the Dow Jones average stands. Bloomberg carries advertising on its pages, which gives the company some income. But if you want to follow the prices of the German ten-year bond and compare it to the price of the Danish two-year note, you'll have to pay about $20,000 a year to Bloomberg. Long before the Internet, nontechnology firms have tried to segment the market. Salesmen have long talked about getting new customers started on a ground floor, introductory priced product, and then "taking them up the escalator" to a richer deal (and a bigger sales commission).

Think of the seats at Wrigley Field in Chicago. A field-level seat might cost $25, a mezzanine $20, and if you want to sit with the "bleacher bums" and really enjoy yourself, you only have to pony up $10. Why is segmenting important? Two reasons. First, by being able to charge low prices (without going broke), a firm can attract a bigger potential audience. Then it can try to entice those customers who might be willing to pay premium prices. A student discount at Wrigley could attract college students, who might eventually purchase a season box. Likewise, a software company that sells an expensive video package might be willing to sell a stripped down version at a cheap price, confident that serious users will be willing to pay more, once they have viewed a "demo."

As an investor you must avoid information technology products that cannot charge higher prices, and are stuck with low-priced, unprofitable services. The Internet is crushing the price of information. At no cost I can find out which hotels are best in Paris and how my stock in Brand X is trading. Five years ago my consulting firm was paying about $10,000 per year for a faxed English version of a Japanese newspaper. Now I can read it free every evening. If a firm's information, delivery, or organizing system is not special, it will have to charge at "marginal cost," which means no extra profits. When considering an Internet stock, for example, ask yourself, is anyone paying an extra fee? Look for companies that have something special that others cannot steal or copy. If a competitor can jump into the market easily and start stealing market share, that market is invadeable and you should draw a big question mark over the firm's earnings forecasts. In 1998 a new company called Priceline began a reverse-auction on the Internet for airline seats and hotel rooms. The prospective customer bids a price, and the airline decides whether to accept it. The firm successfully won a patent for the process, giving them some security—if the public likes the concept. Their spokesperson *Star Trek* star William Shatner gave the idea a futuristic gloss, but we do not yet know whether the company will survive the millennium.

BROAD- AND NARROWCASTING

To divide and conquer the consumer, information technology firms figure out how to "narrowcast," that is, tailor their service and target the consumer. For years, mail order companies, credit card companies, and political candidates have targeted their sales pitches, and even their prices, by zip codes. Zip codes gave them a pretty good idea of a family's income, tastes, and spending patterns. Though it sounds somewhat spooky and nosy, the technology has leaped far ahead. Investors should examine those software companies that teach others how to do this. "We can predict that you're straight or gay, whether you like sports, and a hundred other things. You may be a forty-year-old white male, but you may act like a sixteen-year-old Hispanic woman," explained the CEO of Aptex Software, which was a spin-off of a defense contractor.

Presumably, the middle-aged man with teenage tastes would succumb to advertisements aimed at the youth market. Narrowcasting can be expensive, of course. The trick is to develop computer programs that sort through data files cheaply and quickly. A Boston delivery service called Streamline, Inc. uses special software to predict when a customer may be running low on the oatmeal or facial tissues needed to get through the New England winter.

The automobile industry has struggled with narrowcasting ever since Henry Ford said that people could buy their Model Ts in any color they wanted, so long as it was black. General Motors later pounced on the idea of narrowcasting and market segmentation by establishing brands from Chevy (entry level and working class) to Pontiac (aimed at young sportier crowd) to Oldsmobile (middle-class families) to Buick (doctors) to Cadillac (really popular doctors). The Japanese car industry went even further. Mazda nearly drove into bankruptcy court in the early 1990s when it offered buyers one hundred different choices of steering wheels. Information businesses have a huge advantage over automobile companies when it comes to narrowcasting. Mazda actually needed one hundred different dies, plastics, paints, etc., in order to fulfill customer requests. Yahoo's "personalized" business page, for example, spends hardly anything in order to deliver to your computer screen a customized news page based on which industries interest you. And there's no leftover inventory piling up, if it turns out that more viewers want to read about dining rather than about diplomacy. In economic terms, information firms have declining marginal costs, that is, once they pay off the start-up and programming costs, it costs them virtually nothing to send out another e-mail, or produce another CD. Compare that to Mazda, which must actually build a new car out of steel, plastic, and palladium-based catalytic converters in order to sell another sedan.

By figuring out how to "broad"-cast and then narrowcast, firms can rein in the biggest possible number of profitable customers. No goal is tougher nor more lucrative because they are fighting for one of the scarcest commodities: our attention. "Attention is the hard currency of cyberspace," write Thomas Mandel and Gerard Van der Leun, authors of the book *Rules of the Net*. In a society where millions of people are diagnosed with Attention Deficit Disorder, you can understand why Intel chairman Andrew Grove named his book, *Only the Paranoid Survive*. Bombarded with enough data to make a Renaissance man crawl back into the Middle Ages, we are constantly pushed and pulled by gleaming, glaring, and pulsing lights and sounds.

We are not alone, though, as we stumble through this fantasyland. In fact, we usually depend on our coworkers, family, and friends for guidance. This raises yet another crucial point for investors to understand: By converting a broad audience to their service, technology companies can get their hooks into their friends, families, and neighbors. Most of us struggling to keep up with computer technology rely on either experts or aficionados for help, whether it's a professional engineer in our office, or a twelve-year-old whiz kid down the block. Bob Metcalfe, founder of 3Com Corp., gets credit for "Metcalfe's Law," stating that as a firm connects any number (n) of digital devices to its network (n squared), the value to the company increases exponentially. In other words, if you connect more people, you share more information and thereby boost the value of your network tremendously.

While I am not writing this chapter to endorse eponymous "laws," Metcalfe's observation helps explain a confusing phenomenon: Why do so many firms on the Internet give away their products? The segmentation idea explains part of the strategy: Get them hooked for free, then sell them a better version. Metcalfe's Law suggests that the more your product gets around, the more it will be talked about, and the easier new users will find using it. If my friends have downloaded from the Internet an audio program for free and can explain it to me, I can instantly follow their lead, without being intimidated (the technical term for this process is "positive network externalities"; a more conventional term is "find and follow a smart neighbor"). Then, someday, I might actually be willing to pay for a version. With my Sunday newspaper, I often get free samples of detergent, as well as free samples of Internet software. Usually, I use the soap and toss out the software, unless I have heard about it from somebody else. Because it costs virtually nothing to allow people to download free software (low marginal cost), vendors are willing to do it, as a marketing tool. Further, they are eager to find collaborators and alliances among other technology firms that can promote their products.

The signals we get from our friends count quite a bit. Marketing firms employ "cool-hunters" to snoop out future trends in everything from clothing fashions to pop music. Just as our personal alliances make a big difference, so do corporate alliances. Almost every week, we hear about another Internet firm hooking up with a software firm or a conventional media company. In November 1998, America Online announced a stunning $4 billion merger with Netscape Communications, makers of the Internet browsing system. Perhaps the biggest blunder in the Internet's short history was PointCast's decision not to accept an offer to hook up with Rupert Murdoch's media empire. PointCast fell from the highest flyer of 1997 to a sad footnote in a year, a story well told by Ken Auletta in the *New Yorker*. Without a big partner to subsidize its "free" software, PointCast faded away from the forefront.

While we dwell on high-tech firms, we should not forget that their benefits go to low-tech and non-tech companies, too. The rise of on-line booksellers has created a new demand for old books, the "backlist" books that publishing companies cannot afford to promote or publicize. While scrolling through Borders.com's website to learn about Tom Wolfe's novel on Atlanta, you might happen upon a new edition of *Gone With the Wind*. Suddenly, the publishing company sells a copy that it otherwise would not have sold. Therefore, the value of the inventory and copyrights of publishers and record labels goes up. They are "free riders" profiting from technology they had nothing to do with. Because intellectual property does not generally rot or rust, it can often be repackaged and sold again. In 1984 a recording of Mozart packaged in a dull cover that looked like Army duds sold just two thousand copies. Nine years later the same recording appeared with a flashy cover and title and sold fifty thousand copies. Sometimes the old stuff may be more valuable than the new, especially with new methods to distribute it. Years ago while living in Cambridge, Massachusetts, I would fly from Logan Airport and walk past a counter where one could either take a Legal Seafood lobster "to go," or direct a clerk to mail it for you. This morning via the Internet, to paraphrase Groucho Marx, "I bought a lobster in my pajamas . . . " The lobsters have not changed much over the past fifteen years, but it is a whole new profit center for lobster sellers. In 1998 the Boston Consulting Group estimated that retailers sold $13 billion of goods on-line. I do not know how many lobsters were included, but the crustaceans better be worried. In economists' term, they are suffering from the negative network externality of the Internet.

As investors we must hunt for firms and industries that benefit from the Internet without footing the bill. My advice: Ride on a free rider.

KEEPING UP

The lightning fast speed of high technology digital products can only be exceeded by the explosive growth and then collapse of companies in the business, with PointCast providing a good example. The corollary of Andy Warhol's fifteen minutes of fame is "Here today; gone today." Warren Buffett quipped that he would give the following final exam to business school students: "I would take an Internet company and say, 'How much is it worth?' And anybody that gave me an answer I would flunk." While Buffett expresses puzzlement, the stocks take an express trip to the moon. From January 1, 1998, to January 1, 1999, Yahoo jumped 584 percent and Amazon.com 966 percent. I do not think that investors should panic if they have not yet bought shares. There have been plenty of times since the early 1900s to make money buying Ford, GM, or Daimler-Chrysler stock, even if you did not ride with Henry Ford on the Model T. For those investors who feel too squeamish about the ultrahyped digital age to invest their savings, remember this: If the technologies live up to their hype, you will benefit from being a user, even if you are not an investor. Without owning stock in Boeing, you have probably found their aircraft a convenient way to get around. Someday your life may be saved by a new drug you have no financial interest in. You may shop for a Thanksgiving turkey on-line. In a simple example, University of California, Berkeley, professor Brad De Long points out that if he forgets to turn off his four-bulb chandelier while leaving town for a weekend, his dining room will have received as much artificial illumination as an average pre-1850 household did in an entire year (they spent about 5 percent of their incomes on candles, tapers, and matches). You do not have to be receiving dividends from Pacific Gas and Electric to feel good about indoor lighting.

For those who want to jump into the investment fray, this chapter has described some critical guidelines. Of course, it is hard to beat Nicholas Negroponte's advice: Get a kid. A child can act as your personal "cool hunter," snooping around for the latest fashions and computer components. Plus, they will do you the favor of mocking you *before* you have a chance to step, badly dressed, outside the front door.

3

KABOOM!
The Time Bomb That Will Shatter Mutual Funds

SOMERVILLE, MASSACHUSETTS

Shari Maloney wove through the sales lot of the Ford dealer, like a Boston Celtic driving for the basket. A used T-bird almost ran over her black pumps when she paused to look at her wristwatch. Only forty minutes left in her lunch hour to sign the deal and drive her shiny new Mustang off the lot. She'd test driven the BMW 3-series and even a low-end Corvette, but they were too flashy and would strain her finances. If she bought the Corvette, she'd have to cancel cable television to squeeze by the monthly payments.

She trotted into the showroom and nearly pinned Frank Berrill to the wall with her enthusiasm. His Pepsi tipped over onto the brown laminate desk, but he didn't care. Shari's purchase would put him over the monthly quota and earn him an extra two hundred bucks.

"All I need, Miss Maloney, is the down payment and your bank statement to satisfy my credit manager. While we talk, I've got the boys washing and waxing. She's a beaut," he said, wiping away the Pepsi puddle with the sleeve of his pilled sweater.

"Got it right here," she beamed while unlatching her purse and pulling out two sealed envelopes. "Here's the check for $2,000 from my money market account and here's the mutual fund statement. Just came in today's mail."

Berrill took a rusty pocketknife out of his drawer and slid the knife's edge across the envelope. He frowned.

"Something wrong?"

"Check looks fine. But last week when you signed the credit form, you wrote that you had $12,000 in the mutual fund."

"So?"

"This here paper says you only have $4,000. Must've been a bad week. I can't let you drive that Mustang off the lot without boosting your monthly nut. Sorry, Miss Maloney."

Newsflash

The Senate kicked off today the most bitter set of hearings in years, as small-time investors claimed that mutual funds bamboozled them into investments without disclosing that their funds were not insured. The stock prices of mutual funds have been punished as the Federal Reserve Board wrestles with congressional proposals to shut down even the most famous funds in the business.

"I had no idea my money wasn't safe," said Bertha Hanson, one of today's witnesses. "After all, I bought my fund at a bank. The teller even gave me a blender when I opened the account. I signed the form on a desk with a big 'FDIC' plaque on it. Aren't banks insured by the federal government?"

Experts warned that many mutual funds could bleed to death in the next week, as class-action lawyers advise their potential clients to sell now so that they can hop on the bandwagon of lawsuits. . . .

Raise your hand if you have invested money in a mutual fund over the past three years. Congratulations, you are a commoner! Twenty years ago, Chevrolet launched an advertising campaign with the jingle, "Baseball and hot dogs, apple pie and Chevrolet." Over the past ten years, the Fidelity and Vanguard companies have earned the right to use a similar ditty, as the number of mutual fund accounts in the United States leaped from 16 million to about 100 million, almost quadrupling the dollar amount to $4 trillion. Nearly half of households have jumped in the pool, including 80 percent of families earning over $75,000 a year.

Perhaps you have noticed that in lunchrooms and breakfast nooks around the country, Americans are squinting at the stock pages of the newspaper before tackling the sports page. I am pretty confident that our millionaire baseball and basketball stars do the same.

While attracting more eyes, the business section of the newspaper (on-line and paper versions) is getting fatter and longer, as over seven thousand mutual funds fight for our attention with advertisements, compared to just a few hundred in 1970. Stodgy old banks have had a tough time competing. While bank deposits have grown by less than 1 percent each year, mutual fund assets in the 1990s rocketed ahead at a 20 percent annual pace.

This chapter will explain how the mutual funds achieved their explosive growth and what dangers await them in the years ahead. Their rising fees and slumping performance put them at risk in the new "scissors economy," where consumers routinely cut out the middleman. In addition, we will spell out guidelines for avoiding the "kaboom" in mutual funds.

As mutual fund advertisements becomes as common as those of Coca-Cola and McDonald's, they penetrate our psyche and develop into virtual icons, bestowing them a sense of stability and security. "Brand" identity is worth billions of dollars to their share prices. The Franklin Funds portray a portrait of Benjamin Franklin, that great Philadelphian—though the funds are based in San Mateo, California. T. Rowe Price displays a defiant, long-horned ram, though I've not seen any lately in Baltimore, Price's home base. Decades ago, banks and insurance companies learned to use strong, reassuring images. Prudential's "piece of the rock" looked as solid as Gibraltar, and Allstate's "good hands" looked like God Almighty's. Ever wonder why bank offices tended to use Georgian or classical architecture, complete with mighty fluted columns? The buildings looked as safe and secure as, well, a safe. Victorian architecture looked too spindly legged to support a bank. When I was growing up, a local bank tried to buck the trend by actually constructing retail branches that looked like flying saucers, which, at the grand opening, would touch down in strip mall parking lots via helicopter. The image did not inspire confidence, for a bank that could arrive by air could literally fly-by-night—with your money.

Despite their public relations and financial success, mutual funds are not banks and they are not Coca-Cola. You can be pretty sure that a can of Coke will taste like Coke regardless of the stock price. And you can be sure that a bank will return your deposit since it is backed by the federal government. Today's mutual funds may be risky or they may be safe, depending on what investments their managers make and how their clients behave. A mutual fund that purchases highly rated U.S. Treasury bonds is fairly secure, but one that buys stocks in new, untested companies is rickety. Though even the Treasury bond fund could plummet in value if, for example, interest rates shoot up. From January until December 1998, investors in emerging market mutual funds lost about 25 percent of their money, while those who bet on funds that invest in natural resources watched over 20 percent disappear. Even with a strong U.S. economy, real estate mutual funds lost about 15 percent of their capital. The word "mutual" does not by itself guarantee anything. Think of the *Titanic*'s maiden voyage as a mutual vacation. This kind of confusion is treacherous. History buffs might recall that the failure of the Bank of the United States helped launch the Great Depression. Why? People assumed that any bank with that name must be an official government agency. Thus, when it sunk, investors feared that the U.S. government became insolvent. The panic began.

The biggest blowup of recent years came when Nobel Prize–winning economists got mixed up in a dangerous limited partnership called Long-Term Capital Management. Only wealthy people and firms were permitted to invest with this Greenwich, Connecticut, fund, which almost bankrupted Wall Street by recklessly placing enormous bets on thinly traded instruments like Danish mortgages and Russian bonds. The fund borrowed staggering sums of money, twenty-five times its capital, and thereby controlled over a trillion dollars worth of investment positions. In August 1998, their leveraged positions simultaneously cratered, wiping out 90 percent of their capital. In retrospect, mom and pop investors should be thankful they were not invited to jump into the high-flying investment pool.

HOW MUTUAL FUNDS TOOK CONTROL

Mutual funds have made no one wealthier than the founders and owners of the mutual funds themselves. In fact, over the past five years, you would have made more money by directly buying stock in the mutual fund *companies* than entrusting your dollars to funds they manage. While the S&P 500 jumped almost 200 percent in the five years up to July 1998, T. Rowe Price's stock price galloped by over 800 percent, Alliance Capital's by over 400 percent, and Franklin Resources' by over 300 percent. Despite playing on a crowded, bloodthirsty field, their operating margins resemble fat monopolists rather than scrappy warriors. That near-monopolist Intel enjoys a similar 30-plus percent margin as the mutual fund industry. What a good business!

How do they do it? First of all, mutual funds face what economist call "declining marginal costs," meaning that it costs them less and less to manage each additional dollar they gather from investors. They have already paid for their computer screens, buildings, and personnel. When you send in an extra, say, $20,000, they keep around $300 in annual fees, but it won't cost them very much at all to throw your remaining $19,700 into their pool. The Internet has cut their costs even more, since mailing a prospectus is far more expensive than asking a customer to push a button or two. Compare that business model to General Motors, which actually has to build a new car every time a new customer comes along, forcing it to buy more steel, more nuts and bolts. The stock market likes financial and information service businesses where profit percentages fatten each time someone walks in the door, and business owners do not have to buy any new supplies in order to serve them.

The mutual fund industry took advantage of other curves that graced their business plans. Most helpful has been the powerful trend for pension plans to shift from "defined benefit" to "defined contribution." Simply put, old-fashioned "defined benefit" plans promised a certain dollar payment during retirement regardless of inflation, stock market performance, etc. In contrast, "defined contribution" has promised that the employer will kick a certain amount of dollars into investment funds on behalf of an employee; those funds then grow (or shrink) during that employee's working life. These plans, including the 401(k) system, have given employees greater control over their retirement savings, inspiring them to learn much more about the financial markets and about the investment funds that hold their future retirement savings. This is an awesome responsibility, made more complex by the barrage of advertising that workers receive during "open season," those limited weeks during the year when they may switch their 401(k) holdings from one fund to another. The *Washington Post* devotes a weekly column informing federal employees how their investments have performed and dispensing helpful hints. Twenty years ago "open season" referred to duck and deer hunting; now those two words send people running not to their gun closets but to their accountants.

Woody Allen said that 90 percent of success is just showing up. Certainly the mutual funds were in the right place at the right time. They boasted other advantages, as well. For example, mutual fund managers can peek behind those curtains that are closed off to individual investors. If you try to call the chief financial officer of Disney, you will more likely speak to Mickey Mouse than to the actual official. But if Fidelity calls the CFO, they will receive a substantive reply. (Still, the SEC puts strict limits on the kind of information that a company's management can disclose to *any* investor.) If you telephone the chief tobacco analyst at Bear Stearns, he might not return your call. But if Fidelity calls for his view on the tobacco market, he will show up with charts and figures. During my tenure as a managing director of the Tiger hedge fund, I was amazed at how quickly and gladly the Wall Street analysts would leap to our fortieth-story offices to give us their opinions, hoping that we would buy stock through their brokerage divisions.

Since mutual funds are big customers of Wall Street brokers, they may also receive sweetheart deals when companies first sell stock to the public, known as "initial public offerings" (IPO). Say that an IPO stock looks very popular, so that the market will push up the price during the first day of trading. The brokers will give their best customers the right to purchase shares at the opening, letting them quickly pocket a fat trading profit. Here again, you are unlikely to get such a kiss from your broker.

In the last few years, financial firms have tripped over each other trying to merge and acquire money managers and mutual funds. By merging, major players could take advantage of economies of scale and beef up market share. Minor players, in return, pocketed huge capital gains, selling out to the highest bidders. Nonetheless, by consolidating, major players beefed up their market shares, and minor players sold themselves to the highest bidders. Between the spring of 1996 and the spring of 1998, over one hundred deals took place, totaling $11 billion. Zurich bought Scudder Stevens, while the Franklin Templeton Funds bought the Mutual Series Fund Group and its parent, Heine Securities. "No matter what they paid," said one analyst about Franklin Templeton's acquisition, "it's going to pay off in the long run." Unfortunately, the performance of the Mutual Fund Series sagged after the purchase, lagging far behind the S&P 500 as of early December 1998. Investors worried that superstar investor Michael Price, chief executive of the Mutual Fund Series, lost interest in the funds family after the sale. "Price was a wizard, a bargain hunter who reveled both in finding companies that were flat on their backs and in forcing companies to boost value for shareholders by changing management or spinning off businesses," wrote prolific investment columnist James K. Glassman. The wizard gave up his chief executive post in November 1998.

Despite the mergers, the economics of mutual funds sound solid. Marginal costs heading toward zero, special access to market secrets, tens of millions of devoted followers. So why do I hear creaking?

STAR PLAYERS STRAIN MUTUAL FUNDS

Despite the jump in share prices, mutual funds feel the proverbial noose tightening around their necks. Just as Lenin remarked, "When we go to hang the capitalist, he'll sell us the rope," the mutual funds are stringing up each other. To feel the spirit of the battle, take a look at the somber "game faces" of the Kaufman

Fund's co-managers, under their advertising slogan "Tough Guys Finish *First!*" Though each fund fights to carve out a brand image, most fail to engender brand *loyalty* among the customers. The frenzy of advertising and one-upsmanship convinces customers that they should jump from one fund family to another in order to ride the back of the latest winner. In 1996, for example, funds that earned a four- or five-star rating from the Morningstar agency attracted 85 percent of the new money, up from 60 percent in the early 1990s. For one-third of the funds that year, investors actually withdrew more money than the funds took in. Investors have grown more impatient over time. In 1970, investors held on to their mutual funds for over ten years; now the average turnover is about 2.5 years. Why would investors rather switch than wait for a better year? For one thing, star fund managers have gained followings like those of sports heroes. By placing their names and faces so prominently in advertisements, the funds have given those individuals tremendous leverage. They often jump ship when a better offer comes along. And their followers often follow. Imagine a center fielder leaving the Boston Red Sox for the New York Yankees, and Red Sox fans in Southy packing up their bags to move to the Bronx! The Red Sox would have to whitewash all of the billboards, and Wheaties would have to touch up the cereal box. That is the situation mutual funds have created for themselves, disrupting their operations and raising their costs. In 1997, Thomas Marsico, who compiled an impressive record at the Janus Funds, jumped into an alliance with Nationsbank Inc., and quickly had enough investors to launch two new funds, with $2.7 billion under management within a year.

Some superstars jump out of the mutual fund industry completely and launch "hedge" funds (private partnerships limited to wealthy investors), which may pay them 20–25 percent of the return, while allowing them more leeway over the portfolio. Jeffrey Vinik, who managed Fidelity's Magellan fund a few years after Peter Lynch retired, began a hedge fund in 1996 and quickly attracted $1 billion from wealthy investors.

Economists pull out their hair in anguish, wondering "Why don't investors realize that it does not matter who manages the portfolio?" Nobel Laureate William Sharpe has shown that 85–90 percent of a fund's gains have nothing to do with the specific stocks chosen, but are simply a result of a fund's style. "Style" does not refer to whether the portfolio manager wears a cravat, but where she invests your money. Often the style is described by size. *Large-cap* funds generally invest in big companies with market values over $5 billion. These are usually the household names like AT&T and General Electric and generally pay higher dividends than less established stocks. *Mid-cap* funds find companies with market valuations between $1 billion and $5 billion, while *small-cap* funds search for companies valued at under $1 billion. *Sector* funds focus on specific industries like technology, energy, or health care. *Value* fund managers try to spot stocks that are trading sluggishly, and are underappreciated by the market. *Growth* funds are more aggressive, seeking firms with strong earnings and momentum. *International* funds may focus on particular continents, or may diversify by buying stocks from around the world. Sharpe's research showed, though, that you should spend more time picking the style than picking the particular manager. In other words, your international equity fund will rack up a strong gain only in years when other international equity funds do well, regardless of which superstar pulls the levers. This gives us *Rule Number 1 for Mutual Fund investing: Pay attention to style and diversify among styles.* If you need a steady stream of cash to pay your bills, you must lean toward large-cap funds and bond funds.

The star system may also drive managers to take reckless chances with your money. Like an egotistical baseball player swinging for the fences when he should instead try to hit a single to get on base, fund managers often take more risks to generate higher personal bonuses. These twenty-somethings—80 percent were in high school in 1987—do not know how long the gravy train will last. Hence they have an incentive to get paid out sooner rather than later. An academic study with the provocative title "Of Tournaments and Temptations" shows that managers who are performing badly begin swinging for the fences toward the end of the year. Those with strong first quarters will tend to coast. A dishonest manager might even try to manipulate the market for a prized stock at the end of a quarter. Let's say that Joey runs the Crooked Bros.' Small Cap fund and that his fund holds a big stake in the Yuppie Yogurt company. On December 30, Joey might throw all of his free cash at Yuppie Yogurt in order to drive up the price so that the December 31 results show Yuppie Yogurt as a big winner. The trend toward such seasonal attacks and retreats has grown stronger as investors have proved more sensitive to performance rankings. These tactical upshifts and downshifts make sense for Joey's personal career, but does it make sense for his clients? *Rule number 2: Check the volatility of the funds.* How widely do they swing from month to month? Two funds might, at the end of the year, return the same 20 percent, but you would sleep more soundly with the fund that did not nearly drown halfway through the year. Companies like Morningstar routinely calculate volatility ratings.

SALT LAKE CITY, UTAH

A gleaming red logo burst onto Jim Brent's computer screen, followed by a booming baritone that sounded like a throwback to a 1940s radio broadcast:

"Good morning Jim Brent. Are you ready to invest?" announced a cartoon figure dressed in a tuxedo.

"Yeah, I'm ready, all right," the squinty-eyed Brent replied, while standing in front of the television in his boxer shorts and torn T-shirt, looking nothing like Marlon Brando in A Streetcar Named Desire.

"Good, your mutual fund manager awaits your instructions, Jim Brent!"

Brent scratched his shorts and picked up his mutual fund statement. "First I have a question."

"Yes, Jim Brent. I am prepared to transmit your question to your fund manager!"

"All right. How come you're taking 1.5 percent of my money? When I signed up, the fee was only 1 percent."

"Just a moment Jim Brent, while I—"

"Hang on. How come my actively managed fund lost out to the S&P index by 10 percent—again?" he sneered.

"Just a moment Jim Brent, while I—"

Brent was ready to roll and started smiling at the arrogant icon on his computer screen. "How come the price of your company's stock is going to the moon, but the value of my shares in your mutual fund is falling into the toilet?"

The screen started blinking and suddenly the images collapsed into a black hole. A split second later, the tuxedoed twerp was back.

"Good morning! Are you ready to invest Jim Brent?"

Brent sat back in his checkered couch and put his arms behind his head.

"Yeah, I'm ready now."

"Good your mutual fund manager awaits your instructions!" proclaimed the eager voice again.

"Are you listening closely, Mr. Computerized Mutual Fund Manager?"

"Your mutual fund manager awaits your instructions!"

"Good. Take every cent in my account, sell every crappy share in every lousy mutual fund I've got, and send me a check. Today. And send me a receipt with a copy to my lawyer. You thieving bastard!"

The television blinked a few times. "We will transmit, Jim Brent. But our records do not show that you own any shares in a company called 'crappy . . .'"

THE SCISSORS ECONOMY

Comedian Jackie Mason did a riff on Starbucks coffee that reminds me of the mutual fund industry's faults. Mason asked, How would you react if someone came to you with the following business plan: Set up a coffee shop that charges four times the prevailing prices, serve the coffee in a flimsy paper cup, charge hefty fees for a refill, and then have the nerve to post written instructions directing the customer to clean the counter when he is done! On top of that, the shop would provide stools with no back support. Despite Mason's attack, Starbucks has done just fine. But consider this indictment of mutual funds: They charge excessive fees; they don't care much about your tax liability when they decide to sell stocks; and they don't perform any better than you would on your own. Is this a business that deserves extra-large profit margins?

During the 1980s and 1990s, many baby boomers learned to become "do-it-yourselfers" in areas beyond their professional training. I, for one, never imagined I would assemble furniture. After all, the spice rack I constructed in my eighth grade wood-shop class was not sturdy enough to hold up a standard container of Morton's salt. Yet in my twenties I, like most of my neighbors, started screwing together IKEA dressers and drawers, while try-ing to follow the Swedish instructions. When I was in college, my preppie classmates would grab the new L.L. Bean catalogue when it arrived in their mailboxes each season. L.L. Bean had, long before, cut out the middleman, the retail store. But now, on the Internet, L.L.Bean can cut out the post office and downsize its own battalion of telephone operators. In the 1980s and 1990s people have grabbed metaphorical scissors and cut out the middle-man from nearly every part of their lives. Each year travel agents squeal as airlines and cruise lines squeeze their commissions. Toll booth collectors belong in the Smithsonian, as "smart cards" leave them behind in a cloud of exhaust smoke. Even bank tellers are heading for the endangered species list, as virtual banks with no branches, no vault, and no lollypops for kids advertise on the Internet. "We had a big old vault in our old building, but we used to keep stationery in it," reports the chief financial officer of Telebank.

Technology, government deregulation and individual entre-preneurship have put scissors in the hands of consumers, creating the scissors economy. Almost 50 million computers in about 50 mil-lion households put financial research just a click away from investors. Fifty million is about the same as the number of house-holds that own stock. No longer do we have to wait for our local stockbroker to get back from his lunch break in order to buy or sell shares. Direct trading has cut him out of the picture. Even on-line discount brokers can be cut out by purchasing shares directly from corporations. In 1994, the SEC loosened the rules for Direct Purchase Plans (DPP) and Dividend Reinvestment Plans (DRIPS), permitting you to telephone, say, Mattel, in order to buy shares. Not only do you save on commission charges, but you might get a souvenir from the company. The U.S. government has jumped into the act, too, handing scissors to investors who want to purchase bonds. The "Treasury Direct" program lets you telephone the Federal Reserve toll-free and buy bonds, adding a much smaller fee than the .72 percent that many mutual funds would tack on. The minimum amount for buying Treasury bills and notes has dropped from $10,000 to $1,000.

I never imagined I would be trading stocks from my home. Hedge fund manager James Cramer has argued that retiring baby boomers will devote some of their free time to handling their own finances, *without* the help of mutual funds. But why will they bother? Retirees surely would rather visit their grandchildren, play golf, and travel on the Love Boat, than sit in front of a computer screen, wouldn't they? Remember, retirees are physically much younger than they used to be, and their own investments are much more important to them than they were to their fathers and mothers, who enjoyed defined contribution pension plans. Most sixty-five-year-old retirees today feel more active and energetic than they did as sixty-four-year-old workers. Moreover, they have a greater stake in managing their financial resources. Managing your money does not take all day, unless you are trying to beat the market as a daily trader. By redirecting a few television hours to their investments, retirees will still find plenty of time hit the links or the tennis courts.

MUTUAL FUNDS LAG THE MARKET

Mutual funds could avoid being snipped by the scissors economy if they could prove that they are worthy middlemen. After all, we still go to restaurants, even though we could eat at home. Remember Smith Barney's television commercials with the haughty and professorial John Houseman grunting, "We make money the old-fashioned way. We *earn* it." The mutual funds have a tough case to make. William Sharpe and Burton Malkiel (in his best-selling book *A Random Walk Down Wall Street*) have shown that mutual funds will generally fail to beat the market when they try to pick stocks or pick the "right time" to enter or exit the market. Since 1992, only 30 percent of mutual funds have surpassed the S&P 500 index (since 1995, less than 10 percent have). And it is almost impossible to guess which 30 percent will succeed in the future. Studies have demonstrated that while terrible funds have a somewhat greater than even chance of remaining bad, "great" funds have only a fifty-fifty chance of remaining great. Over the past twenty-four years, the average equity fund returned about 11.6 percent, compared to 13.1 percent for the S&P 500. That difference looks modest, but turns out to be staggering. A 1.5 percent shortfall means that $10,000 grows to $155,500 in a stock-picking fund, but $217,100 in a simple index fund.

That's why I recommended index funds in my 1995 book, *From Here to Economy*. I was not alone in that advice, of course, as the Vanguard Index 500 fund collected about $8 billion in 1997, followed by the Schwab 1000 Fund and T. Rowe Price's Equity Index Fund. These tidal waves into index funds pushed up the relative stock prices of large companies represented in the indices. That helps explain why the big stocks that compose the S&P 500 outperformed the small stocks for the past few years, even though prior academic studies had discovered that small-cap stocks usually beat their bigger brethren. Because small differences expand dramatically over time, you should heed *Rule Number 3: Pay attention to fees, for they may make the difference between a good mutual fund performance and a bad one.* Take a look at a fund's expense ratio, which pays for overhead and salaries. Few funds can justify extraordinary expenses.

"Wait a minute, Buchholz. If investors are plowing dollars into index funds that are managed by mutual funds, why is that a bad sign for mutual fund companies?" Because the index funds charge much lower fees. A fund can charge about 1.5 percent for an actively managed portfolio, but the highly competitive index arena has squeezed fees down to less than .50 percent. It is a commodity. There is no reason to pay a higher fee than the lowest credible bid, any more than you should pay a big premium for Farmer Joe's eggs. You can applaud John Bogle, Sr., the now-retired chairman of Vanguard, for establishing the low fee structure when he launched his pathbreaking index fund in 1976. Bogle boasts that he is personally a tightwad, which redounds to the benefit of his customers.

While most of us would luxuriate in a trip to New York's Plaza hotel, paid for by an expense account, Bogle takes a different tack. When the clerk suggests an "economy" single for $250, Bogle counters by requesting a windowless former broom closet for $89. Bogle freely admits that the industry cannot justify a high fee for an index service that could be performed by a trained, albeit well-organized, seal. As the bidding war for index fund dollars squeezes fees, mutual funds try to recoup by jacking up fees for their actively managed products. Fees for equity funds are almost 20 percent higher than they were ten years ago; while bond fund fees have climbed a little over 10 percent. This, in an era when consumers have seen technology-based industries slashing prices while still boosting performance.

While people used to see mutual funds as heroes, they now see disappointing service, says Don Phillips, president of Morningstar: "I think the fund industry is too busy counting its money to hear what the public is saying." Mutual funds suffer from other flaws that help explain their substandard history, and some of those flaws are quite dangerous. For example, as more money comes in the door from investors, most funds are forced to buy more stocks. They cannot refrain from buying; they cannot hold much cash (unless they advertise themselves as money market funds); and they cannot sell stocks short, even if they believe that stock prices will fall. Remember, Jeff Vinik left Fidelity because in 1996 he committed the sin of buying Treasury bonds on behalf of a stock fund. The press portrayed his portfolio decision as "cheating" investors—they put money in the fund to buy stocks, not bonds. This one-way directive is like a robot without an off switch continuing to throw logs on a blazing fire. Precious metals funds must buy precious metals even when commodity prices are dropping, which explains the 45 percent plummet in the share value of Fidelity's Precious Metals and Materials fund in 1997.

In addition to the one-way robot problem, mutual funds find it even harder to beat the market as they grow larger. Why? They become the market. Fidelity, with its $360 billion (and rising!) portfolio often accounts for 10–20 percent of the trading on the New York Stock Exchange. It is like Siamese twins racing to the top of the stairs. You will need super fast film to detect which one wins the photo finish.

Larger funds face another hurdle: They can no longer hunt for neglected small stocks that fly below the radar detectors of other analysts. Buying a promising small stock would have virtually no impact on the annual performance of a large fund. Can't the fund buy a whole lot of shares in SmallCap Inc. so that the stock's performance becomes more important to the fund's portfolio? No, because if the fund buys many shares, it will drive up SmallCap Inc.'s share price, immediately wiping out the bargain. Moreover, bigger funds need to stay in large liquid stocks, just in case their shareholders start withdrawing money. That pushes major funds into buying stocks of companies with market values over $500 million. Big funds will more likely own Microsoft than the ten emerging companies that may depose Microsoft in ten years. The successful mutual fund Safeco Growth provides a neat example of how the size of the fund impacts the size of the stocks in the portfolio. Safeco grew from about $200 million in 1996 to $640 million in 1997 to $1.7 billion in May 1998. As the fund expanded, small-cap stocks got pushed out, from 90 percent of the portfolio in September 1997 to about 50 percent a year later. The point is not to predict that Safeco's performance will suffer, but to show that larger funds face more hurdles. For these reasons, John C. Bogle, Jr., son of the Vanguard founder, argues that funds should close themselves to new investors after they have taken in about $1 billion. In a speech he jokingly called "Don't Buy My Fund," Bogle recommended a more "truthful" version of the Securities and Exchange Commission's boilerplate disclaimer: "The performance cited represents past performance which undoubtedly will *not* be repeated if we are as successful selling this fund as we hope to be."

But wait, there is more discouraging news. Unlike individuals, who answer only to themselves and their spouses, mutual fund managers often feel like the twisted rope in a tug-of-war between their bosses, pension trustees, 401(k) plan sponsors, the shareholders of the fund, and the investors in the fund. For example, the marketing department will corral fund managers into sales meetings and into television studios to help sell the "product," which distracts them from their research. As I stated earlier, the focus on quarterly statements and end-of-year results often pushes a fund manager into buying or selling particular stocks for no other reason than to dress up the portfolio's appearance. For example, at the end of a rough quarter, a fund manager will find it easier to explain his performance if his portfolio is chockfull of popular stocks and shorn of less noted ones. Therefore, he may buy those popular stocks at the end of the quarter, even if they are "expensive," that is, their prices have already rallied to their potential. This is like the risk-averse financial officer who pays a premium to retain a big accounting group, even if a less prestigious firm could have performed a better job for less. (They used to say that no one ever got fired for buying IBM computers or IBM stock, until both hit the skids in the late 1980s, only to bounce back again.)

These seasonal pressures created the "January effect," named by Wall Street analysts who noticed that stocks would frequently rally in January, after portfolio managers dumped their dogs in December. But in recent years, the January effect has slipped back to December, then to Thanksgiving, as managers sought to coast through the final quarter of the calendar year. By 2000, Wall Street's January effect will retreat all the way back to Yom Kippur, a fitting symbol for the Jewish day of atonement (which usually falls in September or October).

Mutual funds employ other methods to dress up their performances. For example, they will simply discontinue a fund with a fetid performance so that the fund does not weigh down the overall performance of the family. It is like slaughtering the black sheep of the family. Using another trick, a family may merge two funds together, but keep only the name of the successful fund, again erasing the history of the failure. This trick trips up investors because it mixes up styles. Heartland's Value Fund recently absorbed the company's Small Cap Contrarian Fund, bringing total assets to $1.7 billion. Did the Small Cap Contrarian investors know that they were pouring money into a value fund? Robertson Stephens's Partners Fund, which invests in small U.S. firms, recently swallowed up its Developing Countries fund. Did investors in Developing Countries figure they would end up with American small-cap stocks?

Sometimes the calendar gives funds some room to redress their bad performances. Mutual funds rejoiced at the start of 1998 because they could drop the dismal 1987 performance from their ten-year averages. These changes give us *Rule Number 4: Do some homework to make sure the mutual fund is not being revamped or repackaged in a way that changes its style or invalidates its past performance.*

"Hopping on the bandwagon" is a familiar phrase to laypeople. "Momentum trading" is the financial translation, which many mutual funds seem to encourage. Unfortunately, momentum investing does not work very well, except in the case of small, neglected stocks finally catching the spotlight. The great economist John Maynard Keynes sometimes argued for momentum trading through an analogy to a kind of beauty contest. In the pageant, "the competitors have to pick out the six prettiest faces from a hundred photographs, the prize being awarded to the competitor whose choice most nearly corresponds to the average preferences of the competitors as a whole; so each competitor has to pick not those faces which he himself finds prettiest, but those which he thinks likeliest to catch the fancy of the other competitors, all of whom are looking at the problem from the same point of view." In sum, the fundamental value of the stock does not matter much; instead you should try to choose the stock that would most attract others.

The first time I mentioned Keynes's idea to legendary investor Julian Robertson, he bristled with contempt. Robertson's approach, which helped him rack up a stunning record in the 1980s and 1990s, was to find those companies that others did *not* see value in, but which had the best management and the best prospects for future growth. He would rather buck the trend and let the public finally come around to his point of view. Judging by his outstanding record, they usually did. (Of course, Keynes had an impressive investing record, himself, and from time to time had to use offices at King's College, Cambridge, to store commodities in which he speculated.)

Finally, I should note that mutual funds confound an individual's tax planning. The new capital gains tax rates legislated in 1997 allow even top earners to pay just a 20 percent tax rate, provided they have held the stock shares for twelve months or more. If you sell the stock sooner, you will pay ordinary income tax rates, as high as 39.6 percent. Unfortunately, your mutual fund does not know or care very much how sensitive you might be to paying these capital gains taxes. While most individual investors would rather hold on and let their investment build up tax-free until the last moment, mutual funds prefer to lock in the gain and sell, triggering taxes sooner. In the past twenty years, managers must have swallowed steroid pills because they have grown more aggressive and more focused on shorter-term trading. Consider: In the 1960s, managers annually turned over about 40 percent of the stocks in their portfolios. Now the average is twice that, permitting IRS tax collectors to take a bigger bite of the winnings. "I'm proud to be paying taxes to the United States of America. The only thing is, I could be just as proud for half the money," said entertainer Arthur Godfrey.

Capital gains taxes are unusual because *you* decide when to pay them. By turning over that decision to a fund manager, you may be giving up a bit more than your freedom. Even if you reinvest all of the dividends and capital gains, you will have to pay taxes. *Rule Number 5: Beware of a tax trap, where funds turn over their portfolio rapidly, generating ever higher taxes for you to pay.*

ALL HOPE IS NOT LOST

I have delivered a rather damning indictment. Mutual funds charge too much, trade too much, manipulate too much, and add to your tax bill too much. Is there anything good to say? First of all, I have no argument with low-priced index funds. I will gladly confess to using them and recommending them to others. Competition has squeezed their fees downward, which works out nicely for their customers. Even actively managed funds do have some advantages over individual investors, which would make them worthwhile, if their fees dropped significantly. As I mentioned earlier in this chapter, you and I have a difficult time telephoning top CFOs or accessing the regular conference calls that CFOs have with Wall Street analysts. Big mutual funds might not have inside information, but they tend to hear public information as it is divulged and can therefore react sooner. Furthermore, they can better judge and possibly anticipate earnings "surprises" than most of us can. How do they anticipate surprises? Sounds like an oxymoron, no? Wall Street hums with "whisper" numbers, the soft-spoken unofficial estimates that analysts and company employees are contemplating in the days prior to an official quarterly earnings announcement. They are generally not printed. Unless you are listening closely (or vigilantly tracking Internet sites), you probably will not hear the murmuring. In my experience, these two advantages are worth a little something, but not the typical equity fund's 1.5 percent fee. If they were worth a lot, then mutual fund returns would be leaving index funds in the dust, rather than sucking up their exhaust fumes.

What about stock funds run by superstars? Can I easily dismiss Warren Buffett, as a man who simply got lucky for decades? What if Buffett decided to open a mutual fund? Would he not deserve an extra fee? Tough questions. Just as Laurence Olivier played Hamlet better than Mel Gibson, I would admit that every so often a truly gifted investor comes along. The problem is, you cannot predict in advance who that person is, and by the time you gain confidence in their genius, their fees or premiums have grown too high. A huge burden of proof rests on the shoulders of anyone suspected of investing genius. Being a gifted investor demands possession of many disparate qualities, just as Keynes prescribed for a great economist: "He must be mathematician, historian, statesman, philosopher. . . . He must study the present in light of the past for the purposes of the future . . . as aloof and incorruptible as an artist, yet sometimes as near the earth as a politician."

I have a cheapskate friend who orders a trial subscription to *Barron's* each year just to get his hands on the investor's roundtable, where some of the reigning princes of Wall Street reveal their best stock picks. Since *Barron's* is published over the weekend, their advice often moves the market on the next Monday. But not for long. A study of twenty-three years of roundtable predictions showed that my friend is wasting his time: The recommended stocks do not perform any better than those chosen at random.

A joke describes Albert Einstein at the pearly gates of heaven. Another man appears, and Einstein asks his IQ. The man replies, "180." "Wunderbar!," says Einstein. "We can discuss quantum theory and string theory." Another man enters, stating his IQ as 150. "Good," says Einstein, "we can debate world peace and the UN." Another man shows up, admitting to an IQ of 85. "Really!" says Einstein. "What's your forecast for the Dow this year?" Brain power alone does not yield high returns, although an intriguing study suggested that the average SAT scores of a manager's undergraduate institution may have a slight bearing. Why would this be true, since other studies show that IQ is not a reliable indicator? Perhaps graduates of better schools are better networked to hear whisper numbers. Perhaps graduates of better schools are better organized or are hired by better run businesses. They apparently churn stocks less often than competitors with less illustrious backgrounds. Ironically, though, this standard would not have predicted the spectacular records of Warren Buffett (University of Nebraska) and Peter Lynch (Boston College). Jealous colleagues would happily turn in their Yale SAT scores for Buffett and Lynch's undergraduate educations and the fortunes they have brought them.

MINSK, RUSSIA

He remembered when his Leninist teachers told him that communism's problem was sixty years of bad weather. Boris Bensky could chuckle at those memories. Now his wizened but not wise teachers peddled apples in the street. He was a peddler, too, but a retired peddler with smooth skin at the age of thirty. While they lugged boxes of fruit, he had peddled something better than apples. Yes, smuggling a single stockpile of plutonium out of the country, down to the Ukraine and through the Black Sea would pretty much pay his bills for the next, say . . . ten thousand years!

Retirement can be boring, though, even for a Russian with $8 billion U.S. He loved the arts and even donated $50,000 to the Minsk symphony so that he could strut in his new Armani tuxedo, but he liked to live minute to minute, not one opus at a time. That's why he traded mutual funds—aggressively. Why not be aggressive? Just as he'd smuggled out

the plutonium, he squirreled his assets away in safe U.S. dollars. He fig-
ured the Russian ruble could only sink over time. Even if he lost 75 per-
cent of his money, he'd still have over $2 billion, which was probably more
than the Russian government. Besides, he grabbed his fortune by going on
the offensive. Why suddenly turn into some slowpoke Beardstown lady!

Staring at his computer screen, he got tired of watching the Semper Fi
Growth Fund, managed in Boston, bounce around with just a 10 percent
gain. After all, he'd given it two weeks to show some upward momentum.
Enough was enough! He would punish them. Boris's finger didn't even
shake when he pushed sell. Nor did it flinch when he pushed the numerals
4,000,000,000 and 00 cents. Mark McKennan did flinch. His freshly
printed Harvard MBA hanging behind him, Mark had never seen a sell
order for $4 billion flash across his screen—and he was in charge of the
trading desk for Semper Fi's Growth Fund. How could a $4 billion "sell"
come in at once? Mark tore the headphones off his flushed face and ran
down the hallway to the president's office. If he sold $4 billion of Semper
Fi's small- and medium-cap holdings, he'd set off an earthquake in Silicon
Valley. Just before rushing into the president's office, he ducked into a cor-
ner and pulled out his cellular phone. He rang his wife at home. "Honey,
quick—run to the laptop—and sell everything but Dreamworks." He fig-
ured that after the market crashed, Spielberg would make a terrifying
movie.

WHENCE THE KABOOM?

Over the next few years as more people realize that they can
take care of themselves, or that low-cost index funds can take care
of them, many mutual funds will be wiped out of business. In 1998,
pinched profits and a turbulent market drove almost three hundred stock funds out of business. Investment manager Martin
Zweig has talked of selling his fund company, as has Nicholas-
Applegate Capital Management of San Diego. Just as we have seen
consolidation in banking (whatever happened to the local Bailey
Building and Loan from *It's a Wonderful Life*?), hardware stores,
pizza parlors, and coffee shops, we will see ever fiercer competition among mutual funds. At some point, it simply does not make
sense to stay in business if you have to manage stocks at a .30 per-

cent fee, instead of today's 1.5 percent. Note that consolidation will not mean higher, oligopolistic pricing, anymore than Home Depot has pushed up hardware prices (quite the opposite). But it will mean Going Out of Business/Lost Our Lease signs in front on many mutual fund storefronts. Not a comforting thought. And if you have invested in a fund that has shut down, your mailman will show up with not just a refund, but your share of any capital gains taxes the fund incurred while selling off its holdings.

On top of the profit squeeze will come periodic, possibly frantic, withdrawals from investors who worry about the viability of particular mutual fund companies. Would you place an order for lumber from a hardware store that may be closing down? Probably not. For the same reason, many mutual fund investors will take back their money, until they are sure which funds will survive. This is a hot and spicy soup to swim in.

"There you go again, Buchholz. But savers did not panic and withdraw their funds when banks consolidated in the 1980s and 1990s," an optimist might reply. Two responses. First, their savings were insured by the federal government. Second, many S&L savers did, in fact, line up to take back their funds in the 1980s, even with government insurance. One more factor adds a touch of Tabasco sauce. Foreign investors in our mutual funds can confound the funds, as well as U.S. regulators. Our hypothetical Boris Bensky was not involved in the U.S. banking industry ten years ago. Moreover, he could not instantaneously withdraw huge sums via the Internet. Let's face it, today you are investing side by side with Boris. I do not mean that as an anti-Russian slur, but we can't escape the fact that his financial priorities are a bit different from, and a lot more volatile than, the Dilbert in the next cubicle, who is in your 401(k) pool.

Rules for Avoiding the "Kaboom" while Still Taking Advantage of Mutual Funds

1. Diversify not only among fund companies, but also among *styles*. Recall William Sharpe's discovery that 85–90 percent of a fund's performance is determined by its style (big-cap,

small-cap, international, etc.). You are *not* diversified if you invest in six big-cap stock funds run by six different companies.

2. Check the volatility of funds. Those that have historically returned high annual returns, without wild swings from quarter to quarter, will allow you to sleep better.

3. Pay attention to fees. Funds that already charge low fees are in a position to survive a wickedly competitive battle. In fact, they may spark the fight. Furthermore, low fees will probably make a bigger difference in your financial success than trying to figure out the IQ of money managers.

4. Before you send in your check to the mutual fund, make a telephone call to assure that the portfolio manager has not flown the coop and that the fund's mission has not been redirected because of mergers or bad performance. Why throw money into a turbulent institution? The stock market brings enough of its own storm clouds.

5. Don't ignore your income-tax burden, because your fund probably will. Owning some tax-free bonds will shelter at least some of your unearned income, even if your equity mutual fund generates capital gains. Stay away from funds that trade more often than the average. They push up your tax bill, and push down your portfolio's performance.

6. If you can afford to take some risks, don't forget high yield ("junk") bond funds, as well as foreign bond funds that buy from major, liquid countries (mostly the G7).

Five Rules for Investing in Individual Stocks, If You Avoid Mutual Funds

1. Look for companies with strong management in businesses that can earn profits, even when the economy slows.

2. Look for companies that sell products and services with some competitive edge, a brand name or proprietary product that

permits them to raise prices. Commodity businesses will almost always feel pricing competition.

3. Don't trade too often. The stocks you sell have a greater chance of bringing you profits than the stocks you buy instead, especially when you consider commissions and capital gains taxes. A recent study of individual stock traders found that women tended to outperform men—not because they chose better stocks, but because they showed more patience and did not chew up their investment dollars on commissions and by dumping stocks too soon.

4. Hold some cash, and don't let brokers bully you into buying. Two-thirds of their recommendations are "buys," and only 1 percent of the time do they outright urge you to sell.

5. Spin-offs sometimes offer great opportunities, but are often too small for funds to buy. When AT&T spun off Lucent Technologies and TCI spun off Liberty Media, few funds expected the stock prices of the spinoffs to multiply so many times, leaving their parents behind.

CONCLUSION

Whenever some neophyte actress gets burned for the first time by a Hollywood studio, her friends remind her, "That's why they call it show *business*." As stable as the Prudential Rock and as hopeful as the Fidelity sunrise, you should not forget that your friendly "family" of mutual funds is driven not by familial love but by an aggressive sales force looking for their annual bonus. Nothing wrong with that. Adam Smith pointed out about 225 years ago that the butcher does not carve a flank steak for you because he likes your smile. Nay, it is his self-interest that keeps the blade a'chopping.

Only you know your own self-interest. If you are a terribly disorganized, undisciplined person, then please find some solid mutual funds. They will send you a regular, well-displayed report. And if you misplace it under last night's dinner dishes, they will send you another. If you are a careful, disciplined individual who likes to spend some time deciding on investments, you can wean yourself of mutual funds, if you please. I suspect that you will.

Will Rogers once said that he was more concerned about the return *of* his money than the return *on* his money. The "Kaboom!" for mutual funds will threaten both. Be vigilant. The Prudential rock may look awfully solid, but is that the rock you want to tie yourself to? A rock can be a deadly weapon or a protective shield. You might recall from a literature class Prometheus's fate. He was bound to a rock while eagles pecked at his liver.

Prometheus should have gotten out of the market while things were going well.

4

RED, WHITE, AND BLACK, YELLOW, AND BROWN

A Darker America Demands a Darker Portfolio

SAN FRANCISCO, CALIFORNIA

Cindy Lu's room was too still. Hunched over her computer, the sixteen-year-old needed just a few more seconds of silence. She couldn't afford any missteps. She tossed her long black hair over her shoulder and looked behind her back at the rusty door handle, just to make sure no one was watching. How could she live another month in the cramped apartment, with aunts and uncles barging in each night, snatching food from the fridge and sucking all the oxygen out of the stuffy place. The smell of dried fish, once a homey aroma, was now a stench to her. She looked out the window, crusty with chipping caulk, and wondered whether she could get to Oakland tonight. Would Shawn be alone tonight?

The sound of the slamming door drove a surge of electricity through her spinal column. As she fumbled to find the delete key, her mother's chapped hands swooped down and snatched the laptop from her shaking hands.

"Disgusting!" her mother sneered at the photo of the black teen whose gleaming smile flashed on the laptop screen. "Is this that Shawn who *called you?" She pronounced his name by twisting her mouth into a spitting position.*

"Mother—"

"Don't speak! Do you want to go to Stanford? Or do you want to move to Oakland and live in the shadow of a bridge for the rest of your life?" Her mother's graying eyebrows arched up to her hairline, like seagulls flying off into the horizon.

"Mother—"

"Don't speak! Don't you dare speak until you have woken up at five A.M. like your father and me so that we could save money for your college. Don't you dare speak until your hands are bleeding when you get to the subway to come home from work."

"Mother—"

"Don't speak! Your cousin Amy just got a letter inviting her to study at Stanford. I told you last week that the dean of Berkeley had called her, too. No one has called us. No one but this . . . person," she said as she threw the computer onto the cot. The image of Shawn shook and then faded into the pixels.

Cindy jumped onto the cot and caressed the computer, trying to bring back the face of a secret friend. She wiped a tear off the screen. She couldn't compete with her cousin, she couldn't rinse off the guilt that her parents poured on her each night, and she couldn't wait to leave the narrow, dingy room that seemed so much scarier than the dark night of Oakland.

ARLINGTON, VIRGINIA

Cyril Cole led a double life. Always darting around. Couldn't tie him down. Couldn't fence him in. An unbridled electron. He was hungry. Not that kind of hungry—his stomach was full, as he tossed burritos down his throat while racing his T-Bird from meeting to meeting. No, he was hungry for success. And a double life would deliver it to this young black man.

When he arrived at his office, on the ground floor of a Legal Services clinic, he ripped a can of Pepsi from a six-pack. Couldn't wait for ice or a glass, he jumped into his Naugahyde swivel chair with such enthusiasm that the well-oiled chair spun him around twice before stopping. He logged onto the computer, which told him that a lady in Kenilworth,

Illinois, just placed an order for a crystal vase. A white lady, sixty years old, drives a three-year-old Mercedes or Lexus. A Wasp, with some Irish blood. How did he know? The demographic program he devised immediately flashed to Cyril a "probable profile." How did the program figure it out? Well, that's a secret that Cyril would soon sell to IBM. Suffice to say, that the program noticed that Ms. Mary Boyson responded to certain background patterns in the shopping menu. Cyril knew that his Harlem clients would never have responded to the muted tones that turned on Mary Boyson. And now that Cyril knew Mary Boyson's tastes, he could direct other shopping ideas to her computer.

Okay, so Cyril Cole sells gifts over the computer and has a method to figure out the ethnicity of his customers. What is the double life? Mary Boyson thinks that Cyril looks like her. Mary's computer will now receive a customized thank you, which will appear in a font and pattern that she finds appealing. In addition, Cyril Cole's CC Inc. will transform itself into the CC Boutique, a name that Mary will like. Finally, Cyril's face will morph itself into that of a Caucasian, who could be Mary's Waspy nephew from the Northwestern University crew team.

Needless to say, when Cyril gets an order from the southside of Chicago, they get an urban Cyril, who looks just a little bit like Michael Jordan.

Cyril doesn't think America has a race problem—just a race to take advantage of the ethnic stew.

Newsflash

In a stunning "David versus Goliath" revelation, CBS headquarters in New York—nicknamed Black Rock—has just been rocked. Rocked by news that Black Entertainment Television, a fifteen-year-old company, has just bought CBS, once called the "Tiffany Jewel" of the media. CBS executives haven't felt so nervous since the voice of Edward R. Murrow broadcast live from a shaking air-raid shelter in World War II London. Corporate bigwigs had grown used to black entertainers dominating their white colleagues, ever since Oprah Winfrey trounced Phil Donahue in the rating wars of the 1980s. But few expected that black executives could muster the managerial drive and financial capital to pull off this coup.

* * *

If Jesus Christ were a jealous man, he'd be green. Jealous of Michael Jordan, who has achieved more fame than just about anyone in history. His name recognition in Asia and Africa probably surpasses Jesus of Nazareth's. Of course, he has product endorsements and movie contracts that Jesus could not accept. He performed his marketing miracles, not with selfless missionaries and dedicated disciples, but through self-interested marketers and agents wearing, not sandals, but Nike shoes. Where is the Jesus action figure? The cereal tie-in? The Happy Meal toy from McDonald's? The Pope may have his Popemobile and a best-selling book, but has he built a durable franchise that can sell for twenty-five times earnings?

People like Michael Jordan, Colin Powell, and Bill Cosby form the leading edge, and the most glittering edge, of the incredible darkening of America's complexion. It might seem easy to dismiss them as mere tokens of our racial mix. You can hear the skeptic's jaded voice: "So what if minorities dominate sports and entertainment? Didn't Kareem Abdul Jabbar reign over L.A. in the early 1980s, while Mayor Tom Bradley ruled City Hall? Surely, whites still outnumber nonwhites in the average workplace—places where workers eat from a lunch box rather than from fancy menus at Spago's, where L.A. Lakers dine with movie moguls."

In fact, minorities are becoming majorities. Blacks and Hispanics represent just 18 percent of middle-aged Americans, but 33 percent of the youngsters. While whites retire to wrinkle in the Florida sun, blacks and Hispanics are taking their places on the workshop floor. In thirty years, white babies will be a minority in the country's nurseries. Add a fast-growing Asian population, and you can see why Caucasians must surrender their dominance of world markets in the twenty-first century. These numbers will transform American markets—everything from housing to television to clothing. Only a fool would try to pick stocks for the long run without understanding the new kids on the block. Yes, justice should be colorblind. But your portfolio should not be.

Most conversations and writings about "race in America"

focus on poverty and discrimination by Anglos against others. But despite their dominance, Anglos will lose their grip on the nation's pocketbook and cultural tastes. In 1997, President Clinton announced that he wanted a "national conversation" on race. While he conversed and "shared pain" with others, minority business people around the country were busy figuring out how to launch new ventures, expand their market share, or drive up their stock prices. They provide about 2 million jobs in the U.S. economy. Between 1987 and 1992, the number of black-owned businesses shot up by almost 50 percent, compared to about 25 percent for the overall average. Chinese entrepreneurs created over 60 percent more firms in that period. Most of these brave souls, whether struggling in garages, storefronts, or strip malls, do not have time to dwell on their social plight or pass along their social pain to others. Their success has launched a plethora of new magazines, in print and in cyberspace, including *Black Enterprise* and *Emerge.* They are riding on a fast track that they themselves laid; a track they hope will lead to gold.

Most Americans grew up learning the phrase "melting pot." But now that the ingredients are changing so dramatically, so will the ultimate taste of the stew. To extend the metaphor, a 1960s melting pot, cooked with the influence of a 90 percent white population, will produce a different flavor than a 2030s melting pot. In the 1960s, a Hispanic kid in a public school may have started the school year by packing a burrito for lunch. By Columbus Day, she carried peanut butter and jelly with the rest of her friends. Nowadays, an Anglo girl is just as likely to ask her mom to pack a burrito, or even sushi. Quite literally, Americans are eating with their hands more than ever before. While the Anglo culture emphasizes finger foods only for lunch (i.e., sandwiches), African, Hispanic, and Asian cultures encourage breads and roll-ups at almost every meal, whether tacos, burritos, moo shu, or Ethiopian injera wraps. These food trends show up in the stock market, not just the supermarket aisle. Families are tossing into their shopping carts $1.8 billion of hand-held foods, frozen and refrigerated, about 50 percent more than in 1995. When I first accompanied my daughter to lunch in her preschool, I was stunned by the variety of foods compared to what was available during my youth in the 1960s. I recall three basic choices: peanut butter and jelly, bologna, or ham and cheese. All on white bread. Every once in awhile a kid would bring in some leftover meatloaf, which, by way of a jump shot, usually landed in the trash for two points. No one considered bringing yogurt, bagels, burritos, or sesame noodles. What was couscous? A cheese quesadilla? (I must say in support of the 1960s that the full-fatted, sugar-drenched sweets like Yodels, Ring Dings, and Devil Dogs remain superior to today's more healthy but less tasty snacks.)

The new melting pot shows up on movie and television screens, too. In 1995, the Walt Disney Co. released the animated film, *Pocahontas*. Drawn to appeal to all children, the Indian ingenue Pocahontas had a glowing bronzed skin tone that everyone from a black girl to a Chicano girl to a well-tanned white girl could identify with. Her slightly almond-shaped eyes no doubt won over some Asian fans, too. Disney's marketing team tried to excite young people around the world in a *Pocahontas* frenzy. In shopping malls, the film's advertising posters seemed as ubiquitous as exit signs. Coloring books sprouted up beside supermarket checkout counters, elbowing aside even the *National Enquirer*. My daughter was just under two years old at the time. Even before the film debuted, though, she spied a poster, pointed her tiny finger and pronounced with a smile, "Poca Lady."

In this chapter I will lay out investment themes that derive from the new ethnic dynamic in the United States economy. Our new cultural mix is not just a cultural issue, but a financial one as well. Two sectors that will benefit most are those media firms and real estate companies that aim their products at immigrant and minority communities. As immigrants get more secure in their new country they often develop a strong appetite for owning a house or an apartment. Investors can bet on that appetite intensifying. Later in the chapter we will also see why a burst of multicultural media themes should entice investors, whether in Spanish-language soap operas or in firms that own broadcast rights to international soccer games.

The images and sounds of a new America will challenge the

economy and the financial markets. When Ronald Reagan spoke of America as a "shining city on a hill," you could almost hear Kate Smith belting "God Bless America," in unaccented English and without syncopation. Reagan's city will shine even brighter in the twenty-first century, but it may swing to hip-hop, fusion jazz, or a samba, rather than Kate Smith's stentorian hymnal.

Before sitting back to admire the shining city and before jumping to investment themes, we must first take a look at the raging controversies that surround the ethnic swirl in America. First, the social pathologies and controversial social programs that enrage many Americans. California's bitter debate on the English language incited many previously apathetic voters to show up at the ballot box. Second, the hot debate over immigration. Third, the problem of falling wages for lower-income workers. These problems leave financial markets uneasy and will force the Republican and Democratic parties to rethink their demographic strategies.

SOCIAL PATHOLOGIES: THE BLACK UNDERCLASS

Even as we greet black entrepreneurs and a burgeoning middle class, we cannot avoid the more depressing side of the coin. For the past twenty years we have been bombarded by so many statistics on social failings that we have become jaded and fearful of racial stereotyping. Nonetheless, we should not let our eyes glaze over when we hear frightening statistics like over 65 percent of black children are born out of marriage, and often raised without fathers even nearby. Has it always been this way? No. In 1970, this was true of only 36 percent of black children. (While a number of pundits point out that white illegitimacy has climbed as well, they are still far below the debilitating proportions for blacks.) Kids from single-parent homes are most likely to drop out of school and follow in the footsteps of their parents by giving birth out of wedlock. While we can report good news for black education levels and black entrepreneurs, the disintegrating family structure is tearing the black population into two groups: Some will work and participate in the U.S. economy; others are condemned to their own world of poverty and neglect, a world that might as well stop spinning, since there is little hope for progress. Black males on average die about seven and a half years earlier than whites, due to a combination of health risks, poverty, and urban violence.

The downward spiral among some segments of the black population will no doubt encourage political protests and a rebirth of radical activity in the decades ahead. Former Black Panther Eldridge Cleaver's death in 1998 should have reminded us that out of despair can come bullets and blood. Leaders like Jesse Jackson and former Urban League president Vernon Jordan have become pillars of the establishment, whose televised voices no longer speak the language of the ghetto. Who will be the next Malcolm X to threaten mainstream America (including middle-class blacks)? Just a few years ago, black kids throughout the country starting wearing baseball caps with a large X sewn on the front. It turned out to be a good advertising gimmick for Spike Lee's biographical movie, but not a new political movement. Of course, even Malcolm X could not keep his message purely radical and insulated from mainstream cultural influences. When he declared that "We didn't land on Plymouth Rock! Plymouth Rock landed on us," he sure sounded revolutionary. Turns out he was quoting that urbane, not urban, bon vivant Cole Porter.

The Swedish economist Gunnar Myrdal tackled the emerging problem of a black underclass in his classic text, *The American Dilemma*. The book burst out in 1944, at a time when about half of black workers still toiled on Southern farms. But even Myrdal's pessimistic portrayal could not predict the collapse of the black economy during the 1960s and 1970s. When Myrdal wrote his book, a greater proportion of blacks held jobs than whites. But by 1974, the black labor participation rate had dropped to 6 percent below white levels, and it has slid further since. In urban areas, especially, the crime rates rocketed, with drug dealing sometimes presenting young men with a lucrative alternative to menial work.

I will not attempt to squeeze a tsunami of books, papers, and ferocious debates into a subchapter of this book. This is not the place for a thorough diagnosis or plan of action. Instead, let me make just a few points:

- First, the U.S. government in the 1990s finally overhauled welfare spending and forced welfare recipients to work. The timing was exquisite, since the U.S. job market was taking off, driving down the jobless rate in 1998 to the lowest level in about thirty years. We will likely have to wait five years to judge whether welfare reform really changes the depressing psychology of dependency. The great Austrian psychoanalyst Viktor Frankl, who struggled to maintain dignity in Hitler's concentration camps (while surviving the murder of his parents, brother, and pregnant wife), concluded that he could find a purpose only in work. Likewise, only in work will the sons and daughters of today's welfare recipients find a purpose.

- Second, we must remember that young minority workers will be taking over the jobs of many retiring baby boomers. We have an enormous incentive for the new workers to achieve and succeed. Writing off our native population simply means that we will depend even more on foreign workers to produce our goods and services, which generates a bigger trade deficit, putting more downward pressure on the value of the U.S. dollar.

- Third, while middle-class America generally condemns welfare payments for those who have made a "career" of staying at home, we should remember that middle-class retirement programs like Social Security and Medicare are, in their funding, welfare. That is, current workers pay to subsidize retirees. From a black perspective, those retirement programs are a rip-off. Why? Blacks earn less and die sooner. Chapter 1 cited a Rand study showing that on a per capita basis a black worker will, over the course of his life, contribute between $2,000 and $21,000 to whites, from his earnings. How can we defend this "gift," when the average black family's net assets equal . . . zero.

In short, the United States must help alienated blacks to reenter the job market, must create a fairer deal for future workers, and must make sure that future workers have useful skills.

SAN DIEGO, CALIFORNIA

Rita Benfado polished her nails a bright red, trying to cover up the edges she had bitten off. She thought about trimming them, but figured she might need them to claw out the eyes of her daughter-in-law.

"Aren't you ready yet, Mama?"

"Don't rush me, Tina. This is importante," Rita tried to say firmly, though her voice quivered.

"I don't know why you bother voting. All our friends have already voted, and they'll make sure the proposition loses. Besides, you'll get claustrophobia in that tiny booth," the skinny daughter-in-law whined, before muttering under her breath, "You may not even fit."

Rita didn't work anymore. She mostly sat in her living room, underneath a crucifix and a photo of her dead husband, staring at Spanish-language television. She especially enjoyed the Mexican soap operas that came into her apartment over cable. Sometimes she'd watch the news in Spanish and then in English, just to see whether the Anglo newscasters told a different story than the Chicano personalities she trusted. For fifty years she'd lived in California but never considered voting. Even though she came here legally, she trembled at the thought that some sheriff might lock her up or stick her on the trolley to Tijuana. Oh, she knew her rights; she just didn't trust her right to her rights.

But last week she got fed up. It all started with those sheets of pink and blue papers her neighbors shoved under her door. The ones that warned that the State of California was going to make Mexican-American kids to learn English in school—or else flunk out. She immediately called up her son and demanded he drive her on election day. The arthritis in her hips made it too tough to climb aboard a public bus. Sure, the wealthier neighborhoods had those kneeling buses that bow down to the handicapped. But Rita hadn't seen a new bus in the barrio, except one that got lost or stolen.

When her red nails pulled the voting booth curtain securely across the rod, her handed trembled with rage. She stared at the ballot. How dare they! How dare her protesting neighbors condemn their children to the barrio. She pulled the level marked "English—or flunk" with gusto—and with the thrill that at seventy-five years old she was doing something that her family thought was illicit, but she thought was damn right.

IMMIGRANTS: GIVE ME YOUR HUDDLED MASSES YEARNING TO WORK

Few topics will split a room as swiftly as immigration. Which is nothing new. America has resented immigrants ever since Pocahontas shared a canoe with John Smith (if you believe the Disney version). The aristocratic Franklin Roosevelt hurled the best barbed line at nativists. He began a speech to the Daughters of the American Revolution with the greeting, "My fellow immigrants . . ." My late grandfather, who was born in London, came to New York at the turn of the twentieth century. He told me numerous tales of the ethnic mix of immigrants. In a double-dose of bigotry, New Yorkers would disparage Italians landing on the shores by saying, "Ah, Italy. A short swim from Africa." Most nativists today excuse the great waves of immigration during the nineteenth and early twentieth centuries. But times have changed, the argument goes, and so have the immigrants. "Sure, we accepted Italians, for they brought Toscanini. Germans delivered Eisenhower, and the Irish George M. Cohan, who wrote patriot American songs like 'Over There' (the Yanks are Coming!). Most important, they all came here to work."

In fact, those groups did come to work. My grandfather told me that when Irishmen rolled down the gangways in New York, they were greeted with the following question: "A hook or a club? A hook or a club?" This was the New York job market's way of asking whether the men wanted a job as a longshoreman or as a policeman, the two choices for the Irish. Boss Tweed's Tammany Hall would "discover" new job openings every time another vessel pulled into the harbor.

Today's immigrants certainly do *look* different. Between 1915 and 1965, waves of white Europeans scurried off the ships, composing 75 percent of the approximately 11 million total immigrants. Since 1965, over 85 percent of the 18 million newcomers have *not* come from Europe. In recent years, Asians and Mexicans have each made up about one-third of the huddled masses yearning to be free. Together, Caribbean, Central, and South Americans add up to about one-fifth. Illegal immigrants would bloat the Mexican statistics even further, by a few hundred thousand annually. Today's arrivals face frightening social hurdles, as did prior generations (which helps explain why about 30 percent of the turn-of-the-century immigrants turned home again). In Neil Simon's play *Brighton Beach Memoirs*, the immigrant mother recalls the day her ship crawled into New York harbor. She knew the family would have trouble in America when they passed by the Statue of Liberty: "That woman didn't look Jewish." She looks even less Filipino.

Looks alone do not make Americans wary. Here's the real rub: As the American economy grows more technologically and economically advanced, the unskilled immigrant has fewer and fewer ways to make a living here. Further, his chances of "catching up" to natives moves further and further into the distance. In past decades, uneducated immigrants could descend into coal mines, as many Poles did. Or sew buttons, as many Hungarians did. Or push fruit carts, as many Italians did. Or even sweat in the fields, as most blacks continued to do until World War II. But those jobs are gone forever. Most Americans now work in the service sector, where they must read and speak English. Those who still work in manufacturing must develop technological skills, not just the ability to aim a riveter. A recent study showed that 85 percent of the new jobs created in California in the 1970s and 1980s required a college education. The millions of Mexicans headed north past Tijuana cannot fill them, so they get jobs cutting the lawns of the educated.

Harvard professor George J. Borjas has compiled rather damning statistics on this debate, showing that recent immigrants start out with much lower relative wages than previous immigrants, and are more likely to show up on the social welfare rolls. Most striking, old immigrant groups actually came to the United States *more* highly educated than the native population. Prior to 1970, almost 40 percent of Americans dropped out of high school; they were not such an intimidating group to compete against. Within fifteen years immigrants' wages caught up, and within thirty years they surpassed the natives. By 1990, immigrants from the 1950s earned almost 20 percent more than their native neighbors. Education counts. The State of Israel will likely see extraordinary progress with its recent wave of Russian immigrants, who pack more Ph.D.s, petri dishes, and violins than any other people on earth. A Tel Aviv taxi driver is more likely to know the answer to Fermat's equation than to know how to get to the airport.

Sadly, recent U.S. immigrants start off with wages over 30 percent behind native workers, and they seldom catch up. To use a sports metaphor, a 1950s European immigrant coming to the United States was like a high school football player moving across town and trying out for the team. Nowadays, it's like a high school player suiting up and trying to compete as a running back against the Green Bay Packers' defensive line. He seldom makes a forward gain, and the bruises do not heal.

Some ethnic groups do perform better than others on Borjas's tests. Even within Asians, the differences are staggering. For example, Laotians who came to the United States prior to 1980 earn about 28 percent less than natives, while Chinese earn about 2 percent more. Of Latino immigrants, Guatemalans earn 22 percent less, while Panamanians earn 11 percent more. Then again, Panamanians start off much wealthier and better educated than Guatemalans. Differences arise in social areas, too. Some ethnic families fall onto the welfare rolls more quickly, while others fall apart faster, leading to out-of-wedlock births. About 16 percent of Cuban immigrants received welfare in 1990, far below the 28 percent rate for Dominicans.

Many immigrants actually do come to the United States eager and ready to tackle our modern, technologically advanced economy. The immigrant pool displays a shallow end of unschooled masses and a deep end of professionals. At the deep end, 24 percent are college graduates, compared to about 20 percent for natives. By and large they thrive and are more likely to show up as college teachers and scientists than natives. It is their unprepared brethren who drown in the shallow end of the pool.

"Drowning" is a relative term, though, for a poor peasant from Mexico. Would he rather "drown" for $5 per hour in Texas, than suffer for $5 per week in his home village? Would he rather live in a cramped apartment in Laredo, where he may hear about a job laying bricks at a new strip mall, or live in a hut on a dirt floor back home? The steady flow of humanity from Mexico—even during years when the U.S. economy weakens—suggests that "drowning" in America is not such a terrible alternative. Therefore, we can expect more and more poor people to seek their fortune, or at least their subsistence, in America. Media images of the United States continue to entice and enchant foreigners. Our movies tend to portray our country as a violent land, but a land where people live in big houses and drive fast cars. Long-distance telephone costs have collapsed in the past few years, permitting even the poorest immigrants to reach out and touch some relative back home. And since airfares and boat fares have fallen over time, the violent but thrilling American Dream seems closer than ever.

The ultimate test, I think, takes place with the children and grandchildren of immigrants. Econometric analysis is both too crude and too precise when predicting the future. We can make a point estimate to the nearest one/one millionth, but sometimes we can get the plus and minus signs mixed up. Twenty years ago, President Jimmy Carter's economists warned us that we were quickly running out of oil, based on economic and geologic forecasts. The price of oil has mostly slid downwards since that claim was made and President Carter declared "the moral equivalent of war" against oil dependence. The truth is, we do not yet know whether the boat people, foot people, and airplane people of the 1980s and 1990s will instill such a strong work ethic and a drive to learn that their offspring will lift themselves into the mainstream, if not higher. In many cases, they do, and with such energy that new stereotypes and jokes are generated: "How do you know a Chinese gang broke into your house?" the riddle goes. "You find that they've done your kid's homework." While most of us try to shun stereotypes and broad generalizations, it is hard to ignore the fact that Asian students have achieved a plurality at the University of California, Berkeley.

In cities like Chicago and Los Angeles, new, positive stereotypes of Hispanic entrepreneurs are emerging. Along Twenty-sixth Street in Chicago, Hispanic jewelers, clothiers, and restaurateurs together generate sales tax receipts second only to the glitzy and ritzy "miracle mile," along Michigan Avenue. How can nonimmigrants invest in these stories? As we will see later, targeted investments in real estate and the housing market make sense. Successful immigrants quickly improve their housing conditions, creating new demand in that sector.

Despite the marvel of prosperous Hispanic entrepreneurs, we should also pay attention to the dire warnings pronounced by La Raza, the largest Hispanic advocacy group in the United States. La Raza reports that the percentage of Hispanics enrolled in pre-school fell between 1985 and 1993, and that second generation Hispanics are dropping out of school in *greater* numbers than their parents did. Second generation children may very well be assimilating to U.S. society, but I am afraid that too many find it more socially rewarding to assimilate to the level of "Beavis and Butthead," rather than to the Learning Channel.

Skeptics like Borjas may be proved wrong in the end, but they have gathered enough evidence to tilt our government policy toward those immigrants who bring skills with them, rather than those who will likely depend on our social welfare system to keep them fed and clothed. Make no mistake, though, the United States can and should accommodate more people in the next century. If we close off our borders to new workers, especially those with skills, our aging residents will simply import more goods and services from other countries. While that is not a bad thing, foreign workers do not contribute to our Social Security system, do not pay taxes to maintain our national defense, and do not give a damn what happens to "us" in retirement.

WINNERS AND LOSERS

There is another "us." When immigrants cross the borders to enter a country, we hope they come to take jobs. But from whom? Happily, the job market is not a "zero-sum" game, where someone who fills out a job application looks to throw somebody else out of work. The U.S. economy has created 28 million jobs since 1981, driving the unemployment rate down to staggering levels, beyond what almost any economist thought possible. Because we take our paychecks and either buy things or lend the money to others, our jobs tend to create jobs for others. With more workers, the country can create more potential income. From a boss's perspective, a bigger stack of completed job applications gives him more choices, and perhaps, the ability to offer lower wages. California farm owners have generally been quite pleased to find more potential grape and lettuce pickers over the years. As a consumer, I do not complain when my grocery store manager hangs a "sale" sign on those grapes and lettuce heads. My women friends are quite happy to pay Korean immigrants $10 for a professional nail manicure.

Nonetheless, some people may lose when immigrants flood into the workforce. Who? Natives who have the same skills as the immigrants. In the sad case of the United States, unskilled blacks suffer most when unskilled Latinos and Laotians come on the scene. Workers without much education were being squeezed anyway in the past twenty years, watching their earnings slide by perhaps 10 percent in the 1980s, as consumers started buying foreign goods and as manufacturers figured out how to roll more goods off the assembly lines with fewer bodies. No one knows exactly how to allocate the "blame" for the plight of the ignorant. Still, studies show that immigrants drove down the job rate for low-skilled natives by more than 2 percent in major cities, while driving down their wages by 2.5 percent to perhaps 5 percent. The upshot: When someone drops out of high school, they are dropping into a heated competitive race with the last man off the boat from Rangoon.

Even Hispanics living in the United States are troubled by immigration, since they immediately see the danger to their wages. According to a CBS/*New York Times* poll, 36 percent of Hispanics thought immigration should be kept the same, while 31 percent wanted it cut back, and only 25 percent favored letting in more foreigners. As California absorbs more and more immigrants, the state's gap between rich and poor increases. Moreover, the cost of educating and aiding immigrant families imposed a nearly $1,200 annual cost on each nonimmigrant California household in 1994–1995.

Our econometric analyses have trouble picking up a "softer" variable. Namely, genius. When our studies aggregate immigrants together, like steerage-class passengers on the *Titanic*, we cannot figure out whether one of the passengers might make a disproportionate difference in the world. Roosevelt's address to the Daughters of the American Revolution delivered his around the same time that the U.S. government permitted a certain shaggy scientist into the country. If Albert Einstein had stayed in Germany, Californians might be casting votes on a "German-only" referendum. Likewise, our military leaders Admiral Nimitz and General Eisenhower derived from immigrant German stock. And if Great Britain had repelled the son of an American mother, then Winston Churchill would not have been able to rally a tired England from despair and save her from despotism.

In recent years, a Cuban-born engineer named Roberto Gozuita created a fortune for millions of American stockholders and thousands of workers for Coca-Cola. A Dominican named De la Renta brought fashion elegance both to the high-brow and the bargain shopper. Since a bigger population raises the absolute number of geniuses—whose great works can bestow riches to millions—perhaps we can accept the risks discovered by aggregated studies.

By tallying up the costs and benefits, though, we do not get any closer to solving the moral and political questions. So what if we may lower the average wage by letting in more people? When a husband and wife have a baby, they lower their per capita income. If that same couple adopts a milk cow, their per capita income will go up. Since most couples prefer to have kids than cows, we must presume that per capita income is not always the prime goal of families. Or societies. Frankly, I am proud of the generosity we showed to those who escaped Vietnam on leaky boats; and rather ashamed that Franklin Roosevelt turned away the 936 desperate souls on the *St. Louis* in 1939, suggesting we did not have enough room.

POLITICAL DANCES

Mainstream politicians cannot decide whether to scratch their chins or mop their brows when confronted with America's ethnic challenges. The number of minority congressmen and mayors has moved higher in every decade. A few years ago, New York, Los Angeles, Detroit, Chicago, and Washington, D.C., all had elected black mayors. The Congressional Black Caucus and the Hispanic caucuses can frequently use their leverage to swing critical votes. But the behavior of white party leaders is more complex. The Republican Party, despite its appeal to blacks in the post-Lincoln, pre-FDR period, has struggled to attract minority votes. Republican opposition to the 1964 Civil Rights Act did not help. Cuban-Americans may applaud the GOP when its leaders denounce Fidel Castro, but the overwhelming proportion of blacks and Hispanics still cast their votes with the Democratic Party. Only one black Republican serves in Congress today and all but three of the eighteen Hispanics in the House of Representatives are Democrats. Republican pollsters tell their bosses that blacks are just as conservative as whites on social issues and more likely to attend church and favor school prayer. Former congressman Jack Kemp has continuously tried to turn Republicans toward black voters, but he has few followers in the party leadership.

In the next few decades, the GOP will have to win over a large proportion of either Hispanic or black voters, or else find its number of potential supporters dwindle. Their strategists assume that as minorities grow wealthier, they will turn toward the Republican party, as have many white ethnic Catholics over the past twenty years. Perhaps. But so far Jews have defied the tendency to leave the Democratic Party as incomes rise. Republicans will begin to make a stronger drive to sign up Hispanic voters by emphasizing their commitment to religious values and to free trade with Latin America. It will not be easy, though in 1998 gubernatorial elections Jeb Bush of Florida and George W. Bush of Texas each reeled in huge numbers of Hispanic votes.

Conversely, Democrats risk taking minorities for granted, as the Warren Beatty film *Bulworth* explained. In addition, Democrats must figure out how to justify to their black supporters a liberal immigration policy that ends up hurting low-wage laborers. We will likely see a fierce battle by Democrats to hold on to Hispanic voters in California, while the GOP focuses on signing up Texas Hispanics. An economic recession in the next decade could easily spawn new political parties that would try to appeal to those clinging on to the bottom rungs of the income ladder.

HOW TO MAKE MONEY FROM THE NEW ETHNIC AMERICA

Countries with open doors tend to do well. Investors with open eyes can, too. Just as nations succeed by borrowing ideas and innovations, so should individuals. The United States may have the reputation for Emersonian self-reliance, but if we had relied solely on ourselves, we would still be eating berries at Walden Pond with Henry David Thoreau's relatives. British settlers did not discriminate in stealing ideas. Following Milton Berle's logic of comic thievery, they stole only from the best. They fitted their boats with rudders developed in China; their sailors employed nautical trigonometry developed in Egypt, using number systems created in India; and their messengers read with letters invented by Romans. When they arrived in America, they were more than happy to grow maize and shoot wild turkeys.

America's cities frequently lead cultural and business trends because they create the most dynamic social climate, with cultures intermingling, clashing, and merging. In Chicago, a city that used to have more Greeks than any city but Athens and more Poles than any city but Warsaw, Catholic Mass can be heard in twenty languages. Chicago's eclectic clang brought forth stunning architecture, inventive theater, and yes, it even gave birth to Louis Armstrong's blues.

Investors in retail goods should roam the cities. When I saw the logo for Tommy Hilfiger on the backs of black kids in south central Los Angeles several years ago, I knew it was time to buy the stock. The "next" fashion trend for youths usually starts in urban centers, particularly minority neighborhoods. Seldom do white suburban boys launch new clothing styles. I attended a racially mixed elementary school near Asbury Park, New Jersey, in the late 1960s. My fourth-grade Little League team photo, for example, shows five blacks, five whites, and a black coach. (I asked my mother to sew the number 24 on my uniform to honor my hero, Willie Mays. A Dodgers fan, she reluctantly obliged.) As I flip through my class photos from those years, I must admit that the white boys all looked like they just got out of bed and put on Beaver Cleaver's hand-me-downs. The simple checked shirts and straight-legged pants came right from the 1950s with not a single concession to bell-bottoms, gold chains, or tie-dying. The black boys, however, looked like Michael Jackson in his youth—flared pants, wide belts, and leather vests. While they looked cool, we looked clueless.

The new ethnic America will, of course, change more than clothing. Investors looking to profit by this change should look especially at opportunities in the media and housing.

LIGHTS! CAMERA! ACTION! INVESTMENT!

If you could turn through financial records as swiftly as you can flip through television channels, you could figure out which powerhouse earned more money than ABC and CBS in 1997. The answer? The Weather Channel. The venerable CBS network lost money in 1997. So did the once dominant ABC network. As a result of cable and satellite technology advancements over the past twenty years, the television audience has splintered, bringing emotional, if not financial, depression to the major networks but creating untold opportunities for new ventures. In many cases, our multicultural population drives these changes.

I have watched Black Entertainment Television expand its franchise since I invited founder Robert Johnson to a White House breakfast about eight years ago. In starting up his business, Johnson identified a target audience and designed a network that would provide jazz entertainment, stand-up comedy, and news that just could not be found on major stations. He then approached TCI, a leading cable company, for investment capital and advice. TCI's president John Malone showed the foresight to invest in the project, and now Johnson is a very wealthy entrepreneur with new plans to enhance BET's reputation and profitability.

When Rupert Murdoch, an Australian by birth, showed the audacity to set up the Fox network to compete against CBS, ABC, and NBC, most experts laughed. They have stopped laughing. Like BET, Fox immediately saw the potential in urban minority viewers. Soon Fox's program "In Living Color" set new standards (not necessarily higher standards) for sketch comedy, with a mostly black cast. One of its few white actors, Jim Carrey, then hit the jackpot with starring roles in movies. Fox's ratings among blacks and Hispanics soared, bringing in advertising revenue from companies trying to target minority consumers.

Nowadays, Fox frequently sneaks ahead of one of its more-seasoned network competitors in the national ratings. In highly ethnic areas, even greener upstarts than Fox can bloody noses at CBS, NBC, and ABC. In Los Angeles, KMEX (note the call letters) pushed itself to a number-one ranking among eighteen- to thirty-four-year-olds during the six P.M. time slot. The station targets Hispanics by providing relevant news and entertainment programs, but also helpful tips for new immigrants such as how to light a furnace (many in the audience grew up without a modern heating system). A company called Univision owns KMEX, as well as stations in Miami and Chicago, which also pull in high ratings with imported Latin soap operas and soccer matches. Advertisers that especially want to find immigrant customers include firms in the travel, long-distance calling, and money-transfer industries.

Chinese stations will also boom, as they deliver local news, as well as news from Asia. Chinese television in San Francisco discussed Hong Kong's recent chicken flu epidemic long before its English competitors. The diversity of Asian languages does create an obstacle, however. KTSF in San Francisco broadcasts news and drama in everything from Mandarin, to Korean, to Vietnamese, to Tagalog, to Hindi, in addition to a live one-hour Cantonese newscast each weeknight. Other stations deliver the Filipino Channel, Native American Nations, TV Asia, and World African Network.

Major U.S. media companies have been slow to catch on and catch up. Since the Big Three networks were developed on the concept of *broad*casting to a broad, common denominator, they have trouble figuring out how to *narrow* cast among one hundred to five hundred different stations. That gives minority-oriented companies a unique chance to make money through their programming, but also sets them up as potential targets of corporate takeovers. In 1998 Sony/Tristar, in conjunction with Liberty Media (a TCI spinoff), bought the Miami-based Telemundo, which attracts a very large Hispanic audience.

Thirty-eight million Americans do not speak English in their homes. Tom Brokaw, Dan Rather, and Peter Jennings can talk as loudly as they like, and even show up in gleaming high definition television; still they will not squeeze the potential from the ethnic markets. Investors in foreign-language programming have discovered that minority Americans often watch a great deal of television. Hispanics spend over fifteen hours each week viewing Spanish programs, and ten hours viewing English shows. Miami leads the pack, with households typically watching seventeen hours in Spanish. Entrepreneurs are working furiously to appeal to this growing audience. While about two-thirds of American homes receive cable television, only 57 percent of Hispanics currently do. As cables and wires wend their way through more Hispanics homes, Spanish-speakers will become an even larger potential market for advertisers, who now spend only about 1 percent of their annual $40 billion television budgets on the Spanish market. That number will rise. For the first time in its twenty-nine-year history, ABC has begun broadcasting Monday Night Football in Spanish.

Advertisers have been reluctant to jump into foreign languages, because it costs more money to produce new commercials. Several advertising tactics have emerged. McDonald's, for example, mostly dubs its English commercials with foreign languages. Colgate-Palmolive simply takes those commercials it produces for Asian countries and broadcasts them on U.S. stations aimed at Asian-Americans. Oxford Healthcare goes the next step by promoting its HMO plans with originally produced advertisements in Chinese.

While I applaud entrepreneurship and programming diversity, I see no guarantee that these forces will raise the "quality" of television. Alas, foreign tastes are no more sophisticated than domestic tastes. Those rosy eye-glassed Americans who expect erudite dramas based on Octavio Paz's Nobel Prize–winning stories will likely be disappointed. After purchasing Telemundo, Sony/Tristar announced its first projects: a "female action detective" show and a "buddy, buddy male cop" show. Next thing you know they will introduce a Spanish-language situation comedy about a talking horse. And Señor Eduardo will be no more refined than his American predecessor from the 1960s.

MI CASA ES SU INVESTMENT

After the Great Depression, Bill Levitt, Donald Trump's father Fred, and my grandfather, Samuel Lewis, built tracts of homes along the East Coast for families who were climbing into the middle classes. David Halberstam's book, *The Fifties*, paints a memorable portrait of the most famous suburban development, built on a tract of land called Island Trees. When realtors noticed that Bill Levitt's new site had only "two scrawny trees," the name Levittown took hold instead.

Homebuilding was an exciting entrepreneurial adventure, led by far more colorful characters than the "company" men in gray flannel suits who populated other sectors. The real estate industry has always seemed more dynamic, more risky, and more prone to boom and busts. The caroming careers of Donald Trump and Leona Helmsley make that clear. Just when Trump published his self-confident book *The Art of the Deal* in 1988, his empire collapsed. Stingy bankers took a scissors to his credit cards and cut his monthly spending allowance to mere-mortal levels. His father, Fred, was not quite so wild in his day. My grandfather confided to me that while Bill Levitt and he used to play cards each evening, they could never persuade the elder Trump to gamble.

Multicultural America will keep the housing market hopping in the years ahead. Most conventional projections for the next few decades suggest a housing slowdown, as America ages. The standard hypothesis argues that baby boomers will sell their family homes and spend their retirement years in smaller homes or apartments in sunnier climes. Since housing prices shot up in the 1970s and 1980s when boomers bought their first family homes, it would seem logical and symmetrical for prices to slide down as their kids move away and the boomers start hunting for shuffleboard courts. The scenario may be right—for middle-class white families. Still, even they are buying expensive retirement homes that may cost nearly as much as the family home they are selling. They may get rid of four extra bedrooms, but they choose a huge master suite, a Jacuzzi bath, and a "country kitchen." Moreover, many retirees are not moving into *older* houses that are already part of the housing stock. Those senior citizens who "earned" big capital gains in the stock market are increasingly buying newer retirement homes and condominiums. When they dump their old house and buy a new one, they are not reducing overall demand for U.S. housing. Investors need to closely watch their behavior to see whether the conventional forecasts prove wrong. (See Chapter 1 on the baby boomers.)

Even if middle-class whites retire, leading to a sag in real estate prices, investors will be able to make money by focusing on real estate that caters to minority groups, especially immigrants. In California, one frequently sees Mexican-American workers pouring concrete and laying bricks at construction sites. In the years ahead, many of these laborers will buy the homes they build. Between 1995 and 2010, the number of foreign-born residents buying homes will jump by over 50 percent, compared to the period from 1985 to 2000. Foreign-born residents who entered the country during the last twenty years have only now scrimped and saved enough to consider buying. In addition, low long-term interest rates are making housing more affordable. Presuming the Federal Reserve Board does not lose its grip on inflation, mortgage rates should stay attractive.

The average immigrant's American Dream usually includes a home. Though most start their lives in America by renting, or sleeping on a relative's sofa or floor, they hope to move out. Let's take a look at young adults (aged twenty-five to thirty-four) who immigrated between 1975 and 1980. In 1980, only about 20 percent of them owned homes, compared with over 50 percent of native-born young adults. By 1990, though, over 55 percent of those immigrants had bought their own homes, narrowing the homeowning gap with natives to about 12 percent. Over the next fifteen years, Fannie Mae (which lends to home buyers) expects 3.6 million immigrant households to form, generating over 20 percent of the growth in households.

With these dynamics in place, investors should be searching for home-building and real estate development firms that aggressively court the Hispanic and Asian populace. Since these immigrant groups tend to settle in California, Texas, and other parts of the south and west, investment vehicles should not be too hard to find. Investors should also focus on housing *services*, companies that provide financial advice and real estate brokerage, for example. Minorities, especially blacks, often shun real estate brokers, instead relying on word of mouth, newspaper advertisements, or simply cruising through neighborhoods to discover For Sale signs. Those realty corporations that can win the trust of skeptical minorities (who believe that the industry discriminates against them) have the opportunity to win new profits.

MELTING POT, SALAD BOWL, MOSAIC?

Only a tenured professor would waste time debating whether the new America looks more like a melting pot, salad bowl, or a mosaic. It is more fashionable these days to emphasize bowls and mosaics since they convey a sense of separateness. But what is fashionable for intellectuals may be dangerous for common laborers. We hear too many stories of young immigrants, and even native minorities, refusing to "sell out to white culture" by studying hard or learning standard English. Blacks may deride a studious classmate as an "Oreo;" while Chinese may hurl the epithet "banana." *The Washington Post* interviewed Hispanics in Omaha, Nebraska, and discovered a disheartening story even in America's heartland: "When I'm around Chicanos, I feel ashamed to speak English," said a twenty-three-year-old girl who came to Omaha to join relatives. "Instead of helping you, they make fun of you," she explained in Spanish.

Presumably, these insular attitudes do not prevail among the one-third of Asians and Hispanics who marry outside their ethnic group. We should not underestimate the power of love and intermarriage. Consider: Joseph Kennedy, Sr. sympathized with the Nazi Party, while representing the United States as Ambassador to the Court of St. James. If he were still alive today, he would sit at the head of the family's Thanksgiving table surrounded by grand-sons-in-law Edward Schlossberg (a Jew), Andrew Cuomo (an Italian), and Arnold Schwarzenegger (an Austrian benefactor of the Simon Weisenthal Center). More likely, the old Irish patriarch would die at seeing his Waspy ambitions foiled by their likes. Still, the Kennedy clan will look far different in 2030 than it did in the 1930s, when Joe Kennedy took his family to London.

Even with festering social problems, America's minorities will pack a bigger wallop in the economy. Already, the combined pocketbooks of blacks and Hispanics hold over $800 billion in buying power. That is over three times the spending of the Pentagon, which analysts have often fingered as a leading force in shaping the U.S. economy. Minorities are, at the same time, packing a bigger wallop in our culture. You do not have to learn to rap, dance to hip-hop, or study the art of feng shui (designing your surroundings to achieve balance and harmony) in order to profit. But here is an ancient Chinese hint to astute investors: Feng shui teaches you should not keep your back to a window, for you will miss the exciting street scene below.

5

RISING SUN, RISING STOCKS

How Japan's New Buying Spree Will Deliver New Investment Opportunities

DETROIT, MICHIGAN

The countdown began at four o'clock in the morning. That's when Jim Rayfield's eyes opened to squint at the glaring red numerals on the Sony clock radio. He'd never opened up someone else's mail before. Hell, his father delivered mail for the post office. That was the only lesson Jim remembered learning from his father before he changed delivery routes and changed families.

Jim could hear his heart beat along with the whir of the electronic clock. He looked over at his wife, Sheila, who somehow managed to shake off the stress.

Could an FBI team or an Alcohol, Tobacco & Firearms gang burst in and arrest him for prying open someone else's mail? Jeez, he thought, what if they uncovered his teenage arrest for shoplifting from thirty years ago? No big deal. For guys in Detroit it was a rite of passage, like white suburban teens getting braces on their teeth.

Let's not turn this into a federal crime. It was his daughter's mail, after all. Call it fatherly pride. Jim had spent twenty years lifting head-

121

lamps on the GM assembly line. No real education, beyond a couple of night classes that the foreman had suggested.

Then one day last week he comes home to an envelope with maroon letters spelling "Harvard." Still, he couldn't make out whether or not they were inviting his daughter Monica to join the freshman class. He started sweating and wiped his brow with the back of his hand and smudged the envelope. What the hell, he'd just reseal it.

Slipping his pinkie into the corner, he inched his leathery finger across. When it reached three-quarters across, he pulled the letter through the opening. The first Rayfield in human history would be packing for college. And Harvard at that.

Since that day, he hadn't slept through the night. First, it was guilt for opening up the letter. Then it was dread at the outrageous tuition. One year's tuition was almost as much as his take-home pay. Jim spent a week negotiating with the credit union for a loan. The credit union finally gave him a thumbs up. He'd have to work a lot of overtime, and even so, he'd be paying off the debt up until his retirement. But now that he'd figured out how to pay for Harvard, he could reseal the letter.

He slipped it under Monica's door. Her alarm was set for 6:30 A.M., so she could make soccer practice. The countdown had begun. He quietly dragged a chair outside her bedroom door so he could wait for the squeals and screams when she opened the envelope.

FITSUI BUILDING, TOKYO

Mr. Mori wanted to choke Mr. Kato to death, but he couldn't bear to touch his partner's skin. Maybe a belt would do. On second thought, maybe he should put aside his heartbreak and just go ahead with the merger.

Mori was tall for a Japanese man born during World War II. He had to duck when he entered the late-night tempura stands in the Roppongi district. But, then again, he'd grown used to bowing, as he inched his way up the Fitsui corporate ladder over the course of forty tedious years.

Mori walked into the boardroom, looked at Kato and the rest of the directors. His slow, deep bend from the waist spoke sarcastically, signaling his anger. He may be chairman, but somehow he felt less powerful today than when he was a dronelike salaryman, riding the subway into

Tokyo at 5 A.M., and returning to the suburbs at 11 P.M.

He had no choice, his board told him. The Fitsui Motor company would crumble within ten years, unless Fitsui found more workers to staff the assembly lines. Unfortunately, Japan's workforce, like Mori himself, was aging too fast for the job. And robots could only do so much. He remembered the paint fiasco, when the robot painters spun out of control, spraying each other with one layer of primer, two layers of epoxy, three layers of clearcoat, and a nice sheen of wax. He had to implement the plan that would eventually close down expensive Japanese factories.

Faced with a shortage of laborers and an overflowing warehouse of robots gone haywire, the board told Mori to look west. General Motors enjoyed a young workforce in Latin America, and its Detroit plants could be shifted to the Plains states, where unions were weak and workers more docile. Mori knew that his beloved Fitsui would ultimately be no more than a label and a holding company shell. As a result of his signature today, the hands of Japanese craftsman would no longer touch the cars that would roll off the assembly lines, even though they would bear the honorable Fitsui label.

Mori didn't care too much for America or for the English language. He shared the snobbish view of America as a refuge of the shallow and the weak. But in college he had once taken an English course in which the professor forced them to read T. S. Eliot. Mori thought, as he unsheathed the ink pen in the board room, it is we who are the hollow nation, and we are the hollow men.

GOLDEN TRAILER PARK, OMAHA

Francine Gumm checked to see if he was breathing. She couldn't tell by looking at his chest. She leaned her young, but deeply lined cheek next to his. Nothing. She knocked over a chair as she frantically searched for her handbag and the makeup mirror that hid within it. She'd seen this done in the movies. She held the mirror to his nostrils and looked—for what? For fog? Nothing again. Wait. There it is. A wisp of life crept across the mirror.

Relieved, she threw her plump self onto the bed. The hospital nurses told her nothing about caring for a newborn baby. And mother nature wasn't coming to the rescue either. Was she supposed to have a mother's *intuition that told her what the crying meant? And whether to worry about breathing when he slept? Maybe the soccer moms—the suburban moms with husbands—got a secret message. She sure didn't. She hadn't a clue. Mother nature had abandoned her just as her own mother had.*

Scattered around the crib were last week's newspapers and a yellow wrapper from last night's dinner, a Mc-something or other that her friend Josie had dropped off. Francine glanced down at the classified section, on which she'd circled four classified job ads with dark red ink. The jobs all sounded pretty similar with all the right code-words: "Bright, hard-working, entry-level . . . " But who would look after Jake? She needed one of those jobs she'd heard about on the network news, one that provided child care. That meant a big company, with lots of employees, lots of moms, and lots of people trying to make ends meet. Those kind didn't come to Golden Park often. Most bolted their doors in the 1970s and never opened again.

Francine craved sleep. She had sung a made-up lullaby to Jake, but there wasn't anyone to sing to her. So she picked up the television clicker and zapped . . .

Newsflash

In an announcement that has shocked Wall Street and ignited protests from Washington to Detroit to Watts, the chairman of Fitsui Motors has revealed that the Japanese firm has just purchased 52 percent of the outstanding shares of General Motors, the world's largest automaker. This is particularly alarming because it follows another bombshell, Sony's purchase of Disney/CapCities ABC.

The Congressional Black Caucus has condemned the plan because Fitsui has also announced that it will close plants in Detroit and shift them to Nebraska and to Mexico. In late-night conference calls, Wall Street analysts suggested that Fitsui was trying to avoid unionized labor. One investment banker close to the deal hinted that Fitsui wanted to move General Motors operations away from urban centers, code words for African American populations . . .

Like characters in an old episode of the "Twilight Zone," Jim Rayfield, Mr. Mori, and Francine Gumm find themselves rolled around by the mysterious modern economy. You can almost hear Rod Serling's voice as they each turn on the radio or the television to hear the latest news that will shake their families and shape their futures. It's easy to see the immediate winners and losers in this episode. Poor Jim Rayfield will lose his job, and his daughter Monica may miss her chance to get to Harvard. Meanwhile, Francine Gumm may actually gain the opportunity to work in a shiny new factory in Nebraska that will offer child care for her infant son. And embittered old Mr. Mori will live out his retirement feeling guilty for shutting down Japan's domestic auto plants and moving them to the West.

The scenario puts enormous question marks over U.S. economic policy and our financial markets: Will the U.S. government permit the takeover of our flagship firms? Should it? Few blinked when Daimler Benz merged with Chrysler in 1998, despite their warring World War II histories—building armored vehicles for the Axis and the Allied powers, respectively. Unlike the Japanese, though, the Germans do not have a reputation for huge trade surpluses and for blocking U.S. imports into their country. Another question mark: How can investors navigate through the confusion, as stock prices bounce up and down amid the turmoil? Like Scrooge in *A Christmas Carol*, investors must ask themselves whether they are destined to see this scenario unfold, or whether they can do something to avoid it.

WHY JAPAN MATTERS

One thing is certain: Any investor who ignores the 1990s meltdown in the Japanese economy will find his portfolio ground down to dust in the next ten years. Japan has suffered a bigger stock market collapse than the 1929 Wall Street crash. Japan's banks have racked up far more bad loans than the disastrous U.S. savings and loan crisis of the 1980s, almost $1 trillion worth, compared to "just" $165 billion for the United States. Japan has turned its heralded lifetime employment on its head; now shamed workers face lifetime *un*employment. Japan's economy skidded to such an abrupt stop in 1998 that its interest rates fell to astoundingly low levels, actually less than zero for certain government bills. Imagine, the government paid Japanese investors to borrow government money. While U.S. ten-year Treasury bonds yielded about 5 percent for bond buyers, in 1998 Japanese government bonds averaged about 1 percent, after dropping as low as 0.66 percent (in early 1999, yields climbed back above 1.5 percent). During a decade when other countries sometimes worried about creeping inflation, Japan has been plagued only with *de*flation, that is, falling prices. Back in 1989, the land on which the Imperial Palace sits in Tokyo was worth more than the entire state of California. Just a few years later, Tokyo land investments emitted the same decaying stench as Florida swampland did in the 1930s. In 1987, for example, Tokyo housing prices jumped by 57 percent. By 1991 they began a danger-ous slide that has lasted eight years.

The Japanese have called the nasty deflation "price destruc-tion." It's not only prices that get destroyed, though. More Japanese people are killing themselves. In 1997 as personal bankruptcies hit seventy thousand, 3,600 Japanese committed sui-cide, driven by shame and financial despair. In August 1998, one of the individuals, a forty-eight-year-old president of a small sheet metal company, attached a hose to his car's tailpipe and inhaled the exhausts while sitting in his car. Tucked in his pocket, a suicide note apologized "to all our employees for the slump in our busi-ness." Japanese culture has its own poignant and noble way of viewing suicide. The heralded short story writer Akutagawa Ryunosuke left a suicide note in 1927 noting that "I do not know when I will summon up the resolve to kill myself. But nature is for me more beautiful than it has ever been before." Many who refuse to file for bankruptcy and avoid suicide, simply pack up their belongings and move to another part of the country, hoping to leave behind their misery and shame. With such suffering, we should not be surprised that Japan has scrolled through more than a half-dozen prime ministers during a period when the United States has had just two presidents.

So what, you might ask. Other countries have suffered a rough ride, too. Does anyone care that the average Mexican's real income was lower in 1997 than in 1977? But the difference is staggering: Unlike Mexico, Japan has been loaning the world, especially the United States, trillions of dollars. Japanese financial institutions own about $275 billion of U.S. Treasury bonds alone. And by buying our government bonds, Japan kept U.S. interest rates from rising.

In short, Japan's massive cache of savings helped permit the United States to grow in the 1980s and 1990s. Now our banker is bankrupt. Picture Jimmy Stewart's character in *It's a Wonderful Life*. When his Bailey Building and Loan went belly-up, the whole town shuddered and stumbled into a downward spiral. They were left at the mercy of Lionel Barrymore's icy, greedy, and villainous banker, Old Man Potter. Japan's near-collapse threatens to pull down the United States as well if, for example, Japanese banks are forced to sell off their U.S. holdings in order to bring all their money back home.

Time is running out for Tokyo, and the "mandarins" at the Ministry of Finance are desperately trying to prepare a new game plan for the twenty-first century. (Though "mandarin" is usually associated with Chinese bureaucrats, this term is commonly used in Japan to denote the apolitical and often arrogant professional ministers.) Ministry of Finance officials traditionally acted as if they came down from heaven, for they usually attended the prestigious Tokyo University. Like the samurai class of yore, the mandarins commanded deep bows from private industry, who were often at the mercy of bureaucratic directives. Because elected members of the Japanese Congress (the Diet) have virtually no professional staff, even popular leaders wielded little authority. The 1990s economic calamity, though, has tarnished the Ministry's image. They are mortal after all, and perhaps far less, according to their critics who accuse them of not just arrogance but corruption and incompetence. The Ministry of Finance, after all, pushed the government into raising sales taxes during 1996, in the middle of a recession, further accelerating a downward spiral. Moreover, Ministry officials covered up the financial fraud of Japanese banks, trying to thwart investigations by the U.S. Treasury Department and the Federal Reserve Board. They are fighting to protect their hegemony in a world economy that moves too quickly for bureaucrats to control. Critics suggest that Japan would be better off if the bureaucrats took a page out of the history of the samurai warriors who, during the Tokugawa era (1603–1868), put down their swords and instead devoted themselves to less dangerous pursuits like composing poetry and refining the traditional tea ceremony.

Whether or not the Ministry of Finance leads the way, Japanese society will eventually develop a multipronged strategy to reverse its dismal decline. The strategy will arise through discussions among leading corporations, Japanese financial institutions, and foreign investment bankers, who will share their experiences helping to restructure U.S. businesses in the 1980s. Like any good football playbook, there will be an offensive and a defensive strategy filled by Xs and Os. The players are not running backs and defensive tackles; they are high-tech firms, old line manufacturers, and free-agent workers. American investors may feel that they have the luxury of sitting in the grandstands high above the combatants, but their portfolios are tied down on the playing field. Too many professional pundits have dismissed Japan as an historical relic, without much hope and without much import. After describing the economic and social forces impinging on Japan, this chapter will guide readers to those investment sectors that will profit from the new Japanese playbook. Health-care services, defense aerospace, and oil and gas drilling firms could emerge as big winners for those who understand how Japan will transform.

FACTORS FORCING JAPAN INTO ACTION

A number of factors have forced the Japanese government to develop a new playbook for the next century. First, the Japanese people are aging faster than sushi in the sun. Investors should pounce on Western health-care firms that enter the Japanese market. The aging populace also means there are not enough Japanese workers to support future retirees. According to Japan's Ministry of Health, by 2010 there will be fewer than two workers for every retiree, about half of the current rate. In contrast to the United States and Europe, Japan simply does not tolerate immigration (which could theoretically help by letting in young foreign workers). The size of the workforce will actually shrink by more than 10 million, almost 20 percent. That means that Japan will not have enough domestic workers to support its economy. If you visited Tokyo any time in the last twenty years, you would have noticed attractive young women bowing to you in front of every office and hotel elevator, saying *Ohayo gozaimasu* ("good morning"). They were extra laborers, who decorated the hallways like fresh flowers at a Four Seasons resort. As Japan's pool of workers shrinks, we visitors can soon say *Sayonara* ("good-bye") to those smiling and bowing elevator greeters. Unless Japan supercharges its productivity, living standards may be virtually the same thirty years from now.

Second, the Japanese ma's and pa's cannot afford to keep the bulk of their investments in Japan. They will send their savings into stock markets elsewhere around the world. Third, Japanese leaders have learned that they simply do not have the dynamic entrepreneurial spirit to keep up with the Americans in the rapidly changing high-tech, computer, and biotechnology fields. Fourth, Japan fears China, especially a growing China that dominates the Eastern Hemisphere and hosts a People's Liberation Army that could overrun the Japanese islands within minutes. With ten times the population, China could amass a bigger army than the entire population of Japan.

Though I will discuss these factors in greater depth, let's jump directly into Japan's playbook and expose the secrets and the not-so-secrets. I call their strategy the *jelly doughnut* plan. The jelly doughnut is a treat you won't yet find in Tokyo (though remember that a Japanese firm owns the 7-Eleven company, which distributes millions of jelly doughnuts each morning in America), but it does nicely describe the government's goals. On a map, Japan looks, of course, like a long stretch of islands. Economically, though, Japan has turned into a plain, dry doughnut. There is a vast hole in the center of the economy, a hole that began expanding in the late 1980s, when Japanese wages jumped and Japanese companies could not afford to manufacture at home. The economy began to hollow out. Japanese automakers built plants in California, Tennessee, Ohio, Malaysia, Thailand, Indonesia, Vietnam, and

China. The Ministry of International Trade and Industry pumped out imposing documents designing the future of Asia—Malaysia would make shoes for Japan to wear and to export to the West, Indonesia would craft textiles, and China would fabricate toys. A few years ago, audio-visual firms like TDK stopped producing VHS tapes in Japan and instead started importing them from their factories in South Korea. And today Japan's biggest imports include Toyota cars built in America.

Sucked into the doughnut hole were millions of Japanese workers who had expected lifetime employment. Until the 1990s, Japanese paper manufacturers probably never produced a "pink slip." By 1990, after the stock market crashed, wiping out 60 percent of its value, the pink slip became a common office item. Ten percent of the manufacturing jobs were erased. I remember visiting Tokyo in late 1993 and being astounded at the incompetence of the taxi drivers. It turned out that some of them were laid-off manufacturing workers who had no idea how to navigate the tricky Tokyo map.

Many of those who kept their jobs were shoved into the darkest corners of the dimmest corridors, with nothing to do but watch the minutes click by. Their bosses were hoping they would take the hint, though many could not afford to do so. A government survey showed that the number of people wanting to change jobs jumped by almost 50 percent between 1987 and 1996. But for many, the only opportunity was an open window.

MISTAKES OF THE 1980S

Japanese investors displayed what I call a "reverse Midas touch." Every piece of gold they touched zapped itself into a baser metal. Remember the headlines from the 1980s, when the Japanese launched a buying spree that bought them the Pebble Beach Golf Course, the Citicorp Building in New York, Universal Studios, and a big piece of the impressionist art market? Almost immediately those investments fell apart. As soon as a Japanese hand cradled a Monet, Park Avenue socialites got tired of lilies. They bought the heralded La Costa golf course in southern California, and suddenly the Hollywood golf set noticed crab grass on the fairways. In 1988, I was working in Manhattan's Citicorp Center when the Japanese landlords took over. They thought they would be able to raise the rents. Hah! We all knew that an imminent office glut would allow us to negotiate cheaper rental fees.

Tokyo officials know that they have no choice but to accept the doughnut structure, that with a relatively old population resembling Florida's pensioners, Japan will never again be the workshop of the world. The key goal, though, is to inject something sweet into the middle. Japan must become the profit-shop of the world, the place where corporate headquarters coordinate workers located offshore. The sweet jelly is the sweet smell of profits. Japan cannot be paid for its handiwork. It cannot expect to be paid for its innovative genius. But it does have a shot at being paid for its deft planning and coordination skills. Investors must pay close attention as the strategy unfolds. It will determine whether Japan walks out of the intensive-care unit, or whether it, like MacArthur, simply fades away.

While enjoying a sushi dinner in Tokyo recently, I asked an official from the Bank of Japan how Japanese firms can compete with the emerging Chinese powerhouses. The answer, as usual, was "teamwork." "We like to say that in a man-to-man game or fight, the Chinese guy would beat the Japanese individual every time," he said. "They're very smart and aggressive. But we know that in a team fight or sport, we'll win each time. The Chinese like to attack each other. They don't have a history of working together. But we Japanese cannot imagine working apart."

Teamwork is not always good, of course. The Gambino crime family often worked well with each other, but toward evil ends. In the past few years, prosecutors in Japan uncovered chronic corruption even among Japan's most prestigious corporations, including bribes and extortion payments to government officials and *yakuza* (mafia) members. Racketeering charges stuck to such names as Hitachi, Yamaichi Securities, and even Mitsubishi, prompting a newspaper headline to paraphrase Julius Caesar, "You too, Mitsubishi!" One comic strip printed in the *Mainichi* newspaper showed a man in jail shouting across the corridor to the other cells, "Mr. Managing Director, is that you?" The shouter's cellmate asks,

"Do you know them?" "No, I just figure I'm bound to hit the mark with one of them."

Japan's government has also engaged in bad teamwork that injured the economy, most especially the disgraced government of Prime Minister Kauei Tanaka, who pocketed a multimillion dollar payoff when All Nippon Airways purchased Lockheed jets in 1974. In 1993, investigators found $50 million worth of gold bars, cash, and securities in the home of disgraced political kingmaker ("shadow shogun") Shin Kanemaru. Aside from outright corruption, the elected governments and the Ministry of Finance continually confused and discouraged the financial markets by toying with new spending packages intended to stimulate the economy. A parade of prime ministers and finance ministers over the years unveiled seemingly huge programs, which turned out to be greatly exaggerated, including double and triple counting. The Japanese use the term *mamizu*, meaning "real water," to separate the hype from the real stuff. White House officials in the Clinton administration have confessed that they usually disregard about 90 percent of the headline figure that the Japanese government publicizes. The hype hurts, however, for it sends the markets on a yo-yo path, temporarily driving up Japanese interest rates and the value of the yen, which tend to dampen the economy. A conspiracy of hype is bad teamwork.

A REVERSAL OF FORTUNE

As I have already pointed out, Japan tried to grapple with the doughnut phenomenon in the 1980s, and executed the worst investment decisions since Napoleon got hungry for Russian wheat. They cannot afford to make the same mistakes again. They will not simply buy "trophy" buildings to enhance their prestige. They have lost face and learned from their hubris. While in the 1980s, corporate leaders became heroes simply for nabbing famous trademarks like Universal Studios, in the next decade only the bottom line will count. The Japanese utterly failed at glitz and glamour. Now, they will go back to basics. They will prefer to buy an anonymous company that holds a promising patent, rather than acquire a household name that is pooping out on its profits and cannot be revived. In the 1980s Tokyo was motivated by arrogance. In the twenty-first century Tokyo will draw its energy from fear.

The "graying of Japan" does not just mean than Japan will have relatively fewer workers toiling in the fields and on the assembly lines. Service industries will feel the squeeze as well. The entire financial system will either be overhauled under the best-case scenario or scrapped in a doomsday scene. Already U.S. firms like Merrill Lynch and Goldman Sachs are signing up huge number of clients who do not believe that the Japanese banks will survive the next ten years.

For example, the Japanese savings rate since World War II has been extraordinary. While Americans feel lucky to stash away 2 or 3 percent of their incomes each year, the typical Japanese family manages to squirrel away about 15 percent. Those savings have fed the world's companies, which have borrowed heavily from Japanese banks. In the 1990s, when countries like Thailand, Malaysia, and the Philippines needed money for roads, rails, and tunnels, they sidled up to the Japanese, who pumped in about half of those countries' $500 billion in corporate loans. But remember, in ten years when the plurality of Japanese retire from working, they will be *drawing down* their savings, not adding to it. Just like Americans who retire to Leisure Village, the Japanese will learn to live on their investments. After all, Japanese pension plans are pretty miserly, and the government's social security and medical coverage are even less financially secure than America's. In Chapter 1 I discussed a recent poll showing that among American twenty-somethings, a greater proportion believe in UFOs than that Social Security will last another fifty years. In Japan, a similar poll would likely show a greater percentage believing in *Godzilla* than in the Ministry of Health's promises. The skeptics will probably be proved right.

With a shrinking pool of savings and an urgent demand for higher returns on investments, Japanese retirees will demand much higher interest rates from banks and corporate borrowers. That will make it nearly impossible for Japanese firms to afford to borrow funds in order to erect new manufacturing facilities in Japan. In 1998 Japanese ten-year bonds averaged a puny 1 percent, but—have no doubt—those bonds will have to pay at least four times that in ten years. Do you know anyone who can afford to retire by locking up their savings for ten years at yields of only 1 percent? Other than Bill Gates and Warren Buffett, few could accept that meager offer, and those who could are not stupid enough. Elderly Japanese will eventually need a stronger currency so that the yen buys more in the world market, another trend that investors could ride.

Likewise, Japan's enormous trade surplus, now about $125 billion in 1998, will disappear. (Note: A trade surplus simply means that a country sells more goods to foreigners than it buys from foreigners.) Why? Take a simple view. Does the Leisure Village community in Carlsbad, California, have a trade surplus with its neighbors? Let's see, residents of the Leisure Village buy oranges, beauty parlor services, golf clubs, and restaurant services. What do Carlsbad residents buy from Leisure Village? I've been to Carlsbad, but I've never seen anyone go through the Leisure Village gates in order to buy a flank steak or a mackerel. Perhaps a semiretired piano teacher there gives lessons, but for the most part the retirement community only imports. A gray, stooped Japan will have more in common with Leisure Village in sunny southern California than with the vibrant, energetic Silicon Valley to the north. This will open up new export opportunities for U.S. firms that have spent the last twenty years in frustration, pounding on the doors of Japanese retail stores, trying to persuade them to carry foreign goods. In the twenty-first century, the rice paper door will open, and foreigners will be permitted to walk on the tatami mats (as long as they first take off their shoes).

When I served in the White House in the early 1990s, Americans still held to an apocalyptic view of the United States and a starry-eyed view of Japan. Many pundits promised that Americans would be relegated to flipping hamburgers at fast food chains that would be owned by the Japanese. They thought that our trade deficit with Japan would forever doom us to relative poverty. And we were deluged with books about the superiority of Japanese management, manufacturing, and finance. After all, the pessimists proclaimed, the Japanese banks represent six of the world's biggest banks. Citibank, the largest U.S. bank, barely got on the list. The pessimists forgot to ask whether those Japanese banks were actually profitable. It turned out the U.S. banks were far better managed. Their stock prices soared in the 1990s, while the stock prices of their Japanese competitors nearly evaporated. By 1996 Moody's Investor Services demoted most Japanese banks to a humiliating D rating, giving their executives something to commiserate about when they visited developing world countries.

The surprise of the twenty-first century will be that the United States may eventually enjoy a trade surplus, while Japan will endure a trade deficit. Soon Japanese pundits will decry the shabby state of their export sector. The mandarins probably wake up in a cold sweat each evening as they contemplate this shift. There is an even more frightening scenario for them, though. What if the Japanese ma's and pa's simply take all of their money out of their yen-based savings accounts and invest them abroad? This kind of "capital flight" is usually seen in immature countries that bungle their finances, for example, in Mexico in 1994, when the peso lost half its value. It would be breathtaking and scary indeed, if Japanese investors simply gave up on their own country. The deep-seated loyalty to the Emperor and the land may only go so far. Nationalism may be for suckers, if it means living on a 1 percent return. That is why Japanese elites are struggling to cook up together the jelly doughnut game plan, which could renew confidence in the country, and certainly open up new investment opportunities to Americans. Toward the end of the chapter we will be examining those sectors that hold promise.

THE BEST DEFENSE

Since a more internationally entwined Japan will be more vulnerable to world events, we must expect a dramatic shift in Japan's international political behavior. In short, Japan will no longer be a pacifist dummy at the mercy of the U.S. ventriloquist. Remember, in the twenty-first century Japan's labor force will be spread throughout the globe, but especially in Asia. Japan cannot sit idly by without military strength in the region, any more than the

United States could sit by while Saddam Hussein captured and bombed Kuwaiti oil fields. Our vital interest in Mideast oil will be matched by Japan's vital interest in east Asian labor. Make no mistake, Washington is headed on a collision course with Tokyo over national defense. But the collision will not result in trade battles as it did when U.S. trade representatives in the 1980s and 1990s routinely threatened the Japanese Ministers of Trade and Industry. Instead, the Secretary of Defense and the Pentagon will try to command the Japanese Ministry of Self-Defense to stand at attention, just when the Japanese want to make new military alliances with their neighbors. This conflict should direct investors toward defense and aerospace-related stocks, as we will discuss.

While General MacArthur became a hero in Japan and successfully implemented a new constitution that prohibited an armed force, except for self-defense, the memory of MacArthur is fading. One of Japan's most prominent political strategists, Ichiro Ozawa, has openly urged a more independent military and diplomatic approach. It is hard to believe that in 1954 the very idea of a *self*-defense force invited protests. Japan must be able to protect its own trade lanes. In October 1997, the U.S. Coast Guard threatened to climb aboard and impound Japanese shipping vessels, as a result of a trade dispute over the management of port facilities. Imagine the humiliation for Japan—cowed by the Coast Guard, an agency better known for throwing life preservers to weekend sailors off Martha's Vineyard than for intimidating world powers. It was like Gilligan and the Skipper pushing aside the *QE2*.

Japan will not allow this relationship to continue, not as she grows more vulnerable to events in China and southeast Asia. Honda and Toyota own fourteen automobile plants in those countries. What if the U.S. Commerce Secretary decides that a plant in Thailand is illegally dumping (that is, selling below cost) cars on the U.S. market? Who can stop him from sailing over on an aircraft carrier and locking up the plant until the Japanese bow and cry "Uncle?" What if the Chinese premier threatened to show such bravado? Tokyo would be at the mercy of Uncle Sam to respond. Fifty-five years of fealty to the United States is about as much as Japan will tolerate. Japan will also push to develop her own energy resources, offering opportunities for investors in the oil and gas sector.

While most officials at the Pentagon would experience heart palpitations at the thought of this shift, the American people may not be so upset. Remember, the United States has been holding its nuclear umbrella over Japan ever since dropping the atomic bomb on Hiroshima and Nagasaki. At the same time, U.S. taxpayers have spent trillions of dollars on defense systems and soldiers in order to pursue the strategic interests of NATO and SEATO, the Southeast Asia Treaty Organization. While the Japanese government in the 1970s and 1980s dumped trillions into subsidies for the steel, auto, and electronics industries, the U.S. government had to maintain its focus on the Cold War and keeping up to speed with the Soviet Union's military advances. American voters still perceive the Japanese as free-riders who benefit from the U.S. military without paying their "fair share." Whether or not this characterization is fair to the Japanese (who do make payments to subsidize the U.S. presence), Americans may not object to Japan "carrying its own weight." Japan's new strategy need not incite anger in America, nor rage among the typical Japanese citizen. Japanese continue to rate the United States, especially Hawaii and the West Coast, among the friendliest places to visit in the world. In July 1998, 33,000 Japanese baseball fans attended "American Ballpark Weekend" at the Tokyo Dome, eating hot dogs and singing along to a videotaped presentation of the late Harry Caray warbling "Take Me Out to the Ball Game."

Now that we have explored the pressures building in Tokyo, we can examine the new game plan in Tokyo to create the jelly doughnut economy.

THE JELLY DOUGHNUT GAME PLAN

The jelly doughnut game plan includes a number of steps that should sound alarms in the ears of Wall Street traders, Washington politicians, and small investors. The first principle of the jelly doughnut strategy is *modesty*, which had been a traditional Japanese skill, at least until the 1980s decade of hubris. Japanese citizens are socialized from birth on exactly how low to bow to different people, how many times, and whether from the waist, shoulders, or neck, depending on their social and familial stature. Modesty will bring Japanese firms back into the merger and acquisition arena, but this time they will be willing to relinquish the obsessive control of decision-making that they exercised in the 1980s. In the 1980s, Japanese takeovers resulted in U.S. managers scurrying to Tokyo for endless meetings before any executive decisions could be made. Those days are over. Japanese acquirers have learned that they have little choice but to show faith in their new partners. For example, in the fall of 1997, Nikko Securities, formerly a powerhouse in the investment world, announced that its London office would control decisions over pricing and personnel. This would have shocked Tokyo ten years ago.

Another strategy of the game plan is to merge with foreign firms that can teach the Japanese how to compete outside the manufacturing industry in financial and information services, for example. On their own many of Japan's financial firms have been appalling failures, plagued by corruption and incompetence. In 1997, Nomura Securities found it nearly impossible to secure a contract to underwrite new bond and stock securities. In a sign of things to come, in January 1999, Japan Leasing Corp. merged itself into the protective bear hug of GE Capital Corp. Around the same time, Paine Webber Group teamed up with Yasuda Mutual Life Insurance Co. to jointly sell mutual funds in Japan. Japanese information services firms are almost absent from the world's stage and wield no influence beyond Tokyo. Compare them to Britain's Reuters or CNN. The *Nikkei* newspaper is Japan's equivalent of the *Wall Street Journal*. Its Washington office is located in the National Press Club Building. If you walk into the *Nikkei* office, though, you feel as if you are in a Tokyo hovel. Papers are piled up, file cabinets look dingy and there is no sign of that vaunted Japanese efficiency. The Japanese have deployed efficiency only in the factories. The service sector is positively primeval. But now the Japanese know this. During the Meiji Restoration, beginning in 1868, Japan also opened up to new ideas and acknowledged that it had fallen behind the West and had to catch up, adopting the slogan "Civilization and Enlightenment!" (*bummei kaika*). Today the differences between East and West are truly tiny compared to those of 1868, but the newfound commitment will be almost as strong.

Several years ago, when I introduced a Japanese acquaintance to the Internet, he noticed that it was almost entirely in the English language. "We are toast," he said. Well, that will be true, unless Japan makes the proper alliances and nourishes them.

The 8-year economic slump has humbled many Japanese. Government and corporate officials comfort themselves by speaking of the "Wimbledon" example. They point out that the British tennis players seem never to win the Wimbledon trophy—nonetheless, England sure squeezes buckets of money from the event through tourism, admissions tickets, and sporting gear bearing the "W" logo. Likewise, Japan is learning that it does not need to utterly dominate every angle of the world economy, but instead to strategically squeeze out its fair share.

A third ingredient of the jelly doughnut plan is to repair Japan's reputation in the Far East, where the brutal World War II occupation of China, Manchuria, Korea, and the Philippines destroyed its credibility for fair play and civility. The idea of pan-Asian cooperation provokes a shudder in those outside of Japan who remember the "Greater Asian Co-Prosperity Sphere" under which banner Japan "liberated" southeast Asia from Europe's colonial powers and promoted "Asia for the Asiatics." In 1931, the Japanese army occupied Manchuria, followed by a declaration that "Manchuko" was a Japanese protectorate. Soon after, the air force bombed Shanghai to protect Japanese residents from anti-Japanese forces. In many cases, Asians outside of Japan would rather deal with white Europeans than with Japanese. Japan is known in the Far East for being more bigoted than Westerners. Thousands of Korean women, for example, host bitter memories of Japanese soldiers taking them hostage and using them as sex slaves. Even today these so-called "comfort women" continue to ask for official apologies and reparations. The Japanese government is notorious for its slow-footed effort to acknowledge atrocities in school textbooks. The People's University of Beijing recently asked Chinese, "When someone talks about Japanese people, what person do you think of?" The most common response: war leader Hideki Tojo.

But again, Japan knows it must change. Since it cannot erase the legitimate historical resentment, Japan will instead try to nourish healthier *financial* relations with East Asia. Japanese officials have been trying to get Asian countries to buy and sell their import/export goods in yen, rather than denominating them in U.S. dollars. Though Japan is the biggest player in Asian commerce, firms still prefer U.S. greenbacks. If the Ministry of Finance can turn the yen into a more international currency, they will create more demand for the yen, and thereby help subsidize an elderly populace that needs more buying power. The Ministry's Council on Foreign Exchange has been plotting for years to promote the yen and push aside the dollar. Japan's economic debacle in the 1990s certainly set back the schedule.

Japan has tried to deploy other tactics for beefing up pan-Asian relations. In 1997, for instance, the Ministry of Finance attempted to organize and endow an East Asian rescue fund, which would be deployed to help Asian economies that skidded into trouble. Foreshadowing twenty-first century tensions with the U.S. government, Treasury Secretary Robert Rubin tried to twist the arms of Tokyo officials into revoking the plan. The Japanese did not budge. The United States would not countenance an international rescue fund that the Japanese could control. The standoff continues today, and is a subtle, but telling signal of trouble ahead. In 1998 Chinese President Jiang Zemin visited Japan, the first head of state visit since World War II. Japan and China both want to show the United States that they have choices.

Investors should watch how Japan conducts its Asian relations. It is trying to learn lessons from the United States in the post–World War II period. The goal is to exercise economic and military influence, but without feeding deep resentment. If Japan can help bankroll its neighbors' business projects, those neighbors may not object to a Japanese aircraft carrier floating off the coast. Already, Japan provides about one-quarter of the foreign investment funds for Asia. Though Japanese leaders are embracing the strategy, the voters are more wary. Over 50 percent of Japanese citizens do not view other Asians positively; they much prefer Americans and Europeans. If Japan succeeds in its backyard, it will expand its game plan to Latin America as well. Already, Japan has grabbed a big chunk of computer and auto sales in South America. American investors would be surprised at their inroads south of our borders. Here again, though, Japan will not repeat the same awful mistakes it made in the 1980s. It is looking for partnerships with Latin America, so that Latins can ultimately provide the manpower for Japanese business projects. That's a switch from the old game plan, which simply sought to stuff as many Sony radios as possible into Buenos Aires bedrooms.

MAKING MONEY OFF THE JELLY DOUGHNUT STRATEGY

Since the stock market bounces about so quickly, it would not make much sense to recommend specific stocks by name that will win or lose from Japan's jelly doughnut strategy. Nonetheless, I can point to trends that will lift certain sectors. The reader can then do research or speak with an investment counselor to identify the specific companies that fit the program. This approach is akin to a doctor prescribing a generic drug, and letting the patient and his pharmacist choose the brand name.

Defense and Aerospace Companies

Though the Cold War is over, and many twenty-first century investors will dismiss the defense industry as a fossil of the last century, as quaint as a World War I veterans' parade, Japan will (along with China) keep the industry's cash registers ringing. In addition to "Civilization and Enlightenment," the Meiji rulers of a hundred years ago trumpeted the phrase "Rich Nation, Strong Army" (*fukoku kyohei*). Since Japan's constitution currently prevents an *offensive* army (the army is called the Ground Self-Defense Force), Japan's equipment purchases and its corporate acquisitions will likely center on *defensive*, defense industry stocks. Remember the Patriot missiles, made famous for shooting down Scud missiles in the Persian Gulf War? (They were initially designed as offensive weapons.) Japan will need to display military strength, without looking like a frightening, nationalistic power. Japan may very well present itself to Asia as the country offering to protect its neighbors from international terrorism. That means Japan will both buy more defense weapons and eventually purchase defense-related companies. Stock investors should not limit themselves to U.S. companies. French and British defense firms have good reputations and may trade at lower stock prices, making them more attractive takeover candidates, or even merger partners with Japan Aircraft Manufacturing Co.

Oil and Gas Drilling and Services

As Japan aspires to enhance its puny military powers, she must also address her utter dependence on imported energy. This is Japan's historically weak underbelly. In 1940, after Japan took French Indochina (Vietnam), the United States and the United Kingdom reacted with an oil boycott, sparking Japan to capture the oil-rich Dutch East Indies (Indonesia). Though official rhetoric spoke of "liberation" and "cooperation," historical documents from 1941 show that Japan expected the Dutch East Indies to fill its petroleum needs, as well as its needs for tin and rubber. Furthermore, "crude rubber, tin, and bauxite would more seriously affect the United States if their supply is cut off," stated the president of the Japanese Planning Board.

Since World War II, though, Japan has enjoyed the Pentagon's protection. The United States, Europe, and some Arab states fought the Gulf War, not Japanese soldiers. After the war, State Department officials traveled hat in hand from Washington to Tokyo to ask for financial contributions. I remember receiving their reports at the White House. Grudgingly, the Japanese had pledged some funds, but then proved slow to actually ante up, angering both capitals. Japan cannot afford to let this fuzzy relationship linger into the next century. Rather than purchasing American energy firms, Japan may very well buy large shares of oil exploration, production, and refining firms based outside North America. This might include Norwegian, Argentine, and Venezuelan companies, many of which are traded on major stock exchanges.

Health-care Services

Japan is beginning to shake off its ethnic ideology, which had insisted that the Japanese are a biologically unique people. Not long ago, government ministers proclaimed that the Japanese had different kinds of intestines than foreigners, and therefore could not tolerate American beef or apples. With an increasingly elderly population, and a faulty health-care system, Japan will be looking for foreign help in the years ahead. Though "health maintenance organizations" have a dreary reputation in the United States, investors should keep their eyes open for discussions between Japanese medical firms and U.S. firms. Already, an American firm has cornered the market in cancer insurance. Japanese insurance and medical firms are not nearly as sophisticated in handling paperwork as their American counterparts. U.S. companies that provide paper-flow, computer, and organizational expertise to the health-care industry will be huge beneficiaries of the jelly dough-nut strategy.

Retail Products

Japan will always pride itself on quality. Even in the early 1970s when Toyotas looked like tin tuna cans, Japan knew her cars would eventually outshine Detroit and Stuttgart. New luxury names like Lexus and Infiniti redefined quality in the 1980s and effectively slapped American and German manufacturers across the faces, forcing Cadillac and Mercedes Benz to reinvent themselves. In the next century, Japan will not have enough workers to satisfy its motor industry's ambitions. As I have already pointed out, Japanese firms have erected factories throughout the Far East and in Latin America as well. This will continue. But at the same time, Japan will search for opportunities to purchase brand names that have good distribution networks, but lesser quality characteristics. Remember that Ford bought Jaguar several years ago and saved that old company's reputation from being forever branded as shiny and sexy but dangerously shoddy. This turnaround role is well-suited to Japanese management traits. Therefore, as our ficti-tious Jim Rayfield example at the beginning of this chapter suggests, a Japanese firm could very well take over a General Motors in order to buff up its (GM's) image and product quality standards. The general advice to the investor, then, is to keep an eye out for old-line American firms with solid distribution networks, good name recognition, operating within a growing industry, but lacking tight management. Japanese investment bankers will be on the prowl. But unlike the 1980s, they will not pay one yen more than necessary.

Purely Financial Bets

Investors who like to speculate on pure financial instruments should think about the Japanese yen, which can be bought in a number of ways, ranging from simple bank CDs denominated in yen to complex futures contracts traded in Philadelphia.

The bottom line here is that the yen may go down in value against the U.S. dollar, but eventually spring way ahead. For the Japanese economy to recover from its dreadful seven-year drought, the yen should depreciate before this century concludes. Japanese exporting companies need a crutch to survive the terrible domestic sales. A cheaper yen will make their goods seem less expensive to foreign buyers.

Nonetheless, this drop in the yen's exchange rate will present a long-term buying opportunity for speculators. Why? When Japan figuratively retires over the next five to fifteen years, its pensioners will require more buying power from foreigners. Remember, Japan will start resembling Leisure Village, whose population buys goods made elsewhere. The Japanese pensioners will need their yen to buy more foreign goods, priced in dollars or Euros, or Chinese yuan. Therefore, the Tokyo government, which has historically kowtowed to its exporters (who prefer a cheap yen in order to make its goods seem cheaper to foreign buyers), will switch allegiances and promote a stronger currency. Playing this game is not for the faint of heart, but it is what made financier George Soros a billionaire.

In sum, investors should embrace a once-in-a-millennium chance to profit from Japan, as the old ways crack. It takes time, but they do. I'm afraid that many pundits have not just condemned Japan to the dustbin of history, but have already closed the lid. The great masterpiece of Japanese literature, *Tale of the Genji*, was written by a courtly woman almost a thousand years ago. The narrator tells a nostalgic love story of the Emperor's son, the "shining Genji." She treats the governors with contempt and wistfully suggests that Japan's best days are gone. She was premature in her prognosis.

Two personal stories may help make the point here. When I first visited Tokyo years ago, I landed at Narita Airport and took the express train into the capital. Along the way I looked out the window to see rice paddies (even as Tokyo metropolitan land prices had soared into the stratosphere, making Manhattan apartment prices look like cut-rate deals on a flooded Louisiana bayou). Have you ever seen farm land between the Los Angeles airport and Wilshire Boulevard? Or on your way into New York from the Newark airport? It certainly looked quaint, but it made no economic sense. Japan added farm jobs in the 1980s, when other countries pursued efficiency. Sad as it might be for camera-toting tourists and rice paddie dwellers, Japan is now importing California sticky rice. Many of those paddies will see pavement.

The second tale of Japanese change comes from Kamakura, a handsome, beachfront town dotted with lovely old Shinto shrines and Buddhist temples. Happily, those religious sites have not been disturbed or blighted by modernity. After touring the temples, I snuck into a traditional Japanese restaurant for *shabu-shabu* (a beef stir-fry dish). I chose the dish from the menu because it had the only Japanese characters I recognized. I folded my relatively long legs on the tatami mat and under the painfully low table. After finishing the delicious fare, I walked around a bamboo wall to the cashier. There, on the other side of the wall, was a slick, modern, fluorescent takeout stand with plastic tables. It turns out, I could have ordered my meal at a microphone on the counter and eaten with all the charm of a fast-food stand at a bus stop. It really was a pity to see. But it does hold a lesson for investors in the decades ahead: Before you sit down with your investment portfolio, do not forget to peek over the walls that you thought were permanent.

6

EUROPE ÜBER ALLES

How European Unity Splinters

DÜSSELDORF, GERMANY

Ronald Meyer did not notice the man in the trench coat who ducked into the elevator just as the doors closed. The man clutched a leather folio with one hand and wiped the sweat off his neck with the other. Meyer focused only on the digital display, telling him what floor the elevator was passing. He sniffed the air and smelled a heavy cologne that made his nostrils quiver. There were just four in the elevator. A lady in a black dress got off at the fortieth floor. The smell lingered. An older man dressed in a sweater and dark trousers walked off at fifty. The smell did not diminish. He glanced at the suspect in the trench coat. They both stepped off as the cab reached the highest floor of the sleek skyscraper, fifty-five.

When Meyer reached his secretary's desk, she stood up. "Good morning, Herr Meyer. Remember you have a meeting with the consortium in ten minutes. Hmm, are you wearing perfume today, Herr Meyer?" she asked.

"Absolutely not," he answered with a sneer. "It smells like a Parisian prostitute out of work."

Meyer walked into the conference room and motioned for the eleven others to stay in their seats. He was the president of DuselBank, but his

146

board of directors asked him to treat the others as equals. So be it. He accepted their orders, but without much grace.

"Monsieur Meyer," said the man bathed in cologne, "I am concerned about our tighter lending policies. This is not working in our French offices. Our clients cannot tolerate all this paperwork and these higher interest rates. It simply will not do. On behalf of DuselBank's French branches, I ask you to desist."

Meyer's face turned from pale to red so fast he looked like a barbershop pole on a windy day. He looked down at the seating chart that his secretary had prepared to figure out who this man was. Christian Bossard, head of Paris operations.

"Mr. Bossard, if you are not tough enough to dictate terms to your branch managers, I suggest you send them to me. I will take care of them. A united, competitive Europe will require sacrifice. It's not all wine and pastry, sir."

Newsflash

There is danger in the Frankfurt air. The local police force has taken up positions with shields, tear gas, and dogs. It looks like they're preparing for World Cup riots and hooliganism. But this is far more serious. The train station has turned into a battle-ground for European economic policy. The train arriving from Paris is jammed with French union members demanding that the new European Central Bank slash interest rates to reenergize France's sagging economy. Meanwhile, the train from Amsterdam is packed with shopkeepers demanding that the bank hike interest rates to cut off the rising inflation rate that is keeping shoppers at home. The Paris train arrives at 10:45 A.M. Amsterdam at 10:55. Two trains crowded with people who speak two different languages, but carry the same kind of money, are ready to rumble.

When asked what he thought of Western civilization, Gandhi replied that it sounded like a good idea. So, too, might a "European community." Looking back at the twentieth century, it is not easy for Americans to imagine it. In 1914 a bullet fired in Sarajevo triggered the greatest bloodshed the world had known, threatening countries thousands of miles away from muddy European trenches. Germany even tried to incite Mexico against the United States, in exchange for promises to help Mexico reclaim Texas, Arizona, and New Mexico. In 1939, Germany invades Poland, which tries to defend against Panzer tanks with the charge of a horse cavalry. In 1945, 38 million lives later, World War II ends, not with a horse's whinny but with the bang of two atomic bombs. Even amid the peace and prosperity of the post-World War II era, raw tensions within Europe threaten common civility. In the 1980s, French President François Mitterrand visits England for a ground-breaking ceremony for the tunnel spanning the English Channel, nicknamed the Chunnel. British protesters, who want to keep the continent as far away as God planted it, shout to the president, "Froggy! Froggy! Go Home Froggy!"

Europe has not behaved with the semblance of a united community since the time it was known as Christendom, under Charlemagne in 800 A.D. Even as leader of the Holy Roman Empire, Charlemagne struggled with the mosaic map he ruled over, dotted with different languages and customs defended by warring tribes. While trying to master the continent he tried to respect its diversity. About languages, he purportedly said, "I speak Italian to my women; French to my chef; Spanish to God; and German . . . to my horse." Fast forward twelve hundred years. Is a continent that demands various electrical plugs simply to play a radio ready to abandon national currencies and pin their hopes on the exact same economic policy?

This chapter will explain how European Monetary Union (EMU) works and how it could enrich investors. In short, on January 1, 1999, eleven European countries abandoned their national currencies and adopted a single currency, the Euro, which is regulated by a joint European Central Bank. At the same time that Europe weaves itself into a single financial web, though, investors must prepare for a dangerous unraveling of EMU, and the launch of a tempestuous economic war within Europe. As Americans discovered in World Wars I and II, the Atlantic does not protect us from Europe's internecine battles. A blowup of EMU would hurt markets everywhere. Therefore, U.S. businesses and Washington should root for EMU's success. At the same time, though, if EMU works as smoothly as a BMW transmission shifts gears, Americans would face new competitive challenges, especially in Latin America. The U.S.'s backyard will quickly become a super-competitive playing field for European institutions. In sum, we cannot avoid EMU, whether it succeeds or explodes.

Though this chapter will intertwine the forces of history, finance, and culture, my ultimate goal is not to design a college course on Europe—but to show investors where to look for profits. To benefit from EMU, I would urge investors to brush up on their Latin and Greek, for countries like Italy, Spain, Portugal, and eventually Greece have the most to gain. Later in this chapter I will discuss why well-managed firms in the Mediterranean region will be attractive takeover candidates and competitors. In addition, this chapter will show investors why companies that can crack into European internet and mail order commerce will show up as winners. Finally, we will see why EMU makes Europe ripe for a junk bond bonanza that will enrich those investment banks and investors who stay ahead of the game.

WAR AND PEACE

Why abandon national currencies and adopt EMU? Fear. Of inflation? Recession? Taxes? No. Fear of Germany. The intricate economic engineering behind EMU is not driven by economics. Sure, EMU requires complex statistical calculations to regulate the European money supply and the new European Central Bank's foreign reserve holdings. That is for the technicians. The raison d'être of European Monetary Union, though, is politics, more specifically, it is an attempt to prevent a united Germany from rising up in the twenty-first century as it did in 1914 and 1939. While politicians in the United States, Canada, and Japan cheered the fall of the Berlin Wall in 1989 and applauded the uniting of East and West Germany, European nations quivered. A few years before, they had quaked when President Ronald Reagan stood in Berlin and implored Mr. Gorbachev to "tear down that Wall." While French leaders, for example, did not like a totalitarian East Germany dominated by the Soviet Union, they feared even more a new Germany, with 25 percent more Germans and 45 percent more land. They could not forget that it was the Germans, not the Soviets, who had marched down the Champs Elysees in June 1940. Now fifty years later, almost to the day, Germany had sewn its economy back together again. In a confidential 1990 memorandum the French Finance Ministry predicted that "at the end of the century Germany will be—even more than today—the dominant economic power in Europe." And what would happen if Germany got too friendly with Russia again, as it did in 1939? The French experience was encapsulated by the officer who after World War II worried that "every time Berlin and Moscow come to an agreement, they arrive in Paris."

What to do? Tie down Germany like Gulliver. In a complete contrast to George Washington's warning that America should avoid "foreign entanglements," Europe deliberately aimed to so entangle Germany's economy that the fatherland would be, if not castrated, at least trussed. France, in particular, had learned that currency arrangements could be translated into political power. British sterling dominated the world before the Great Depression; the U.S. dollar dominated from after World War II until 1971. In the 1980s and early 1990s, the French government frequently fought to prevent the French franc from losing its value against the rock-solid German mark. In August 1993, the Bank of France spent about $55 billion buying up French francs, in a desperate battle to fight off private market participants who were dumping the currency in favor of the German deutsche mark. This fight was a matter of pride, since French politicians and bureaucrats had promised to defend their "Franc fort" policy. Ultimately, the French taxpayers lost out, because the Bank of France could not stop the market's anti-franc momentum. The politicians had to swallow their pride and stomach a weaker franc. But what if there was no French franc or German mark? Presto, no German economic hegemony. Margaret Thatcher recalls that German unification "fuel[ed] the desire of President Mitterrand ... for a federal Europe, which would 'bind in' the new Germany to a structure within which its predominance would be checked."

So far, my description sounds like a secret plot hatched in the labyrinthine gardens of Versailles. Surely, the Germans were duped, hypnotized, or poisoned? Quite the opposite. The German government has been, not just an accomplice but a chief conspirator. Chancellor Helmut Kohl, who reigned from 1982 until 1998, was a three-hundred-pound unstoppable force on behalf of political and monetary union, announcing that "Germany is our fatherland, but Europe is our future." Without Kohl's political heft, the project would have fallen apart (though it began in the 1970s, with the Social Democrat Helmut Schmidt and the conservative French President Valery Giscard d'Estaing). Like the French, Kohl worried that an independent Germany could turn again to nationalism sometime in the twenty-first century. To Kohl, EMU was a preemptive strike, stating that "political union and economic and monetary union are inseparably linked." Of course, such unions are no guarantee of peace, as hundreds of thousands of Dixie and Yankee widows discovered in America in the 1860s.

Kohl's public arguments for EMU were not so blunt as to warn the German people they must be emasculated or else they would turn to Fascists again. Instead, he and leaders throughout Europe focused on economic benefits, for example: It would reduce the foreign exchange costs of traveling from country to country; it would empower consumers to compare prices for the same goods, at a time when a bottle of Bayer aspirin cost 50 percent less in Spain than in Bayer's native Germany; and it would prevent individual European countries from pursuing reckless or opportunistic economic policies.

Despite Kohl's campaign for EMU, the *volk* disagreed. Just because the elected German government favored EMU did not mean that the people liked the idea. The government never held a referendum on abandoning the German mark. Newspapers of the left and the right attacked the program, and the country's most popular newspaper printed a photograph of Kohl holding up a new Euro coin, over a sarcastic caption, "Helmut, you make such a lovely couple." Even in 1998, moments before the official adoption of the Euro, a majority of the people still opposed the program. In February 1998, more than 150 German economists appealed to the government to postpone EMU because European conditions were "most unsuitable" for the project to start. The German Finance Ministry replied that the time was ripe, since a "European culture of stability has come into being."

Obviously, the German people did not oppose EMU because they wanted to prepare for a third world war. On the contrary, they wanted to avoid the calamitous economic *conditions* that led to World War II, namely, the hyperinflation and economic collapse that made Hitler's nefarious foaming palatable. In the 1950s and 1960s, the German central bank (the Bundesbank) had done an outstanding job fueling the "German economic miracle" that rebuilt Germany's industrial might from the rubble. Why throw out a perfectly oiled monetary machine and replace it with an untested scrum of continental self-interest?

Germans remember the bad, old days before the Bundesbank. After World War I, Germany suffered with excruciating reparations and a hyperinflation that sent them stacking currency notes in shopping carts, as German prices soared by over 300 percent per month, requiring about eighteen hundred printing presses to supply all of the cash. Since prices moved more quickly than paychecks could be written, bosses paid their staff twice a day, so that the employees could shop during their lunch breaks. Patrons at restaurants asked for the check when ordering dinner, and bar patrons ordered beer by the pitcher, since the brew got stale more slowly than prices rose. A common joke told of a German lady running to the market carrying a big straw basket full of bills. She put down the basket to get a look at some fish. When she reached for the basket it was gone. But the thief left the worthless money! John Maynard Keynes blamed much of Germany's disaster on French Prime Minister Georges Clemenceau, who exploited the Treaty of Versailles to "weaken and destroy Germany in every way possible."

With the experience of monetary disasters seared in their collective memories, the German people took great pride in their post–World War II Bundesbank, which carefully maintained the purchasing power of the mark. Unlike Italy and France, which had tolerated inflationary forces, the Bundesbank stomped its foot on any whiffs of higher prices. "There can be no hard currency without hard measures," stated a Bundesbank president. While in the 1970s and 1980s, the Bank of France and the Bank of England were under the thumb of political appointees, the Bundesbank stood as an independent force, far away from populist politicians. Even its geographical location signaled independence. I have spent many marks on taxi rides out of downtown Frankfurt in order to visit Bundesbank officials in their austere, isolated office building. In sum, the German people generally opposed EMU because they worried that erasing the mark and stripping the Bundesbank would leave their economic fate to the hanky-panky of untrustworthy, foreign politicians. (On the other hand, large German businesses, especially the banks, tended to like the idea of EMU, since it would save them great sums of money on foreign-exchange transactions.)

Ultimately, the German *volk* lost the argument, and a Going Out of Business sign was hung in the window of the Bundesbank. After all is said, history suggests that the German people do tend to follow their leaders. And so they accepted the European Central Bank (ECB) and the Euro on January 1, 1999, despite objections from the man in the street and from the professors in the classroom. But can the European center hold?

NO EXIT: TENSIONS WITHIN EUROPE

While Kohl encouraged the Lilliputians to tie up Germany, he did some weaving of his own. In exchange for eliminating the mark and turning over control of money to the ECB, other countries agreed to the Maastricht Treaty, which attempts to limit their governments from spending money irresponsibly (by curbing annual budget deficits to 3 percent of GDP and national debts to 60 percent of GDP). Furthermore, Germany won a symbolic victory by placing the ECB headquarters in Frankfurt, home of the Bundesbank. But perhaps the ECB is an enemy invasion of the fatherland. The initial six-member executive board is composed of a Dutchman, a Frenchman, a Spaniard, a Finn, an Italian, and only one German. Germany could be outvoted in a vote tallied in Germany—after all, the United States loses its share of United

Nations votes on the East Side of Manhattan. (In the near-term, Germany takes some comfort that the individuals initially appointed to the board have a hard-liner bent, especially Dutchman Wim Duisenberg, Finn Sirrka Hamalainen, and the highly respected former Bundesbanker Otmar Issing. Still, there is no guarantee their replacements will follow their strong, anti-inflation convictions.)

Later in this chapter, investors will learn that the biggest winners within Europe are the Mediterranean countries, Italy, Spain and Portugal. They can now borrow at the same low interest rates as Germany, since their history of shaky national currencies are made irrelevant.

ECONOMIC PROBLEMS WITH EMU AND
THE LOCOMOTIVE PARADOX

A committee is not always an efficient way of decision-making, as any PTA board member would attest. The diplomacy scholar George F. Kennan suggested that the odds of a committee failing increases by the square of the number of members. For the ECB, even Kennan's odds may be optimistic. Here is the rub: A single currency works well only when countries enjoy, or suffer from, similar economic conditions, because a single currency means that the ECB will set just one official interest rate for the entire bloc. Now suppose Finland, a member of EMU, has a booming economy, with a very low unemployment rate, and the strong economy is starting to push up prices, at a 4 percent inflation rate. Perhaps its Nokia telephone exports and its shipbuilding enterprises are soaring. Meanwhile, Italy is in a slump. Nobody wants this year's Armani fashions from the annual Milan show, and Alfa Romeo cannot find buyers for its sports cars. Prior to EMU, Finland's central bank could try to slow its economy by jacking up interest rates, before inflation got out of hand. In contrast, Italy's central bank could try to add some zip to the economy by cutting interest rates, which would depress the lira, making Italian suits and automobiles cheaper for foreigners to afford. But what is the ECB going to do, when two patients require the opposite medicine? It has no choice but to set one interest rate for its one currency. This is like a primitive hospital that has only amphetamines, even for patients that need sedatives. Someone will suffer. And when they do, the politicians will march on Frankfurt to "reform" the system. But no reform can get around the basic problem, that one medicine cannot treat all diseases. Years ago the television program "Saturday Night Live" featured a regular sketch about a restaurant where, regardless of what the customer ordered, the restaurant served a cheeseburger and Pepsi. It is much funnier to talk about fast food than people losing their jobs.

How will the ECB figure out which medicine to administer? Wim Duisenberg has announced that the ECB will focus both on the money supply within Europe and the *overall* inflation rate. But you cannot look at an overall average without inspecting the underlying range of numbers, any more than a tailor can dress a basketball player by reading that the average man stands about five foot nine inches tall. Federal Reserve Board Chairman Alan Greenspan revealed that he wakes up early each morning and pores over reams of economic statistics while taking a soothing bath. How long will the ECB president have to bathe to study the economic statistics from eleven different countries? We do not know who will serve as president in the future, but he will be a very clean and wrinkled person.

The EMU system faces yet another problem. The Maastricht Treaty requires that countries contain their annual budget deficits to under 3 percent of GDP. But if the economy of a country slows, tax revenues will drop off and social spending will jump, ballooning the deficit. These effects are "automatic stabilizers" for the economy, creating a safety net. In fact, cutting taxes might be a smart response to a weakening economy. But EMU would demand that the government *raise* taxes and cut spending to ward off a growing budget deficit (unless the slowdown is severe enough to fit within the EMU definition of recession, as set forth by the Amsterdam Summit of 1997). In the late 1920s, the gold standard required most European countries to mimic the Bank of France (which, with the United States, held most of the world's gold). When France raised interest rates in 1928, others had to follow, which squeezed their economies and incited speculators to take their money out of Europe. This further undermined those countries, and their governments responded by hiking interest rates and raising taxes, even as the economies were beginning a long, dangerous downward spiral.

I have used the term "locomotive paradox" to describe another potential problem. Germany and France are usually the locomotives of the European economies, especially Germany. De Gaulle even suggested that, after those two countries, the rest of the Continent is decoration. If German consumers are buying, their economic energy spreads across the border, as they vacation in Italy and buy chocolates from Belgium, for example. Similarly, the Canadian economy usually follows the path of its large neighbor to the south. Often, though, there is a time lag between a German recovery and the positive spillover on its neighbors. Here's the locomotive paradox: If the ECB tends to focus on the biggest economy, it may raise interest rates preemptively to head off German inflation, sending rates higher before the neighboring economies really have a chance to get going. Thus, the locomotive does not get to travel far enough to start pulling its cargo (the neighbors), before the central bank slams on the brakes (or the bond market slams on the brakes, in anticipation of a central bank tightening). This problem predates EMU, for when the Bundesbank raised rates, all European rates would go up. EMU does not create the locomotive paradox, but it makes the railroad station a more incendiary place.

THE ANALOGY TO THE UNITED STATES

EMU fans in Europe have a quick rejoinder to American skeptics, which comes pretty close to the playground taunt, "So's your mother!" More precisely, EMU-philes argue that our United States of America has a single currency and a single official interest rate, even though Georgia may be booming while Illinois is busting. The 1982 recession, for example, looked like a Midwestern "rust-belt" recession, while the 1991 recession punished mostly the East and West coasts. Although the same George Washington quarter jingles in pockets and vending machines throughout the United States, its

E pluribus unum motto tells us that there is a lot of diversity. So why does the ECB and the Euro currency face a chorus of naysayers in the United States and the United Kingdom?

A handful of factors tend to determine the success of a single currency zone, or as Robert Mundell called it in a seminal 1961 paper, an "optimum currency area." First, *homogeneity*, meaning similar countries require similar monetary policies. Our earlier example of Finland and Italy depicted a lack of homogeneity. Even more striking would be a comparison of Portugal, a highly agricultural country, with Finland. Margaret Thatcher facetiously points out that the cacophony of languages makes EMU more difficult: "The EU is already fifteen different languages, or fourteen if you count Ireland as speaking English, which is very doubtful." Of course, New Jersey (the Garden State) grows more tomatoes than Alaska. The difference is that the United States has overlaid an identical federal tax and regulatory system with the same income tax, inheritance tax, pension laws, and mortgage deduction rules, apart from relatively minor state laws. As a result, home ownership levels between Alaska and New Jersey are very similar, and households in each are sensitive to their mortgage interest rates. Furthermore, banking systems differ greatly within Europe. A country with strong creditworthy banks may be able to offset a tighter ECB monetary policy (by borrowing in the private bond markets); whereas a country with weaker banks and more firms dependent on those banks will suffer a more severe credit crunch when the ECB pushes up interest rates.

Europe's varied banking industry (France has one bank branch per two thousand people, while Spain has one branch per one thousand) is swirling in merger rumors, as banks try to figure out how to survive in the EMU environment. As I will point out at the end of the chapter, savvy investors should also keep an eye on other financing services, particularly junk bonds.

Second, *labor mobility* makes a single currency more palatable, for if one region's economy dips, workers can take a plane, train, or automobile to a more vibrant area. Here is a key to the U.S. success. California was a shining destination for workers until the early 1990s, when a deep recession sent people fleeing the state for work.

The recovery in the mid-1990s reversed this trend. The Sunbelt of the Southeast lost workers in the 1950s and 1960s to the Northeast, only to attract them again in the decades to follow. A remarkable one-third of young American workers twenty to twenty-nine years old move each year, with 17 percent of those thirty to forty-four packing up. In contrast, Europeans feel hundred-year-old roots keeping them in place. There is some historical self-selection here, since those European families with wanderlust wandered across the Atlantic in the great migrations of the nineteenth and early twentieth centuries. Leif Erikson, Christopher Columbus, and periodic famines and wars did not inspire everyone to follow, after all. Within the European Union, the relatively young Irish population seems most willing to travel, and, of course, Turkish guest workers can be found throughout the Continent, often the target of nationalist abuse.

When an economic slowdown hits one of the United States, it gets an automatic bounce because its workers receive federal unemployment and welfare payments, and the hard-hit state sends less money to Washington. These *fiscal transfers* help the United States operate as a single currency zone. Martin Feldstein calculates that a $1 drop in a state's income is partially offset by a 40 cent change in the flow between that state and Washington, D.C. This safety net explains why no state in the United States has defaulted on its debt during the twentieth century. In the late nineteenth century, before the Federal Reserve Board and automatic transfer programs, numerous states went belly-up. South Carolina defaulted on $22 million of bonds, known as the "whorehouse bonds," which the governor had authorized from a barstool in a brothel.

In Europe the relations between the countries and Brussels (the capital of the EU) are murkier than the relationship between the states and the federal government in the United States today, but less sordid than South Carolina in the 1800s. Consider: European countries have starkly disparate debts weighing on their books as they head into EMU. Italy's government debt exceeds its gross national product, while Finland's debt adds up to less than 60 percent of GDP. Even more striking is to examine the burden of future public pension payments. The value of France's promises to future pensioners adds up to over 110 percent of GDP, while the United Kingdom's total less than 10 percent. Deciding how to share these fiscal burdens within the EMU framework will require some hard thinking (and possibly drinking).

Finally, *flexible labor and goods prices* make a single currency more practical. If a regional economy dips, firms can (temporarily) cut wages and prices, rather than lay off workers or force down nominal interest rates or the exchange rate. Here again, the United States has weaker unions and a more flexible labor market, which helps explain why Europe had such trouble streamlining industries and creating new jobs in the 1980s and 1990s. When former French Prime Minister Edith Cresson served as Agriculture Secretary in the early 1980s, she was once chased off a farm by angry farmers wielding pitchforks when she recommended reform. Cresson has a history of stormy relationships. Though a former member of the European Commission, she hardly promoted a sense of European community several years ago when she accused English men of being rather limp-wristed and disinterested in women.

LOOK OUT! HERE COME THE POLITICIANS

The real sparks will fly when politicians arrive to meddle in the ECB's business. Remember, European political parties tend to come from a wider spectrum than U.S. politicians, with Communist and former Communist parties often taking part in governments. In 1981, Mitterrand began nationalizing French companies, including the banks and the largest corporations. After an electoral thrashing in 1983, he performed a pirouette and began privatizing them again. Mitterrand had a feline knack for multiple political lives. After supporting the pro-Nazi Vichy government as a young man, he served as a center-left cabinet minister in 1946. He even orchestrated a fake assassination attempt on his life, with a drive-by shooting at an outdoor café. The French people forgave this ploy, though the other diners at the café probably did not.

In addition to a wider range of participants, a parliamentary system usually leads to more frequent or at least less regular leadership turnover compared to that of the United States. Italy, for example, has had fifty-six governments since World War II. Long-serving leaders like Helmut Kohl have been the exception.

The point is that the ECB will be circled by vulturelike politicians looking to swoop down whenever the economy weakens and threaten to make the ECB more "democratic" and less independent from elected officials. The politicians' short-term attention spans give them a bias toward looser policies that, in the short-term, can perk up an economy, even at the cost of longer term inflation. Just as medicine comes with "childproof tops," the ECB needs a "politician-proof" top. It will not get it. France has been methodically chipping away at Germany's goal of a thoroughly nonpolitical ECB. In December 1996, the EU Council of Ministers meeting in Dublin created a new "stability council" that would vigilantly watch over the ECB, ensuring that politicians could keep close tabs on the central bankers. Around the same time, Germany swallowed a series of accounting gimmicks intended to make the French budget deficit look smaller. Then, at the Amsterdam Summit in 1997, the Socialist French government of Lionel Jospin squeezed a new "employment chapter" into the Maastricht Treaty, stating that jobs are just as important as price stability. Furthermore, the French have won for the EU Council of Ministers new responsibilities for foreign exchange decisions.

The ECB will suffer from an ongoing wrestling match between Germany and France. The Germans believe in the rule of laws; the French in the rule of men and their political discretion. Who will win? Put your money on the French. But you don't have to listen to me, listen to the Germans. Max Weber, the great student of bureaucracy, pointed to the historical preeminence of French civil servants, for "the Revolution and still more Bonapartism have made the bureaucracy all-powerful." Even that nationalistic, brilliant asylum resident Nietzsche admitted that France "always possessed a masterly skill at converting even the most calamitous turns of its spirit into something attractive and seductive." Germany cannot resist her allure, thought Nietzsche, who respected the long French traditions and angrily denounced all other European culture as a "misunderstanding." Nietzsche's famous contrast of the Greek gods Apollo and Dionysus gives us some insight into the coming conflict between German versus French economic policy. Apollo represented order, logic, and discipline; their motto being, as today's gym rats put it, "No pain, no gain." In true Apollonian fashion, the Bundesbank taught Germany to suffer low inflation in exchange for a strong, durable economy. The French are more like Dionysus, the god of wine, revelry, and passion, and believe, as the yuppie's used to say, "You can have it all." French politicians have been willing to juice up the economy, even at the risk of an inflationary hangover. In the end, EMU not only tries to blend French and German, but Apollo and Dionysus. Who will win the wrestling match between gods? It depends on the terrain. Damon Runyon said that the race is not always to the swift nor the fight to the strong—but that's the way to bet. Likewise, bet on Germany on the battlefield, but France in the parlor.

Let's get beyond the metaphors and Nietzschean musings for a moment. What does it mean for the French to "win" at the bargaining table? In short, an EMU that is increasingly French will over time drift toward looser monetary policy, a weaker currency, a higher inflation rate, and more regulation of the economy. As I pointed out earlier, these effects will not come quickly. The Euro may look stable at the outset (though its value fell 6 percent against the U.S. dollar in January–February 1999, its first two months of trading), since the initial ECB members tend to be hawkish, "hard money" men. These tough guys may even overtighten the money supply to offset the lax fiscal and regulatory policy of politicians. Such a combination could send the Euro's value dangerously higher (as tight monetary and loose fiscal policy did in the United States in the early 1980s). Regardless, the ECB hawks won't rule the roost forever. Eventually, even Greece will join EMU, giving yet another vote to less-than-Germanic monetary discipline.

As for the EMU's oversight of industry, Paul Krugman has predicted that "France will not give up its taste for regulation— indeed, it will surely try to impose that taste on its more market-oriented neighbors." He analogizes the tightly restricted French job market to New York City's rent control. Like New York City tenants, French job holders enjoy generous benefits, and "it is almost as hard to fire those workers as it is to evict a New York tenant. . . . France's policies have produced nice work if you can get it. And, given the generosity of unemployment benefits, many don't even try." Holding on to old regulations gets tougher, though, as the Internet, mail-order catalogs, and other mass marketing ventures undermine old-fashioned rules and relationships. These open up money-making opportunities for investors (see the end of this chapter), but threaten the old way of life. Perhaps the biggest weapon aimed at the quaint, old postcard view of Europe is the network of twenty-one Wal-Marts spread throughout Germany, each with aisles that look as wide as the boulevards of Berlin.

EMU is an explosive cocktail, then, of political ambition, economic dispute, and philosophical rancor. The first year may go smoothly, amid backslaps and handshakes. But consider the following scenario: The politicians grow frustrated with the ECB because some parts of Europe are slumping while other countries are overheating. A few left-wing governments lose their hold on their parliaments and blame the "heartless bankers" at the ECB for throttling the economy. Voters demand more public sector spending, just as the Maastricht Treaty begins to bite down on budget deficits. The aging population of countries like France demand more secure pensions and higher taxes on workers, just as younger countries like Ireland are cutting tax rates. The Euro currency first looks too strong and European exporters complain that they cannot compete with the U.S. dollar and Japanese yen. Then, the Euro swoons, as political fissures come to the surface. Denmark and Sweden delay joining. Citizens of the EMU begin trading in their Euros and nationalist parties in Italy, France, and Germany protest in favor of national currencies. EMU unravels.

Will EMU unravel? As investors, we do not need to believe that the odds of disaster exceed 50 percent; we just need to believe that the odds are higher than the market currently thinks (this is similar to Chapter 9's approach to global warming—as long as the market misjudges the probabilities, there is an investment opportunity). Based on the strong 1997–1998 performance of European bonds and currencies, the market has given EMU a thumbs up, which may be too optimistic, considering the risks and the history of European in-fighting.

THE U.K. STRUGGLE

SOUTHAMPTON, ENGLAND

Lady Margaret Thatcher lifted up her sparkling red dress as she stepped onto a World War II cruiser bound for Normandy. The skies were dark, the seas rough, but her weather forecasters told her that midnight would bring calmer weather, and a safe crossing. A flotilla of vintage boats set off past the Isle of Wight toward Honfleur. The cannons had been dismantled and equipped instead with laser lights. The ancient public address speakers were replaced by digital sound speakers, which blared "Hail Britannia." While General Eisenhower and Montgomery's 1944 invasion received aerial support from C–47 and glider-launched aircraft, Thatcher's mock invasion got aerial television coverage from BBC and CNN helicopters.

Thatcher grabbed a microphone from a young lieutenant: "We will not tolerate a European invasion of Great Britain. Britons must vote against the referendum to join the European Monetary Union. Tens of thousands died in 1944 defending our island from European tyrants. We must defend ourselves once more. We shall fight on television, we shall fight on radio, we shall on the Internet, and we shall never, never give in. . . . "

When Lady Thatcher's flotilla arrived at Honfleur, the misty port with pastel façades looked like a Monet come to life. Thatcher flipped a huge electrical switch, sending red, white, and blue laser lights splashing across the black sky. The image of Queen Elizabeth on a ten-pound note flashed among the stars. "Neither this lady, nor that Lady," she said while pointing to the sky, "will turn."

If EMU does not self-destruct in the next few years, the British Labor Party will likely bring the United Kingdom into the pact. It is a treacherous path for Prime Minister Tony Blair, since most Britons oppose the idea. Ironically, many would see joining EMU and surrendering their monetary and fiscal discretion as a kind of "taxation without representation," recalling the American revolution. I could imagine a Boston Tea Party–like protest with Londoners pouring French wine into the Thames. Since Margaret Thatcher's reign, the United Kingdom has promoted a fluid labor market, where unions cannot block management from restructuring. Tony Blair's "New Labor" has so closely tracked the Thatcherite program that Lady Thatcher spoke glowingly of his candidacy in 1997, even as she officially supported her successor, conservative John Major. As a result of its efficient labor market and relatively low levels of industry regulation, the United Kingdom attracted a disproportionate amount of foreign investment in the past fifteen years compared with its continental neighbors, especially from Japan's automakers.

Nonetheless, Blair veers sharply away from Thatcher, and from the U.K. masses, on the single-currency issue. The British people, who lost lives defending a sheep-raising island off Argentina, are not ready to give up their pound notes, imprinted with the regal profile of Queen Elizabeth. Thatcher is ruthless in her critique. At a private dinner with Thatcher, I was struck by her scathing comments on Europe: "We British and you Americans believe in equity and fairness—traits not shared in Europe." She went on to remind us that "We saved Europe, defeated half—with America—and rescued the other half. We won't get absorbed into Europe now." Of course, Thatcher is out of power and regarded more as a national monument than an active politician. Even so, her views reflect far more than just the Tory right wing. British newspapers routinely report the latest regulatory policies from Brussels, which try to "harmonize" regulations and create industry standards for almost every product. Many of these edicts lend themselves to exaggeration and mockery, including the alleged banning of curved bananas, curtailing the transport of Scotch whisky, and dictating the design of coffins. Perhaps the most egregious and publicized "standardization" concerns the "Euro-condom." In 1991 the European Commission directed its standards agency to develop uniform condom characteristics, leading to newspaper reports about the "Euro-penis." Naturally, all member states claimed that their men could not fit within the EU's proposed dimensions.

The European Commision's credibility took an even bigger

blow in March 1999 when all twenty commissioners suddenly resigned, after a scathing independent report accused them of tolerating fraud, corruption, and mismanagement.

As in Germany, large British businesses tend to support joining EMU. Giant multinationals like General Motors, Siemens of Germany, and Japan's Nissan warned Blair that they could be forced to curtail their U.K.-based factories if Blair continued to opt out of EMU. Before BMW would commit to a $2.5 billion Rover plant near Birmingham, the German automaker requested that Blair pledge that Britain would join the single currency. Will big businesses get their way, against the prejudices of the man in the street? It depends on how well EMU works for the Continent. The Tory government had shrewdly negotiated an option to join EMU at a later date. Now Britain can stand back on dry land and watch whether EMU sinks or swims. If the project brings new prosperity to Europe, Blair and his followers can then confidently jump into the chilly waters and cross the English Channel in a standardized, Euro-sized swimsuit.

HOW THE EURO AFFECTS THE UNITED STATES

American officials naturally give official support to EMU. In private, they are more bemused than enthusiastic. It is a mixed bag for the United States. Naturally, if EMU succeeds at making Europe a more efficient and wealthier continent, the United States would be better off because we would have richer people to sell our goods and services to. European consumers will discover the pleasures of comparison shopping on a continent where German automobiles cost 30 percent less at Italian dealerships. Furthermore, a single currency provides an enormous help to U.S. catalog and Internet merchandisers. One Euro-price for a book ordered from Amazon.com or BarnesandNoble.com saves computer time and space. At first, Europeans may be confused by the new Euro-pricing, until they get used to the new currency. When I land at Heathrow Airport and the captain tells me it's 23 degrees outside, I put on my coat. Then I realize that 23 degrees Celsius means it's a day for short sleeves.

At the same time that EMU helps general merchandisers, particular American exporters worry about new regulations that could limit their sales. For example, the EU now wishes to define "chocolate" as dark chocolate, so that milk chocolate could not carry the label "chocolate." Some corporate executives in Hershey, Pennsylvania are understandably upset. These disputes predated EMU, but the push for European uniformity has intensified the debates.

While individual companies fret about specific regulations, the U.S. bond and currency markets will worry more about the value of the U.S. dollar versus the Euro. Right now, the dollar is king. Just as Jell-O means gelatin, the dollar means money to people throughout the world. The U.S. economy makes up just over one-quarter of the world economy, yet foreign central banks have decided to keep about 60 percent of their official reserves in dollars. Almost 50 percent of world trade takes place in dollars. Even though the European Union's total GDP surpasses that of the United States, foreign central banks keep only about 25 percent of their reserves in Euro-currencies, and only 33 percent of world trade takes place in them. In other words, the Euro-currencies are *underrepresented* in world trade and in central bank vaults. If EMU proceeds smoothly, we could see the Euro increase its market share, putting downward pressure on the U.S. dollar.

A weaker U.S. dollar would tend to push up U.S. interest rates, by fueling inflation and scaring foreign bond buyers. Nonetheless, I doubt that central banks will jump into the Euro without waiting to see whether it survives infancy, and whether the United Kingdom, Denmark, and Sweden will jump onboard. Another factor could slow the rise of the Euro: Individual European investors have not yet invested much beyond their national borders. Germans, for example, have placed just 1 percent of their holdings in foreign stocks, compared with 4 percent for the United States, 9 percent for Canada, and 5 percent for Japan. If Germans develop a similar taste for buying foreign stocks, they would be turning in their Euros for dollars (or yen, or Chinese yuan, etc.), which would tend to depress the Euro's value. With all of these conflicting forces at work, you might as well flip a Euro coin to predict its future value.

STEALING LATIN AMERICA: OUR OWN BACKYARD

BOGOTA, COLOMBIA

When Michael Saxton stepped into the room he knew he was not in Kansas anymore. He'd never been to Kansas, but he was sure it wasn't like this. He was surrounded by screamers and pushers. The screamers were the bond traders who slammed down their headsets in disgust; the pushers were the brokers who wanted to shove a contract in front of you even before offering you a cup of local coffee. Michael was caught in the middle, his first meeting of his first trip to Latin America. He would admit that, but keep secret that it was also his first business trip since joining Cropper & Smith after graduation. He hoped that the altitude would not aggravate his acne.

One of the chief pushers, an old man in a just-pressed pinstripe suit, took Michael's elbow and guided him into a windowless conference room. The man sipped from a mug of coffee, but didn't offer any to Michael.

"I just read your proposal," he said in a thick accent. "Very nice, Mr. Michael. We could use some help with our accounting. Too bad, though."
He shook his head and sipped again.

"Sir?"

"Too bad the Dutch beat you to the punch. They were here last month. One more thing: They undercut you by 25 percent. I hope you enjoy your stay. It'll be a long plane ride back from the Andes." He left the room.

Michael brushed his finger across his forehead. His skin felt bumpy.

Latin America's relationship with Europe is getting tighter, and, if EMU succeeds, Latin American countries will be major beneficiaries. U.S. citizens must keep in mind that South America is neither our "own," nor our "backyard." For one thing, Rio is closer to Portugal than to Des Moines, literally and figuratively. While the United States debated the North American Free Trade Agreement in the 1990s (which still does not extend past Mexico), Europe tried to sew up the Latin banking and telecommunications sectors. "We see a major diminution of the business with the United States and a tremendous increase with European countries," stated a top official at ABN AMRO Bank, a Dutch firm. Meanwhile, the Union Bank of Switzerland predicts that Latin American central banks will eventually switch as much as 30–40 percent of their reserves into Euros, whereas today's holdings are almost exclusively in dollars. In the 1998 Brazilian auction of telephone companies, Telefonica de España took home the biggest prizes, São Paulo's fixed-line company and Rio de Janeiro's cellular leader. Portugal Telecom and Telecom Italia also picked up big cellular regions. Outside of the telecom sector in 1998, the Spanish bank Banco Bilbao Vizcaya purchased a majority interest in Brazil's Banco Excel, while Belgium's Tractebel bought a large power company, and Italy's Parmalat snapped up a dairy company, Batavo. Europe's pursuit of Latin America goes beyond Brazil, of course. Spain's Banco Santander has established a strong network throughout Latin America. Perhaps these aggressive European firms have bid too high and will regret throwing money after Latin corporations. De Gaulle did quip that Brazil had a great future, and always will. More likely, though, Latin America will continue to shed its dependence on the United States. And if EMU succeeds, the pace will accelerate, while U.S. political and financial influence fades. Even if EMU falls on its face, individual European firms will continue their race to Latin America. If Europe invests wisely in Latin America's young population, those energetic young workers can help support the aging residents of continental Europe.

HOW TO MAKE MONEY ON EMU

As I stated in an earlier heading, there is no exit from EMU, no legal map for countries to follow if they want to run away from the project. In that case, an unraveling of EMU would be a disaster for most European stocks, with firms spending a fortune on lawyers and accountants.

Club Med

But what if EMU works well? While I have focused mostly on the German-Franco tensions, neither will come out big winners. The biggest winners are "Club Med"—not the vacation company, but the Mediterranean members of EMU: Spain, Italy, and Portugal. These countries used to pay punishingly high interest rates in order to borrow from the rest of the world. Foreign lenders worried that their currencies would devalue and that they might default on their debt. Just a few years ago, even the Italian government had to pay about 4 percentage points more to borrow than the German government, for example. By getting rid of the lira and bowing to the ECB rather than the Bank of Italy, Italy can now borrow at almost the same interest rates as Germany. By erasing the lira, they erase the possibility of a lira devaluation. That will save Italians and Italian companies billions of dollars. As a result, Club Med firms can afford to borrow and invest in new factories and new products. In a sense, by linking up with Germany, Spain, Portugal, and Italy are inheriting some of the historical credibility of German economic policy. In contrast, Germany is diluting its credibility by jumping into bed with Club Med (over time this will tend to push German rates higher than they otherwise would be).

Well-managed, efficient banks like Italy's Unicredito Italiano and Spain's Banco Santander (each with extensive branch networks) are reaping the benefits of Club Med's suddenly low borrowing costs. Poorly managed banks that have been able to overcharge lenders simply because they were the only bank in town will be driven out of business. Savvy investors should be hunting for Club Med companies (and Irish companies, too, since Ireland will enjoy much lower interest rates under EMU) that dominate their local markets *and* can successfully compete against larger Franco-German companies. And it is not too early to seek out investments in Greek stocks and bonds, since the Euro will likely replace the Drachma in a few years.

Virtual Distributors and Merchandisers

"One price for the same good" will be the motto under the Euro, which will expose the weakness of those local companies that are not competitive enough to handle full-blown competition. Mail-order companies will swoop down and wipe away any over-pricing by local retailers. They also enjoy a tax advantage over local shops; customers pay the value-added tax rate of the mail-order company's country, rather than the possibly higher local rate. Local travel agents, car dealers, booksellers are in big trouble. Those who figure out how to harness the Internet will win.

Junk Bond Kings

Europe has virtually no junk (high yield) bonds. At first that might sound good and solid. "Bully for Europe! No messing around in the gutter!" At a second glance, we see that European firms have missed a tremendous opportunity. Despite the pejora-tive name, over 95 percent of U.S. firms issue bonds that fall into the "junk" category (rated BB or lower by Moody's or Standard & Poor's). Junk bonds have not only fueled such powerful companies as MCI, Duracell, and Time-Warner, but they have delivered supe-rior returns to their owners. From 1980 to 1997, Merrill Lynch's High Yield Index outperformed Treasury bonds by 2.52 percent, while incurring reasonable risks. (Note: The autumn of 1998 was particularly challenging, as Russian and Asian meltdowns worried bond buyers everywhere.)

Until recently, European investors who wanted super-high yields could simply buy government bonds from Italy, Spain, and Portugal. In 1984, for example, Spanish bond yields hit 26 percent, compared to about 8 percent for Germany. Now those Spanish yields have collapsed down to within 0.5 percent of German levels. As more and more Europeans retire, they will be looking for higher yields to provide them with income. The European corporate bond market, which is less than 20 percent the size of the U.S. market, is ripe to take off. Who will win? It is impossible to name names here, but you should keep an eye on the investment banks to see which ones are pushing hardest and most successfully to underwrite junk bond offerings. Then consider investing in those banks that are winning market share in this explosive new market. In addition, the burgeoning of junk bonds in Europe will bring more business to the ratings agencies like Moody's and Standard & Poor's.

Beyond creating big profits for financial institutions, a more diversified bond market will greatly help those young corporations and entrepreneurs who are not burdened by a century of pension commitments. Look for firms with clear profitability targets and strong management incentives, where the managers will not earn much compensation, unless profits and the stock price rises. Remember Dr. Johnson's comment that when a man is to be hanged in a fortnight, it concentrates his mind wonderfully.

CONCLUSION: EMU AS ART AND STATECRAFT

Jacob Burckhardt, the great scholar of the Renaissance, saw the state itself as a work of art; the political and economic system required the same deft hands as Michelangelo's David. It is hard to picture EMU as a work of art, stapled and jammed together by a warring assortment of politicians and bureaucrats. Nor did the EMU project grow from artistic roots. The European Union started in 1951 as the European Coal and Steel Community. Imagine that— a "community" of rocks and metal! Will it end where it began, in rubble? Or will Helmut Kohl's vision of a tamed and tied up Germany prevail? Like King Arthur rolling a round table into his castle, Kohl willingly surrendered Germany's role as the head of European monetary policy. Will history see him as a brave, magnanimous king or a cuckolded fool? The answer may not come quickly. The initial signs may be promising, but events can turn like a Porsche.

Remember, when Britain handed Hong Kong over to China in 1997, the Hong Kong stock market jumped to record highs. Six months later, a market meltdown had wiped out half its value. Nine days after the glorious 1873 World's Fair, the Vienna stock market crashed, spreading panic throughout Europe. In contemplating EMU's future, perhaps we should take some advice from the philosopher Arthur Schopenhauer, who spent his last years in Frankfurt, home of the new European Central Bank: "Treat art like a great man; stand before it and wait patiently until it deigns to speak." And so we wait for Europe's many tongues to speak.

7

HOLD THAT TIGER

How to Play the China Card
Past the Year 2000

BEIJING, CHINA

The Honorable Ho Chin nearly spilled his Coke when he snuck a look at his Longines watch. He'd better swallow that lunch quickly before the even-more-honorable Chao Bang arrived. He bit into the corner of a stubborn pack of mustard. A knock. Ho swiveled his chair away from the door, while slamming his half-eaten cheeseburger into his desk drawer. But Bang didn't knock again. Like an old Communist bureaucrat, he simply threw the door open and spun Ho around in his chair. Ho tried to jump to his feet, but Bang's gnarled but firm seventy-year-old fingers kept him down.

"Did you get the message?"

"I'm ... uh ... getting ready, sir," replied Ho, trying to figure out what Bang was talking about. Had Ho been cut out of the loop again?

"You're not ready. You've never been ready. Not ready for China. You may be ready for some soft Western government," said Bang. "Why don't you wipe that mustard off your face and get a job in Switzerland or Canada?"

Embarrassed, Ho took his sleeve to his lips. Bang was a dying breed. And Ho wished he knew how to speed things up.

Bang turned on a heel, the boots he boasted accompanied him on the Long March with Mao. If you weren't there in 1949, you couldn't gain his respect. So Bang, the devoted egalitarian Communist, sneered and looked down on 1 billion of his own countrymen.

Ho rushed to follow. It was an important meeting. The township council must decide whether to award McDonald's or Burger King the franchise in the new train station.

HONG KONG, CHINA

Lin Fat left the gas streaming out of his stove and then stumbled toward his bed for a good, long sleep. The crash of 1997 had wiped him out. He might as well have dumped his million-dollar stock portfolio into a shredding machine, for the strips of paper would've been worth as much as his bankrupt stock certificates. And Lin wouldn't have to worry about feeding his wife and kids if they all took a deep breath and a deep sleep.

He glanced into the kids' room to take a last look at his son and daughter. He could've sent them to Vancouver to live with his brother-in-law, but at two and three, they were much too young to fly alone. And shame can travel 10,000 miles. He couldn't admit even to his wife that they didn't have enough money for even third-class boat fare to Canada, much less plane fare.

The Beijing government stole his light bulb business. He would have signed on to a fair deal, if the bureaucrats had at least paid him back for the $100,000 he had invested last year in a new processor. But they wanted everything he owned, everything he had built in twenty years, and offered him just a job. Suddenly, he would be just another employee— in his own factory! For just $20,000 a year—the same as everyone else.

Lin gently pulled back the covers on the bed, and he slid his slim body between the sheets. He dared not kiss his wife, for fear that Zhao would wake. He leaned his head against the pillow and closed his eyes.

Police sirens screamed but Lin thought it was a nightmare and kept his eyes tightly shut. When the sound grew closer, he heard Zhao rustle. She rushed to the balcony of their high-rise apartment.

"Oh my god," she yelled. "It looks like a neighbor must have jumped off his terrace." She curled up her nose. "Lin, do you smell gas?"

Newsflash

In an unprecedented and inflammatory move, the Chinese government is preventing the president of the United States from landing Air Force One in Taiwan today. Beijing has warned the United States that Taiwan belongs to China and that China was extending its hegemony to Singapore, Malaysia, Thailand, and Indonesia. Diplomatic experts interpret this declaration as a demand that the president submit his entire Eastern Hemisphere visitation schedule to Beijing and the People's Liberation Army. While this comes as a shock to most Americans, economic analysts in the Far East have been reporting increasing signs that China will use its dominance in the East as an economic counterbalance to the European Monetary Union and to the North American Free Trade Agreement.

A specter is haunting Beijing. It is Russia. The ghost of Mikhail Gorbachev—alive in body, but certainly dead in spirit—frightens Beijing's leaders. China prides itself as the oldest country in the history of the world, but worries that it will not learn from that history. How can the centralized Beijing government survive the onslaught of the twenty-first century's freewheeling technology, politics, and financial markets? After all, the Communist Party strode to power in 1949 with the crudest implements, walking the Long March on worn-out boots. Mao Tse Tung chased Chiang Kai-Shek across the Formosa Strait to Taiwan with bayonets, not with smart bombs. The People's Liberation Army were guided by messengers on foot, not cellular telephones.

But the world has changed. (For one thing, the once rag-tag People's Liberation Army now runs five-star hotels as well as pharmaceutical companies.) China's President, Jiang Zemin, watched on CNN as the forces of technology, politics, and financial markets smashed the Soviet empire into pebbles. He watched in the 1980s as Polish unionists rammed and barricaded government offices, chanting "Reagan! Reagan! Freedom! Freedom!" Jiang watched as East German students chiseled away at the Berlin Wall, encouraged by faxes from all over the world. Hand-held chisels and portable facsimile machines destroyed the Soviet empire, not soldiers or bombs.

While watching Eastern European nationalists carve up the Soviet Union into a dozen fiefdoms, from the once-regal Russia to the seemingly insignificant Tajikistan, China's premier and current economic czar, Zhu Rongji, concluded that Beijing's central government must develop a bold and coherent plan. China, left on its own, would collapse and then break down into fragments. Though 90 percent of Chinese derive from the same Han ethnic group, the provincial conflicts could rip apart China into a kind of Asian Balkans. Anyone who has taken a course in Chinese history remembers that each two-hundred-year dynasty often brought a different province into power. Zhu knew that entropy was not confined to the physics classroom.

The biggest mistake would be for China to sit back and allow Western financial markets to determine China's fate. The USSR was too poor to fight Ronald Reagan's America, militarily or even rhetorically. Like Deng, Zhu believes that Gorbachev's tragic error was to surrender political freedom to the Soviet people *before* overhauling the economic structure. This viewpoint harkens back to the classic Marxist materialist doctrine: The political system must follow the economic system.

Zhu has now committed his life to ensuring that China does not make Gorbachev's mistake. This chapter will show how his plan poses investment opportunities to Westerners, along with treacherous risks to Chinese leaders and businessmen. Stock market investors have numerous tools at their fingertips. First of all, many U.S. and European companies do a great deal of business in China, so that investments in, for example, Procter & Gamble will be affected by China's economic performance. More targeted country funds like the China Fund and individual equities like China Telecom and Asian mutual funds provide a wide open door to let China into your portfolio. But should you? The 1997–1998 Asian meltdown has destroyed many intrepid investors. But the next century provides new opportunities for those who can ride the fearsome tiger.

Our fictional Lin Fat's attempted suicide is not so far-fetched, considering the terrible economic and political pressures building throughout Asia. Though China would not divulge such embarrassing information, during the first quarter of 1998, the economic and social disaster spurred 2,288 South Korean suicides, 36 percent more than during the same period in 1997. A survey showed that under the pressure of economic and financial collapse 26 percent of South Koreans report an urge to kill themselves. Nonetheless, during the second half of 1998, the South Korean stock market rebounded, almost doubling in value. The financial market clearly leaped ahead, even while the man in the street suffered in despair and financial distress.

THE MOTHER OF ALL PUZZLES

To safely guide the Chinese economy in the years ahead, the Communist Party must balance dangerous and contradictory goals. The odds are long enough to blanch the face of the crustiest Vegas bookie. In 1974, a slow-footed Muhammad Ali faced seven-to-one odds against the menacing George Foreman in Zaire's "Rumble in the Jungle." The weight of history and the conflicts of the future suggest much higher odds against Jiang Zemin and Zhu Rongji.

Consider the simultaneous goals that Beijing must strive to achieve:

1. Maintain the centralized Communist Party's control of the political system, while some provinces get richer and others grow poorer and more angry;

2. Generate 8 percent annual growth rate in national income so that you can feed the 1.2 billion population, despite declining farm land;

3. Prevent inflation from rising above 10 percent;

4. Keep the value of the currency (the yuan) stable against the U.S. dollar;

5. Close down technically bankrupt state-owned businesses, which dominate the economy, and provide jobs for over 100 million urban workers;

6. Find jobs for 100 million wandering rural workers, who trudge from field to field;

7. Stop environmental destruction, which sickens millions of citizens and pours raw sewage into the waterways;

8. Preserve political freedom in Hong Kong, while bringing it closer to Beijing's political orbit;

9. Attract foreign investment so that you can continuously upgrade the quality of manufactured goods;

10. Extend China's domination to Singapore, Malaysia, Indonesia, Thailand, while fighting off the United States and Japan, which also seek hegemony.

With these nearly impossible goals in front of them, Jiang Zemin and Zhu Rongji would probably prefer to strap on boxing gloves and kick sand in the face of George Foreman.

But there is no choice; no turning back for Chinese leaders. Remember, to do nothing is to follow the crumpled Soviet blueprint into the dustbin of history. According to Chinese press reports, there have been over eight hundred rural rebellion incidents since 1993, involving groups of over five hundred people. Naturally, Beijing tries to stifle such reports, as well as the actual rebellions. The 1989 massacre in Tiananmen Square put protesters on notice that the government would stand ready to aim and fire. Still, protesters outside Beijing, and beyond CNN cameras, march on.

The paradox for the Communist Party is strikingly clear: China must grow. But growth, in a capitalist world, tends to corrode the bonds of government power. Like a bubbling acid, capitalist trading can destroy traditional authority. People who have the freedom to trade generally prefer progress to patriarchy; a fiber-optic Internet chat line to the Communist Party line.

Traditional Chinese culture sneered at merchants, considering them beneath peasants, who had dignity. Dynasties that reigned before the twentieth century imposed heavy taxes, license fees, and regulations. Of course, Mao's Communist Party tried to wipe out the merchants when it took power in 1949.

A sharp break took place, though, under Deng's dominance at

the 1978 Party Congress. Gradually (and haltingly) Beijing would encourage a merchant class, especially in agriculture. Deng, who as a student in Paris in the 1920s had munched on croissants, was more frightened of keeping China closed to progress than he was afraid of the West. As he put it, "I have two choices . . . I can distribute poverty or distribute wealth." He succeeded grandly, launching an economic revolution that lifted hundreds of millions of Chinese from poverty and sent per capita incomes soaring by over 10 percent per year. At that rate, every seven years households would double their income. While in 1978 the government controlled over 90 percent of farm goods, Deng flipped that number on its head, allowing peasants themselves to sell nearly 90 percent of the crops. During a recent visit to China, I was nearly run over by ramshackle trucks hurtling their way from the countryside overloaded with leeks. Capitalism is messy, and sometimes it smells like onions, but it generally delivers a much higher standard of living.

Not only did Deng liberate workers, he slashed tax rates in a way that would have made Ronald Reagan proud (or embarrassed, since Deng went further than Reagan!). In 1978, Beijing took about 30 percent of national income. By 1995 Deng and his followers had slashed that figure to 10.7 percent (compared to about 20 percent in the United States).

Deng's bravery and flexibility gives potential investors in China *Lesson Number 1: Follow the leaders.* Thousands of years of history can be turned by determined, charismatic leaders like Mao and Deng. Investors must watch carefully to see whether determined reformers like Zhu Rongji continue to pull the levers in Beijing. Any sign that Zhu is slipping from the premier's pedestal should have you selling your China stocks.

THE PARTY'S DEADLY PARADOX

Zhu faces a deadly paradox: A free economy will make China richer but it will ultimately unhinge the party and traditional society. With economic freedom comes this obvious insight that can shatter traditional societies: Only a fool would do a job simply because his grandfather and father did it. And only a coward would do a job because an authority figure told him to. American culture struggled with this idea early in the twentieth century. For example, the movie *The Jazz Singer*, about the son of a synagogue cantor, has been filmed at least three different times, with Al Jolson, Danny Thomas, and even Neil Diamond portraying the renegade. Why sing psalms, when Duke Ellington beckons? Does a Duke outweigh "the Lord?"

Indeed, for a Chinese citizen today, why till the soil, when you can log on to the Internet and till cyberspace? Why read the *People's Daily*, when the *Wall Street Journal* does a better job covering the Shanghai stock exchange?

Make no mistake, in the past twenty years, Western culture has invaded China with more force than tanks and guns could ever muster. Over forty McDonald's surround Beijing. The "Chinese" word for pager is "motorola." It's a simple phonetic word, but a complex miracle of modern global markets. In Beijing you can buy rich Haägen-Dazs ice cream. Imagine: Chinese are rushing to an upscale ice cream parlor, featuring a fictitious Dutch name slapped on a dessert made by company based in Teaneck, New Jersey. When I visited Beijing a few years ago, I noticed a fur coat in the window of a store that catered to the locals. Emblazoned in the fur was the image of Mickey Mouse. For me, this coat is China's Shroud of Turin, for it symbolizes China's supernatural ability to copy icons for mass consumption.

The appeal of symbols like Haägen-Dazs and Mickey Mouse gives investors *Lesson Number 2: Do not limit your portfolio only to those firms that want to sell simple products like bicycle tires.* China's consumers are quickly moving away from the most basic commodities and toward more sophisticated goods and services. Chinese consumers are compressing twentieth-century goods into less than twenty years. In the early 1980s, they bought bicycles; in the late 1980s they bought black and white televisions; in the 1990s, they bought cars, computers, and color televisions. The service industry is also exploding. Private apartments yield real estate agents, mortgage bankers, lawyers, electricians, and computer repairmen. Investors should look for those Western *service* firms that are penetrating the consumer market, not just the manufacturers who are selling scentless soap and shoelaces.

While the portrait of Mao still hangs over Tiananmen Square, the government long ago tore down the images of Marx, Lenin, and Stalin. A visitor to Beijing today gets the feeling that Mao should share top billing with Bill Gates and Michael Eisner (though in 1998 Beijing cracked down on the Walt Disney Company for producing a pro-Tibet movie, *Kundun,* and banned some of its products).

Deng Xaioping did not let this paradox intimidate him. Probably because he underestimated it. During a heralded 1992 tour of China's southern area, Deng pronounced that "to get rich is glorious." Of course, this was the same Deng who in 1989 ordered military troops to fire guns on uppity students in Tiananmen Square, leaving perhaps one thousand dead. Harkening back to Gorbachev's inglorious model, Deng concluded that "Concessions in Poland led to further concessions. . . . The more they conceded, the more chaos." Is it possible to concede only to Western economics, but not to its political impulses? Deng thought so. This is the kind of thinking that permits Beijing nightclubs to adopt glorified Western names like NASA and Apollo, as long as the teenage revelers obey a government curfew and do not take to the streets in protest.

Some optimists in the West seem confident that Deng's successors cannot stuff the proverbial genie in the bottle and cork it. To them, trading with the West, combined with a rising standard of living, is too powerful a force for China to overcome. According to one such analysis, democracy will become "impregnable" when Chinese incomes reach an annual average of $7,000. After all, South Korea, and much of Latin America leaped to democracy when their mean incomes climbed over the $5,000 level. Perhaps. But none of those other countries had the patience and fortitude of Chinese party leaders. Few leaders in the world could have survived the televised slaughter of Tiananmen with so little reaction. If Ronald Reagan was coated with Teflon, Deng Xiaoping had coated himself in impenetrable lead. Unlike American presidents, for example, Chinese leaders do not have to squeeze their agendas into four-year cycles, by which time they must live up to campaign promises to, say, create 10 million jobs or drive the unemployment rate down to X percent. They have time. The typical dynastic cycle was two hundred years. If they feel too rushed, the Chinese leaders would place themselves in the context of a three-thousand-year history. In any event, Jiang Zemin's China is not content simply to allow economic growth to rip apart Beijing's stranglehold on power.

CRACKING THE PARADOX: NATIONALISM

To crack the paradox, Chinese leaders will try to feed a nationalist spirit, hoping that it will give Chinese peasants and merchants alike a reason to care about the state. "Growth plus Nationalism" will emerge as the special formula, a potion that poses investment opportunities and political risks for the United States and Europe.

Leaders remember how Mao Tse Tung's Long March became the Jungian archetype of peasant struggle, transmitted through generations, just as Rosa Parks's defiance in Montgomery, Alabama, became a searing symbol of the battle for civil rights in the United States. The memory of the Long March gave peasants hope and solace, even during the terrible famines brought on by the Great Leap Forward and the demonic purges imposed under the banner of the Cultural Revolution.

Jiang Zemin has impressed American dignitaries by reciting the Gettysburg Address. Those Americans interpret this both as a neat parlor trick and a sign of respect, as when the CIA reported to Washington in 1982 that the new Soviet premier, Yuri Andropov, liked Glenn Miller tunes. Jiang's knowledge of Lincoln is more telling than Andropov's purported foot-tapping. Jiang has carefully studied those iconic moments in history when great leaders risk lives in order to keep the seams of their country from tearing. Perhaps Jiang has his own Chinese Gettysburg Address tucked away for a bloody contingency.

Modern Chinese history is dog-eared with humiliating episodes at the hands of foreigners. From the Opium Wars with Britain in the nineteenth century, which reduced millions of

Chinese to hopelessly addled addicts, to the vicious Japanese occupation of World War II, the Beijing leadership can draw on many brutal memories of foreigners opening up China's door only to slam the Chinese people against a wall. The Chinese in Shanghai have their own Rosa Parks heroines, for along the Bund, with its elegant European porticos, once hung signs proclaiming "No Chinese or dogs allowed." In an ironic twist, a protest in Tiananmen Square once played a positive role in the Chinese nationalist psyche. Back in May 1919, Beijing residents took to the square to protest the foreign domination that followed World War I.

Perhaps the Boxer Rebellion in 1900 best illustrates a nationalist frenzy inspired by foreigners. In the 1890s, flood, famine, and foreigners besieged China. Missionaries arrogantly dismissed traditional Chinese culture, while touting the benefits of new technology like the locomotive and steamboat. Missionaries ridiculed Confucian scholars, who had long taught respect for tradition and confidence in China's role as the world's "Middle Kingdom," surrounded by barbarians. "If we have the telegraph, then *you* must be the barbarians!" Westerners implied. These lethal blows to national pride inspired teenage boys in the northern provinces to proclaim Chinese superiority. They would chant and shadow-box with their so-called "fists of religious harmony," under the slogan "Uphold the Pure Dynasty, Exterminate the Barbarians!" Unlike other discontents they did not seek to overthrow the Empress Dowager and her Ch'ing Dynasty. Instead, they sought to prove their supernatural powers and to suggest that she, too, should not act like a weak mortal under the boot of superior Western invaders.

Eventually, the old empress became entranced with their spiritual and warrior movement, seeing the Boxers as a gift from heaven. The cult spread from the countryside to the cities. Finally, European troops had enough of the Boxers and their deadly guerrilla attacks on missionaries and other Western representatives. Superior European gunfire eventually tamed the Boxers. But their defeat fed a nationalist fervor, leading to the revolution of 1911 and the rise of Sun Yat-Sen's republic.

Jiang Zemin and his advisers have all studied closely the deep historic memories that connect foreign influence and Chinese

nationalism. Their only hope for solving the paradox—and pre-
serving the Communist Party—is to play on those memories like
the strings of a Stradivarius. Westerners have so often embarrassed
and stolen from Asia that the government has plenty of examples
to call upon. In David Hwang's play *M Butterfly*, a Peking opera
singer delivers a scathing parody to his/her French suitor, after he
calls *Madame Butterfly* a "beautiful" story of love and sacrifice.
"What would you say if a blonde homecoming queen fell in love
with a short Japanese businessman?" she asks. "He treats her cru-
elly, then goes home for three years, during which time she prays
to his picture and turns down marriage from a young Kennedy.
Then when she learns he has remarried, she kills herself. Now, I
believe you would consider this girl to be a deranged idiot, correct?
But because it's an Oriental who kills herself for a Westerner . . .
you find it beautiful." The distrust of foreigners resonates most
powerfully in poor, distant provinces that have never heard of
Hwang or Puccini.

This discussion could stay at the metaphysical level for three
thousand years, or at least three thousand pages, but Beijing's leaders know they must nourish nationalism in a practical way, using
all of their tools, from the highbrow to lowbrow, from high tech to
low tech. Remember that in 1971, at a treacherous time of Vietnam
War negotiations, Beijing buttered up Richard Nixon and pumped
up the Chinese public by inviting the U.S. Table Tennis team to
China. After a year of Ping-Pong diplomacy, Nixon himself flew to
China. While his maneuver humanized the West in the eyes of
China (and scared the Soviets), it also lifted Chinese pride. Amid
an army of snapping cameras and rolling film, the American president pronounced that, indeed, the Great Wall was a great wall, a
banal remark he might have nabbed from Noel Coward's play
Private Lives: "Very big, China."

Just as Beijing deployed Western media to enhance its image in
1972, party leaders today use Western technology to boost a
national ego. The government has backed computer game companies that manufacture such hits as "Fighting Eagles of August
First," a bloodthirsty virtual battle between Chinese and American
warplanes during the Korean War. From time to time provincial

governments pick a fight with American consumer goods companies, denouncing such Western symbols as Lipton tea and Coca-Cola. Despite an American advertising slogan that assured us that "nobody doesn't like Sara Lee," the province of Tianjin even gave her a hard time when she tried to buy out a venerable Chinese brand (this despite Sara's arguably Chinese surname).

These attacks more often target U.S. businesses than European, since European political leaders and corporate executives tend to kowtow more deeply to Chinese sensitivities on issues like human rights and prison labor. This bias gives us *Lesson Number 3: Look for European corporate success stories, not just American.* Whenever Beijing gets annoyed with U.S. politicians who denounce China's human rights abuses, Beijing throws another contract at Airbus instead of Boeing.

Beijing's national pride campaign is cheerleading Shanghai's status as the financial capital for the twenty-first century. While rapidly building up Shanghai's infrastructure with billions of dollars of subsidies, China's leaders have announced to the world that Shanghai will ultimately push aside Hong Kong (and Singapore) from its place at the center of Asian commerce. Both Jiang and Zhu Rongji are former Shanghai mayors, giving their commitment very deep roots. With almost 300 million residents living in Shanghai's coastal region, the Shanghai experiment dwarfs any other urban plan in history (more below).

At this moment, Shanghai looks treacherously overbuilt, too eager for new business and for new real estate. When I visited Shanghai a few years ago, officials proudly told me that the crane was the national bird—the construction crane, that is. By some estimates almost 20 percent of the world's cranes nest in Shanghai. During the same week in 1997 when Shanghai announced it would construct the world's tallest building (the World Financial Center), the government admitted that about one-third of the current office space sat empty. Beijing has taken a big risk and its rush to astound threatens a deep recession.

If, however, Jiang Zemin's government can, on Atlas-like shoulders, heave and ho Shanghai up to the pantheon of powerful cities, it will prove to Chinese citizens that China has reclaimed its title, the "Middle Kingdom." Barbarian visitors will once again make "tribute missions" to the Chinese rulers. Furthermore, those discarded racist placards that once proclaimed European dominance along Shanghai's Bund, will surely fade deeper into the collective consciousness.

In addition to the ego boost that comes from bashing Sara Lee and building up Shanghai, Chinese leaders need to prove a military and diplomatic purpose for Beijing. When U.S. soldiers were fighting in Vietnam, and when the Soviet army was placing forty-five divisions on Chinese borders, Beijing could easily make its case, namely, "Not only are we surrounded by foreign devils, but they're holding hand grenades and missiles." With a more peaceful climate in Asia, though, Beijing must show more imagination. The government will continue to rattle the diplomatic cage that entraps Taiwan's 22 million people, and from time to time threaten to invade the island. In addition, China remains immersed in a bitter dispute with Vietnam and the Philippines over the Spratley Islands, a potential source for offshore oil.

While stoking such militaristic embers, Beijing will also try to kindle some warmer relationships. The Pacific Rim's disastrous collapse in 1997–1998 has given China an opportunity to blame Western financiers, while also offering some financial aid to distressed neighbors. Among the most disgusting reactions to Asia's collapse was Malaysian Prime Minister Mahathir's anti-Semitic ravings about allegedly anti-Malaysian Wall Street speculators. It sounded like someone translated the "Protocol of the Elders of Zion" into mangled Malay. Nonetheless, Malaysian leaders used this canard to explain why, for example, their stock market had lost over 65 percent of its value between May 1997 and May 1998, shoving millions of people back into poverty. Perhaps the most pathetic sight, from a Chinese viewpoint, took place in Indonesia, where a run on banks was accompanied by a run on Barbie dolls. By snatching up those Mattel dolls, newly impoverished Indonesian consumers were betting that Barbie would maintain her market value better than the Indonesian currency, the rupiah, which had lost over 70 percent of its buying power. In any event, Beijing has exploited this economic implosion to remind Asians—whether

Chinese, Indonesian, or Thai—that they cannot leave themselves at the mercy of mercenary Caucasian capitalists.

Nonetheless, the Pac Rim countries know that the Chinese flag still waves stars amid scorching red, not a Red Cross. China offers neither a safe nor a charitable harbor for its neighbors to turn to, even in their most desperate moments. Indeed, Pac Rim leaders continually ask themselves, Does China want us as allies, or for dinner?

CHAMPAIGN, ILLINOIS

Tom Franklin loved to pin a nun against the wall, a body check to throw her off balance, followed by an elbow to the chin. Nothing as exciting as seeing that habit tussled.

Of course these were just the metaphors the sandy-haired high schooler thought about when he launched prosecutorial questions at his social studies teacher, Sister Benjamin.

Today the sixty-year-old teacher scribbled on the chalkboard a list of reasons why the United States sells and buys goods with China. Then she leaned against the board while entertaining questions from the adolescents. By the end of a fifty-minute class session, Sister Benjamin's generous posterior usually ended up wearing half of the chalk. Tom's buddy Kyle Landon joked that if you could read backwards, you could use the Sister's butt as a cheat sheet during her infamous pop quizzes.

"Ladies and gentlemen," she said in a squeaky but authoritative voice, "when I look around the room, I can easily see how trading with China helps you. Just look at your feet. Most of your basketball shoes come from China. Your parents probably couldn't afford them if they were made in the America. American workers get paid, maybe $20 per hour. Your Nikes might cost $200 if they were made here."

Tom shot his hand into the air. "Would you have said that about African American slaves in 1860, Sister?"

She glared, knowing that her pale complexion had just turned six shades redder. "What do you mean, Thomas?"

"I mean, sure, it's cheap to buy from China. But it was cheap for northerners to buy cotton from Southern plantations during slavery. After all, the slaves didn't get much money. And it's not like they had 401(k) plans for retirement, did they?" Tom responded.

Sister Benjamin took a deep breath and saw forty eyes staring at her, like tennis fans at Wimbledon, awaiting the next volley. Unlike Wimbledon, though, St. Joseph's Academy had a bell that clanged every fifty minutes. Lucky, that . . .

WHY CHINA'S TASK MATTERS TO THE UNITED STATES

The American people know much more about their local Chinese takeout restaurant than they do about the country of 1.2 billion inhabitants. Yet the United States and China have been dealing with each other since the birth of our republic. After all, the patriots in Boston dumped Chinese tea during their famous and inflammatory party. In 1867, the U.S. ambassador to Peking, Anson Burlingame, led a delegation of Chinese officials to meet President Andrew Johnson. In a highly publicized visit, Americans displayed the same enthusiasm and awe as Marco Polo did when he found China's wondrous silk, chopsticks, and unicorns. During World War II, U.S. navy ships liberated Shanghai and other regions from the perfidious Japanese rule. My father served on a ship that sailed into the harbor, to the cheers of an elated yet wounded and weary populace.

Certainly, when Mao wrested control of China from Chiang Kai-Shek in 1949, U.S.-China relations plunged into a dark abyss, later fueling the McCarthy hearings. How, after all, could the State Department and Department of War (later Department of Defense) have permitted a Marxist peasant to depose Chiang and his Wellesley-educated wife? The bitterness intensified during the Vietnam War, as "Red China" loomed a villainous threat, along with the Soviet Union.

Fortunately, the collapse of the USSR, combined with the reversal in China's hard-core commitment to a Communist economy, softened Sino-U.S. relations. The most colorful symbol came in 1979, when Deng visited a Texas rodeo. He not only smiled to the hollering crowd, but he donned a cowboy hat. As a rule of thumb, septuagenarians do not look terribly menacing while making whooping sounds and waving hats that dwarf their heads. The party leader played his grandfatherly part nicely.

Though the U.S. government no longer perceives China as an enemy, relations remain guarded and occasionally frosty. Under both Republican and Democrat leadership in the 1980s and 1990s, Washington has verbally attacked China for economic reasons, as well as strategic/foreign policy reasons. The blood pressure rises fastest on three key issues: (1) China's exploding trade surplus with the United States, (2) China's periodic threats to Taiwan, and (3) the United States' concerns about human rights and Chinese political prisoners. In contrast to the roar from U.S. political leaders, American businesses generally want calmer, quieter diplomacy so that China does not retaliate by, say, canceling contracts with Boeing or Caterpillar.

President Clinton has himself dramatically shown the complexity and occasional duplicity of U.S.-Sino relations. In the 1992 presidential campaign then-Governor Clinton blasted President Bush for "coddling dictators," specifically for granting China most favored nation (MFN) trade status. Clinton suggested that Bush was tucked in the back pocket of those companies that feared Beijing would retaliate against U.S. firms, if Congress turned down MFN. Nonetheless, after Clinton won election to the White House, he, too, renewed MFN for China, under pressure from American firms. Motorola derives 12 percent of its revenues from China, the world's largest pager market. Ford has invested in several plants that produce trucks and wagons for the Chinese market. The Clinton White House heard these corporate voices loud and clear, and tore up its old campaign literature.

Trade

Politicians frequently denounce China for selling about $50 billion more goods to the United States than the United States sells to China. You do not have to fly to Beijing to figure out why. In 1997, ABC News asked me to comment on the Asian economic meltdown. Instead of packing my bags for a fifteen-hour flight, I directed a camera crew to a Toys R Us and a Best Buy store in Virginia. Almost every toy we turned over was stamped "Made in China." Even Barbie, who looks like a blue-eyed California surfer girl, was apparently born in China. Yes, Virginia, there may be a toy-making Santa Claus, but he probably eats with chopsticks and rides a bicycle to work.

Walk into your kitchen right now and turn over a cheap telephone handset or radio. It will probably read "Made in China." Fact is, U.S. industries long ago abandoned cheap, plastic manufactured goods, leaving China to fight it out with Malaysia, Indonesia, and Mexico. Of course, when China needs to buy sophisticated computers, aircraft, or electrical generators, they must call on either U.S., Japanese, or European companies. Remember, a single Boeing 747 aircraft (costing $175 million) is worth far more to the U.S. economy than the thousands of transistor radios that could fill it up.

Another factor explains the big gap between our exports and imports to China, namely, Hong Kong. Many Chinese and American goods pass through Hong Kong on their way to the final buyer. Unfortunately, U.S. government officials are not so precise when they calculate the comings and goings of goods. Before Hong Kong passed to China in 1997, the Commerce Department often undercounted our exports to China, by listing them as exports to Hong Kong, the stopover point. If you added the U.S. trade surplus with Hong Kong to the U.S. trade deficit with China, the trade imbalance problem would look much smaller.

Nonetheless, American firms continue to ask the U.S. government to protect them from foreign competitors, including Louisiana crawfishermen, who see the Chinese consistently selling their catches for less. The Louisianans do not usually generate much sympathy. But while Chinese crawfishermen may be fair competitors, China's rampant pirating of intellectual property is certainly not fair. I had earlier mentioned a Mickey Mouse fur coat, which would have horrified the Disney publicity department, not to mention Mickey's young fans. It clearly violates international copyright law. In addition, China's notorious CD industry copies millions of music and computer programs, cheating inventors and artists out of billions of dollars. Even though Chinese officials denounce such piracy and government television stations broadcast video footage of trucks crushing pirate CD factories, the

Clinton administration has assailed the government for its occasional complicity.

The Foreign Policy Threat: Taiwan

China would sooner lob missiles at Taipei and invade the island with amphibious vessels than permit Taiwan to celebrate independence. In 1981, Deng announced "one country, two systems" to describe Taiwan (the phrase was later applied to Hong Kong, too). "Two countries" would last only for the few minutes it would take for missiles to fly across a narrow channel of the China Sea. In 1995–1996, Taiwan-China-U.S. nerves frayed dangerously. China displayed her determination and her deadly power by launching missiles that landed just off the coast of Taiwan, during an election season when Taiwanese politicians were flirting with independence. Naturally, the United States denounced the military threat, and President Clinton sent warships within 200 miles of Taiwan. Unfortunately, other Asian nations were either too scared of Beijing or too wary of President Clinton's intentions to applaud the U.S. maneuvers.

Around the same time, the United States had poked at China's eyes in two symbolic ways. First, Speaker of the House Newt Gingrich invited Taiwan President Lee Teng-hui to the United States, while the Chinese government (and Secretary of State Warren Christopher) objected noisily and strenuously. Second, U.S. politicians began a nasty and effective campaign to deny Beijing its bid to host the 2000 Olympics. It's one thing to malign a nation's military intentions, but to the Chinese man on the street, it was unforgivable to malign a nation's sportsmen.

In the past few years, Taiwan has built closer commercial ties to China, and has softened its independence rhetoric. Likewise, Jiang Zemin and President Clinton have tried to display a more cooperative image, leading to Vice President Gore's 1997 visit to China and Clinton's 1998 trek. Beijing has learned how to skillfully play the Western public relations game in recent years. China even tricked an old political hand like Al Gore into toasting the Communist Party regime during his trip.

Human Rights and Arms Deals

Sino-U.S. tempers flare whenever the United States condemns China's "human rights" violations, which it does frequently. China remains repressive and dangerous—to its neighbors and its own people. China defends its behavior by arguing that Chinese people are freer to speak their mind today than anytime before. Yes, but there are no habeas corpus rights, no Bill of Rights, and certainly no Miranda warnings for criminal suspects. Only those with warfare experience could stomach a Chinese prison. Still, say the Chinese and their defenders, people can choose their own jobs, sell their own crops, and marry whom they want. There is even a Ralph Nader equivalent in China—the China Consumers Association lodges complaints against government manufacturers. Plaintiffs have even sued the venerable *People's Daily* for libel. China recently held its first district election for a township chief, complete with debates and secret ballots (a Communist Party member won). Is this enough? Hell, no. Do most Chinese accept these terms? Yeah. I was surprised and somewhat demoralized to hear how matter-of-factly a thirty-year-old woman described to me the "one-child" mandatory birth control command. Even with more wealth than ever, the Chinese government still exploits peer pressure to shame parents into having just one child. As has been widely reported, many couples have practiced gynecide, so that they could raise a male child.

Some American corporations have shut down trade with China, especially when they have received bad publicity regarding, for example, slave labor. But the lure of China is hard to resist. After leaving China in 1993, Levi Strauss announced in 1998 that it would return, arguing that China had improved its human rights record.

Though it is China's human rights record that most offends Westerners, her record on arms sales can also cause shudders. In March 1997, just a few weeks after President Clinton had certified to Congress that China was no longer selling nuclear materials, a top-secret briefing revealed that China was about to sell to Iran chemicals used to produce nuclear weapons. A 1997 CIA report revealed that "China was the primary source of nuclear-related equipment and technology to Pakistan . . . and Iran also received considerable chemical warfare-related assistance from China." Never mind that China had committed to the Nuclear Nonproliferation Treaty in 1992 and the Chemical Weapons Convention of 1993 (reversing Mao's radical and dangerous pledge to spread nuclear weapons in order to defeat Western hegemony). In May 1998 when India shocked the world by detonating three nuclear blasts, American diplomats grew even more nervous about China's intentions in the black market for atomic weapons. As always, China has a defense and defenders, who argue that renegade army officials are responsible for the infractions, and that the U.S. record on arms control is not as white as a Monet lily. While it would be wrong to characterize China as an unreformed, bad actor in the world's arms control efforts, the United States will have to maintain a vigilant watch.

CHINA'S REAL BOMB AIMED AT THE UNITED STATES

About 100,000 American troops patrol the Pacific on land and at sea. Those soldiers and sailors could deter China from reckless military ventures. However, they would be as impotent as Superman in a room filled with kryptonite, if China confronted them with its most dangerous weapon—a vast hoard of U.S. government bonds and currency. Thankfully, the United States is not so vulnerable to China's Exocet or Stinger missiles. But when a foe has $150 billion in its vault, we must be careful. How could it hurt? It is surely not a physical threat, unless you are lucky enough to have $150 billion dumped on your house. Instead, China could threaten to drive down our financial markets by unloading its holdings of U.S. dollars. Such a dump of currency on the worldwide market would send the value of the dollar sliding. Likewise, U.S. interest rates would shoot up, since much of China's cache of dollars takes the form of U.S. Treasury bonds. If Beijing suddenly gave the signal to dump its bonds, their value would plummet, meaning that the U.S. government would have to pay higher interest rates to make them attractive to new buyers. And, of course, higher interest rates would slam the brakes on U.S. auto sales and the housing market. Finally, the U.S. stock market would tumble, since higher interest rates would slow down the U.S. economy, and a cheaper dollar would probably frighten foreign investors into throwing U.S. stocks overboard.

Naturally, such a deadly tactic would hurt China as well. Foreign investors would start selling their Chinese assets for fear that China was reversing its path toward freer markets. I doubt that China will ever drop this bomb on Wall Street—but from time to time Beijing might hint at its newfound financial might, sending nervous speculators scurrying and giving markets a temporary tremble.

ZHUNOMICS: AN ECONOMIC PLAN TO BREAK THE PARADOX

Deng liberated his successors from Marxism when he announced "black cat, white cat, so long as it catches mice." By embracing any color cat, he chased away all dogma. By confessing that he never bothered to read Marx's *Das Kapital*, he cleared a path for the pragmatist Zhu Rongji. Like Deng, Zhu was thrown in prison, stripped of all official titles and of all human dignity during Mao's bloody Cultural Revolution. In the early 1990s, Zhu rose through the ranks and directed the People's Bank of China. When inflation looked as if it could skyrocket past 25 percent in 1994, Zhu engineered a remarkable "soft" landing for the economy. He leaned on banks to cut back their lending and thereby slashed the inflation rate in half, without throwing the economy into a recession. Central bankers around the world marveled at how skillfully Zhu defused the inflation crisis, with just the crudest of financial instruments and the most elementary banking system. The only whiff of socialism from Zhu has come, ironically, when discussing initial public offerings (IPOs) of stock. Zhu declared that listed companies must spend part of their IPO "winnings" helping less fortunate firms. "From each according to his IPO price" is a startling way to rewrite a Marxist directive.

Now, the seventy-year-old "economics czar" must prove that it is possible to successfully and harmoniously spin and twist the Rubik's cube that is the Chinese economic experiment. At the outset of this chapter I suggested that the Soviet implosion constantly reminds Chinese officials how great their task is. After a meeting with Zhu, U.S. Treasury Deputy Secretary Lawrence Summers (formerly a wunderkind of the economics profession) purportedly stated that Zhu must have an IQ of about 200. He'll need every point. If Zhu wins this challenge, it will prove that Chinese bureaucrats were better prepared than their Soviet counterparts. In the 1980s, Soviet leaders were, to be blunt, old, drunk, and ignorant. Zhu and his reformers are none of these things. They are ready to fight the deadly paradox. Here is their plan, which will be a five-year plan if it fails—and a five-hundred-year plan if it works.

Buy Off the Discontented Urban and Rural Workers

According to press reports, three thousand farmers battled police in a violent clash in Henan province, a province where workers earn only about half the income of their wealthier provincial neighbors. With the footsteps of the Long March still resonating in rural regions, Zhu must keep farmers from rebelling. Furthermore, he must keep rural workers from flooding into the cities, where incomes have soared beyond the comprehension of isolated provinces. How do you explain a family friend who drives a Mercedes Benz to someone has never seen anything more sophisticated than a yak yoked to a plow? In March 1998, Zhu announced that he would throw about 50 percent more money into the so-called Grain Risk Funds, which have kept farmers' prices 25–30 percent higher than market prices.

Even if Beijing calms the rural masses, it must worry about urban tensions. The 1998 budget quintupled payments to unemployed workers in the cities. Rather than creating make-work jobs and putting the jobless on the government payrolls, the government prefers to pay them to stay home.

Boost Industrial Sector by Importing Better Machinery

Mao clearly wanted China to be free from foreigners and self-sufficient. In fact, he even wanted local towns to supply their own goods (in contrast to Stalin, who oversaw an economy where, at one time, about 75 percent of all products were made in one giant factory). Mao's disastrous Great Leap Forward—in fact, a giant plunge into famine for tens of millions—forced families to perform their own smelting.

Zhu's agents now recognize that both Stalin and Mao drew different but equally deadly economic blueprints. China must import sophisticated machines in order to produce the high quality goods that other countries want to buy. The new bureaucrats want to consolidate the fragmented and far-flung textile industry, as well as dispose of old mills and spindles. Therefore, China is slashing tariffs and rebating the Value Added Tax on imported machinery, especially in textiles. Those Nike and Adidas shoes will be of even higher quality as a result. By producing better products, China has the best chance of creating more jobs for the 80 million textile workers, an industry that makes up 24 percent of its exports.

Shrink the Government

Supply-side economists loudly applaud China for cutting its taxes to under 12 percent of national income. But to pay for "operation buy off discontents" (see above), Beijing is trimming its own budget and laying off government workers. Zhu will swing the ax at up to 4 million civil servants and fifteen ministries. Clearly, the government is betting that poor farmers and disgruntled urban workers are more likely to revolt than laid-off bureaucrats. Of course, many wily old bureaucrats will find ways to sneak away from the budget cuts, since Zhu does not have complete control of the government. Last year a new bureau, the State Physical Culture and Sports Bureau, managed to pass through Zhu's sieve, for example. Remember, even Ronald Reagan and Margaret Thatcher could not live up to their promises to dramatically shrink their governments.

At the same time as the government dumps workers, it will sell off more state assets, such as China Telecom, a publicly traded stock that is operated by the government. Zhu wants to unveil a balanced budget in 2000, placing China in a tiny but proud band of economically rock-solid countries.

[handwritten margin notes: # CHiNA Telecon]

Jiang and Zhu have even been brazen enough to attack the People's Liberation Army, which runs thousands of companies, from karaoke bars to auto plants to China Great Wall Telecom, which is developing a mobile phone network. Beijing wants the PLA to divest such enterprises to the private sector and has deployed the state-run media to reveal PLA abuses and corruption.

Turn Over the Housing Market to the Private Sector

When a typical American couple thinks about putting a roof over their heads, they assume that they will spend about 25–35 percent of their monthly income. In China, families think that 5–10 percent should be enough, because the government has traditionally picked up most of the tab. In fact, until recently, most Chinese simply lived in government housing, usually a perk for government employees and for those who worked for so-called "state-owned enterprises." Zhu aims to create a "normal" housing market, where people actually pay for the cost of their apartments. The reformers see three positive effects on the economy by: (a) inspiring entrepreneurs to improve housing standards; (b) prodding people into spending more of their salaries on Chinese goods (such as housing), rather than on imported consumer goods that could unhinge China's delicate trade balance; and (c) creating a secondary market in residential real estate. By creating a liquid market, China could better absorb economic slowdowns and expansions. Beijing plans to lift rents to 15 percent in most places, though it expects fierce resistance from those who have gotten comfortable with huge subsidies. As I stated earlier, a privatized housing market would unleash a set service of industries, including finance, real estate, and insurance.

Find a Delicate Way to Slash and Burn State-Owned Enterprises

I mentioned earlier Stalin's love of big factories that made no economic sense. Likewise, there is no virtue in small factories that make no economic sense. Imagine, a system that piles up a surplus of 1.5 billion shirts, 10 million wristwatches, and 20 million bicycles. Let me introduce you to the biggest players in China's economy and the biggest migraine in Zhu Rongji's head: the state-owned enterprises (SOE). Not only do they pile up shirts, watches, and bicycles, they pile up staggering multibillion dollar losses. It might be easier to solve the problem if, à la Stalin, the SOEs could be blown up in one big ambush. But they are everywhere; there are over 100,000 such companies. Only about half of them turn a profit. They are not a single time bomb in the economy; they are spreading, breeding colonies of termites.

The SOEs grab about 70 percent of the loans made by the Chinese government and, in turn, make jobs for about 125 million urban workers. They produce about one-third of China's goods, though this figure has fallen from two-thirds in the 1980s as the private sector has taken off. Like rapidly spreading termites, the SOEs are nearly impossible to manage and rather difficult to reform. Because they provide so many jobs, Zhu must move gingerly. Even he has not been able to concoct a totally coherent plan for dealing with them. Nonetheless, we can expect the following guidelines: (a) Bunch together many smaller SOEs and try to sell a cluster of them to private companies; (b) force foreign companies to take over weak SOEs as the admission price for entering the Chinese retail market; (c) channel government loans to healthier, larger SOEs that might be able to withstand international competition, such as the China Eastern United Petrochemical Group; (d) give managers greater monetary incentives to turn profits; and (e) improve bankruptcy laws so that firms can figure out *how* to go out of business.

No Chinese leader would have the courage simply to poison the SOEs until they die, for no leader could explain this to the 125 million urban SOE workers. Yes, the government has the temerity to shoot at thousands in Tiananmen Square, but they cannot shoot at 100 million. Instead, the government will strive to improve the SOEs, while thinking of them as a kind of "on-deck" circle for employees. That is, eventually, the Chinese private sector will create enough jobs for the SOE workers. For now, they are just swinging bats and limbering up, waiting for their day at bat. You could also see them as a twist on Karl Marx's notion of the "reserve army of the unemployed." Marx thought that capitalism would keep throngs in poverty and on the sidelines, so that their presence would keep employed workers from demanding higher wages. In China the SOEs employ a "reserve army of the *em*ployed," waiting to take jobs that make economic sense.

The rapidly growing private sector suggests that most Chinese citizens are not so addicted to working for the state and will switch when they have the chance. They would be happy to stay away from the central government in Beijing, the PLA, and other hierarchies. An ancient Chinese ode still echoes:

> I dig a well to drink its water, I cultivate a field to produce food,
> At sunrise I go to the field, At sunset I retire to my shelter
> The power of the Emperor reacheth me not.

MAKING MONEY FROM CHINA'S PLIGHT AND PLANS

Richard Nixon's 1972 flight to China spawned many ideas, including a mediocre opera *Nixon in China*. In addition, his visit inspired Western manufacturers to dream of selling deodorant to the billion armpits of China. In many cases, those dreams have failed, often popped by a combination of Chinese bureaucrats and

Western ignorance. Sometimes, those dreams have come true. Coke's the real thing in China, bottling Coca-Cola, Fanta, and Sprite in more than fifteen facilities. If you can get Chinese people to swallow sweet, orange-colored soda, you must be happy with your success. Pepsi is not far behind, with numerous bottling plants and fast-food restaurants. As Chinese incomes grow, their thirst and hunger for luxuries intensifies—yes, I would call a bottle of cola a luxury, when the average city dweller earns about $1,000 a year, and the typical farmer collects half that. Chinese consumers have proven themselves frugal but inventive home economists. On modest incomes, most city dwellers have managed to purchase refrigerators to keep those sodas cool, as well as color televisions. Here are some other sectors where Western investors should pay close attention, and consider placing some bets.

Cosmetics: Hey, Good Looking

Vanity itself is not expensive, even the poor can afford it. But as people get richer, they can afford more prestigious products to beautify themselves. Procter & Gamble dominates the shampoo market in China, charging much higher prices than domestic competitors. Its sales will soon hit $1 billion, no doubt leaving executives in Cincinnati looking younger and more beautiful. For years, Avon saleswomen have rung doorbells all across the United States, but the corporate cash registers have never rung louder than when Chinese Avon ladies descended on Guongdong, introducing direct marketing techniques to the nation, along with Mary Kay cosmetics and Amway. I have not yet seen any pink Cadillacs in Guongdong, but since Mary Kay sales have been so strong, there may be some lipstick-colored rickshaws somewhere. Amway claims to deploy eighty thousand people distributing its products. Aggressive direct marketers have so offended the Chinese government, that in 1998 they cracked down on practitioners, which only led to violent protests. In the Hunan city of Zhangjiajie, hundreds responded to the crackdown by smashing cars and looting stores. According to a newspaper story, two women approached a visitor at a famous temple, dedicated to a fishing goddess. They then pulled out a picture of Amway's president, revealed themselves as Amway saleswomen, and told the pilgrim "We worship him." And we Westerners think the Dalai Lama is holy.

In a true sign of excess, plastic surgeons are popping up in China's cities, in many cases to perform nose jobs—aimed at enlarging, not bobbing the offending proboscis. Investors should keep a close eye on those companies that are cracking into the Chinese market for personal luxury goods. L'Oreal has opened up a second plant in China, and is spending over $1 billion versus just $100 million in 1996. Firms like International Flavors & Fragrances, though based in New York, supply the secret flavor ingredients for everything from Estée Lauder makeup to McDonald's french fries. The trick is to make sure that Chinese intellectual property pirates do not simply copy the formulas and produce their own versions. Of course, Procter & Gamble's success proves that prestige also plays a role; therefore, luxury names will keep their appeal, even if they offer few authentic advantages over generic goods. Remember, in the West, vodka companies battle it out at all price levels, from $10 to $30 a bottle, trying to sell their colorless, tasteless potions. And discriminating buyers will name their "own" brands at bars. Do not expect the Chinese to ignore prestige, anymore than we do.

Meats and Land Down Under

As the Chinese get wealthier, they get hungrier, too. Hungry for more protein like eggs, meats, and fish. The menu in a typical Chinese-American takeout restaurant is still a fantasy for those in the homeland. At the famous Peking Duck restaurant in Beijing, I have seen wealthy businessmen and Communist Party members, not peasants. Even if typical Chinese could afford such rich fare, China's land cannot keep up with the pace of economic demands. With a bulging population, China's ratio of fertile land to consumer is shrinking at a quick pace. Unlike modern-day Malthusians, I see no need to panic, since China has not yet benefited from the ongoing technological revolution in farming. Someday Caterpillar tractors will push aside all the old yaks pulling plows. Then they will eat the yaks. In any event, China can certainly import foodstuffs and feed grain from around the world. While this new wealth-driven demand for food could lift the prices of commodities in the short-run, it will also inspire entrepreneurs to develop more fecund ways to produce food. Someone once suggested that if food prices jumped high enough, some entrepreneur would figure out how to grow corn on asphalt. I have seen agricultural tricks in Israeli deserts that already rival that.

Before they resort to asphalt corn, though, China will look to import more meats and grain, especially from New Zealand and Australia. Chinese demand will keep New Zealand/Australian farm land prices firm, and the equity prices of food exporters in a favorable position, as they revive from the economic slaughter that erased share values all across the Pacific Rim in 1998. A New Zealand veal chop will be a juicy treat for Chinese consumers, and a tasty investment for Westerners.

EUROPEAN COMPETITORS

John Locke and Jean-Jacques Rousseau may have been European, but only the United States seems willing to, from time to time, anger the Chinese over "human rights" conditions. When German chancellors and French prime ministers travel to China, they are not hounded by journalists and parliamentarians urging them to harangue the Chinese leadership over political prisons. Europeans often think of Americans as naïve idealists, but Americans take pride in their ideals. For it was this same "naïve" idealism that President Roosevelt tapped into to justify sending U.S. soldiers to fight Adolph Hitler on the ground in Europe.

The point is that it is U.S. companies that are most likely to suffer from a focus on China's political flaws. In 1996, the Boeing board of directors flew on sleek jets to Beijing in order to urge the government to purchase its airplanes instead of those from the European consortium Airbus. Premier Li Peng used the opportunity to deliver a stern lecture on how the United States brazenly pries into the business of sovereign nations. The premier had not cornered the market on anger and indignation. A recent book called *China Can Say No* features a chapter titled "I Won't Get on a Boeing 777." If the authors won't get on a Boeing, they have little choice but to step into an Airbus, where you can check your political conscience at the gate.

Likewise, high profile U.S. names like Caterpillar face direct competition from Komatsu of Japan, where politicians stay silent on sensitive Chinese issues. Despite being an oligopoly, Boeing/Airbus and Caterpillar/Komatsu compete ferociously in the world market. Investors can spot an opportunity for Airbus and Komatsu, whenever political nerves fray between China and the United States. Stay on the lookout for other foreign firms willing to rush in and take market share wherever the U.S. angels dare not go.

BUY CHINA?

Alas, publishing lags are too long for me to issue a "buy" recommendation for Chinese stocks. However, this chapter has spelled out the key guideposts to follow. For example, is Zhu Rongji firmly in command? He has become a key player, as important to China as Paul Volcker and Alan Greenspan were to U.S. economic glory in the 1980s and 1990s. He will either go down in history as China's Alexander Hamilton, or he will be hanged. In the 1850–1860s, a man named Hong Xuiuquan led a rebellion against the Ch'ing Dynasty, proclaiming himself Jesus Christ's younger brother. Zhu has not made this claim, but he is leading (on behalf of the government) an economic revolution. And he certainly hopes that he has a "mandate from heaven."

Presuming Zhu hangs on to power, we must ask, Has he managed to stem the losses at the SOEs? Are multinationals continuing to build factories and directly invest in China? Has the People's Bank managed to keep inflation under 10 percent? Has China avoided the temptation to launch an attack on Vietnamese oil properties and block the South China Sea's oil lanes, in a desperate bid to capture subsidized energy? If you can answer "yes" to these questions, you can carefully go shopping for Chinese stocks. If not, you would do better flying to San Francisco to buy trinkets in Chinatown.

While shrewdly looking for investment opportunities, you should not lose your ability to marvel at China's amazing economic story since 1978. William Overholt's provocative and optimistic book, *The Rise of China*, reported that in 1993, 40 million Chinese still lived in caves in the northeast. He quotes from Harrison Salisbury that in a village of Gruizhou, "A family of ten owned only one pair of pants and wore them serially. Only when the fog was thick did the women emerge from their huts." For years it was too embarrassing for Beijing to admit how primitive life has been for most Chinese. Now, as the people emerge from huts and from caves, they are almost instantly handed a cellular telephone and an e-mail address. It is as if all of human history has been compressed into a single moment. Forget Rip van Winkle—he only slept forty years! Most of China has been sleeping for four thousand years.

Now she is waking. And it's an awesome, dangerous, and exhilarating sunrise.

8

LOCK 'EM UP
The War on Crime
Goes into Retreat

PHOENIX, ARIZONA

He recognized the squeak and jumped out of bed: 2 A.M. Shaking his wife's bare shoulder, he handed her the telephone. "Sharon, call 911. Someone's opened up the kitchen window." Matt Hopkins quickly stepped to his closet. He whipped out the fireplace poker that he kept next to his boots. He didn't have a gun in the house; Sharon was afraid of them. So he had sharpened the fireplace tool until its point glistened silver. He could fillet a flounder with it if he had to. Or a burglar.

Climbing through the splintered window frame, Josh Hauser scraped his knees, leaving a few drops of blood. He wiped the windowsill with his rubber gloves. Dammit, now the cops can do a DNA match. He wiped the sweat from his forehead, accidentally spreading blood over his face.

Patrolman Randy Simmons got the call from the dispatcher and sped through the working-class neighborhood. Why the hell would anyone break into these sorry houses? He thought. The country clubbers live just a traffic light away.

Matt hesitated, trying to decide whether to tear into the kitchen, his lance in front of him, or whether to slowly approach and try to hit the thug from behind. After a moment he figured that the rickety floors would give him away. Better to charge in, fireplace poker a-blazing. He began a deadly, determined sprint down the hallway.

Hauser heard the phone click, then fast footsteps. He didn't have a weapon. He didn't have a prayer. The lady's purse that he had spied through the window suddenly looked, not ten feet but ten miles away. He stood on a chair and jumped headfirst back through the window frame, rolling onto the Astroturf that covered the back porch. He heard a crack inside his left arm, but quickly rolled to his feet and ran toward the woods. He heard the sound of a heavy projectile land behind him. He didn't look back to see the fireplace poker.

Two days later, Patrolman Simmons showed up at the Texaco station to speak to Josh about his blood type.

Newsflash

This morning, Washingtonians woke up to read yet another grisly story of drug-related death. A twelve-year-old boy was shot in the head after refusing to give up a small bag of heroin to gang members. After a dramatic ten-year plunge in the crime rate, the FBI has recently sent out a classified bulletin to police chiefs throughout the country, warning them that the crime rate is now soaring and headed back to the levels of the late 1970s.

Windows '82 has helped many more people than Windows '95 or Windows '98. Never heard of Windows '82? It's not the latest software from Bill Gates's tool chest, it's the nickname I give to one of the most influential pieces of paper since Lincoln scribbled on his way to Gettysburg. In 1982, the political scientist James Q. Wilson published an article in the *Atlantic Monthly* entitled "Broken Windows." In that slender article, Wilson and criminologist George Kelling achieved a rare triple victory: They devised a theory that is at once simple, memorable, and practical. So what is their compelling point? Leaving vandalized windows in a broken condition invites more damage and danger. Shards of glass tell criminals and decent people alike that the community has neither the strength nor the desire to fight crime. While most criminologists had focused on the most heinous felonies such as murders and rapes, Wilson and Kelling reminded people that small misdemeanors enter a community's bloodstream like a virus and eventually rot the quality of life. Who, after all, feels safe while walking down a street that is framed by boarded-up windows or doors hanging on by a single hinge? Who feels safe waiting for graffiti-covered subway cars in stations that reek of urine? Even if no murders, rapes, or robberies have taken place on that street or subway station, our human instincts smell danger and instinctively pump adrenaline into our veins, flare our nostrils, and widen our pupils. Regardless of the actual crime-rate reports, we want to step faster and farther from this place. If such places look *god*forsaken, who are we to hang around? No surprise that businesses flee as well, creating a downward spiral of fewer jobs, fewer legitimate opportunities, and more crime. If Robert Frost thought that "good fences make good neighbors," broken windows make exceedingly bad ones.

Since 1992, the United States has enjoyed an "anti-crime" wave, with New York Mayor Rudolph Giuliani looking like the movement's poster child. Indeed, Giuliani and his first police chief, William Bratton, displayed the exalted "Broken Windows" article the way that churches post the Ten Commandments. While living in New York City in the 1980s, I was enraged by the "squeegee boys," those red-eyed drug addicts who extort money from frightened drivers in exchange for dirty windshield spray. The perpetrators would prey on tourists and out-of-towners by standing just outside the Lincoln Tunnel. Following the broken windows theory, Giuliani argued that those ostensibly harmless squeegee boys were actually creating a menacing, fearful climate. The police force began cracking down with arrests, symbolizing a new, tougher attitude. It did not hurt that the Walt Disney Company was simultaneously pouring hundreds of millions of dollars into resuscitating a fetid Forty-second Street. As Woodrow Wilson went to war to make the world safe for democracy, Giuliani declared war to make Manhattan safe for Mickey Mouse and his friends. Giuliani may have been more successful.

Other cities followed the zero-tolerance lead. Serious crime rates have fallen five years in a row in most urban areas. A nationwide crackdown has thrown more people in jail, and squeezed the national murder rate down to the lowest level since 1969, while burglaries are down to the levels of the 1970s. To protect yourself against crime, *Lesson Number 1: Live in a community that does not tolerate broken windows and petty crime.* More cops, better cops, more jobs, more prisons, and less tolerance have all contributed to a good story of decent people reclaiming their streets. It is a story filled with heroes and villains.

Unfortunately, the story is not over, and the good news will not bless the front pages forever. Indeed, we can expect a sharp turn for the worse over the next ten years, which will reignite investor interest in crime-related stocks: makers of security systems, developers of gated communities, private prison operators, etc. Why will the good news come to an end? Among other reasons, a new generation of children is about to burst into adolescence and enter the critical age group that commits most violent crime. Nearly 40 million kids are under ten years of age today, the largest cohort of kids since the 1960s. We will have 20 percent more teenagers in 2005 than we had in 1995. And while adolescence is obviously not a disease (though some parents may think it is), we would be foolish to ignore the side effects. These 40 million children, whom demographers call the "baby boomerangers," will be more prone to violence than their parents. They are more likely to come from broken homes, more likely to be illiterate, and more likely to have been eyewitnesses to violent crimes. Of course we should not resign ourselves to misery. We are not predestined or programmed to self-destruct. It is even possible that the crime rate will continue trickling down for another five years. Even so, investors should scrutinize their portfolios. If the crime rate stays down, it will be precisely because communities have invested more in prevention and imprisonment. Crime already costs the economy about $450 billion, according to a Department of Justice study. Private companies that manage prisons will continue to expand their businesses, for example. Investors should watch their stock prices as they negotiate with state prison authorities.

We cannot rush right into stock recommendations, though. Crime is an old and painful issue that has perplexed everyone from Immanuel Kant to Karl Menninger, the permissive psychiatrist who denounced all legal punishment in his 1968 book *The Crime of Punishment.* In this chapter, we will examine the trends in crime;

the "causes" of crime; the profile of felons; and the damage that crime does to the economy. We can then tackle the issue of why crime rates have been plunging, and why they will likely jump in the years ahead. After building this foundation, we can figure out how to handle crime in our financial portfolios.

People who look to invest in downtrodden industries might find crime-related stocks of particular interest. By understanding the dynamics of crime and crime-fighting, investors can search intelligently for firms and industries that will be moved by our most challenging social problem. Towards the end of this chapter, I will argue that firms that develop new crime prevention technologies will find a big audience. In addition, firms that oversee private prisons could come out of their market slump.

THE CRIME SCENE: WHO? WHERE? WHEN?

Between the 1992 movie *Lethal Weapon 3* and the subsequent *Lethal Weapon 4*, the violent crime rate in the United States plunged by 15 percent. Don't look for Hollywood to exploit this favorable trend, since crime has put buttocks in theater seats ever since Thomas Edison released *The Great Train Robbery* in 1903. It is hard to think of a great film that does not include a crime scene—even in *Mary Poppins* young Michael evades police arrest in Edwardian London.

Historical crime trends seem to confound common sense. Most people would guess that hard economic times drive people to crime. Jean Valjean comes to mind. Yet crime fell dramatically during the Great Depression, while skyrocketing amid the healthy economy of the 1960s. Some theorists have argued that urbanization and industrialization feed crime. *Oliver Twist*'s Fagin comes to mind. Yet the crime rate in the United States and England fell during the second half of the nineteenth century, just as Charles Dickens was turning his surname into an adjective signifying dark, sweaty, and oppressive city life. These historical data tell us that we cannot squeeze the causes of crime on a small bumper sticker.

Returning to more recent times, a closer look at the FBI's crime statistics actually reveals two different trends. For adult felons, the arrow points downward toward less crime. For teenagers and children the arrows have plateaued, but at very high levels. Let's examine homicide, since statistics for that crime are most reliable (there is, after all, a body; whereas robbery reports are often susceptible to error due insurance fraud and embezzlement). Among older adults, the murder rate has fallen by about half in the past twenty years. In contrast, the murder rate by teenagers remains about twice the 1980 rate (despite a decline for the past several years). Even murder rates have flaws, of course. Suicides may appear to be murders. Technology plays a role, too. How many would-be murder victims are saved by paramedics and doctors at trauma units? Urban warriors have deadly AK–47s, but urban surgeons have lasers and defibrillators. Despite these fuzzy factors, the plummeting adult murder rate is too steady and powerful to argue with. I am troubled, though, that the teen rate has stayed at lofty levels. There are few things more frightening than an angry and armed teenage population—particularly when their numbers will grow sharply.

The slide in adult crime rates would seem more sustainable if entry-level crime was also falling fast. Alas, shoplifting, automobile break-ins, and pick-pocketing remain at high levels, providing good "training opportunities" for young felons. *Lesson Number 2: Use this current climate of low crime rates to negotiate low rates for insurance and for home/office security systems.* Firms like Brinks are aggressively trying to build up their market share in the home alarm business. As a consumer you have bargaining power. Use it.

Who?

To compose a police sketch of a typical criminal does not take much time. Summing up the annual arrest reports that the FBI collects from sixteen hundred city, county, and state law enforcement agencies gives you the following warning: If you are followed home by a twenty-year-old male, who does not have a job, has been kicked out of school, comes from a broken home, has a low IQ, uses drugs, is impulsive, has a bulky frame, and was not a first-born child, bolt your door and dial 911. That was two hundred years and millions of pages of research condensed. No single feature gives you a reliable prediction. But the composite is scary. Unfortunately, such specimens are not so rare in our society. You could make the composite sketch even more frightening by assuming that the stalker has a criminal parent. While DNA researchers have not located an inheritable felonious gene, sociologists have discovered that the sons of criminals are much more likely to turn into felons, even when they are adopted by decent citizens immediately after birth.

To use some more precise statistics than our composite sketch, we find that 80 percent of criminals are male (including over 90 percent of murderers), with 45 percent of them under the age of twenty-five and 90 percent under the age of forty. Teenage males are especially bent toward property crimes, committing about 60 percent. Few middle-age men find a thrill in riding in a car and bashing mailboxes with a baseball bat or spraying painted designs on the side of a wall. If you chart "age" on an X axis and crime rate on the Y, you will find that rates for almost every crime spike at young adulthood, before going into a nosedive before midlife. While burglary and assault peak early, even gambling and tax cheating tail off before age forty. (Statistics do show that, people need a few more years to shrug off more sophisticated white-collar crimes such as insurance fraud.)

The data suggest that if we locked up every male teenager and released them at forty, we would have relatively little crime. Of course, many critics in the black community would argue that we are well on our way, with about 12 percent of black males twenty-four to thirty-four in prison, and a majority of high school dropouts in prison, on probation, or on parole. Blacks commit about 30 percent of the felonies and just over 50 percent of the country's murders. Blacks are disproportionately the victims, too; in fact, blacks are twice as likely to be robbed as whites.

Young males commit such an overwhelming proportion of crimes, one is tempted to infer that maleness actually causes criminality. This specious logic has some appeal when you take a look at studies that show that about 40 percent of all U.S. males have been arrested by age thirty. And remember, most lawbreakers do not get caught. Studies of less violent places such as the United Kingdom come up with similar numbers. Nor can we blame this on the permissive 1960s, the decadent 1970s, the indulgent 1980s, or Oval Office dalliances in the 1990s. Martin Wolfgang's pathbreaking report of teenage male Philadephians born in 1945 showed that one-third had been arrested by the age of eighteen and 43 percent by age thirty. Even the Amish in Pennsylvania, known for simple living and strict rules, have trouble controlling their youth. So they don't. In a fascinating article in *The New Yorker*, David Remnick reveals that Amish elders let their teenagers run relatively free and fast, even joining Amish gangs, in a period called *"rumspringa."* At gang meetings, souped-up Chevys may park next to horse and buggy. While the teens sometimes get drunk, and occasionally use drugs, they do not commit many violent crimes. Now and then a "drunken buggy-driving incident out on the highway" makes it into the police blotter. The point of *rumspringa* is not criminal but biological. As any high school teacher can attest, there's something to that testosterone racing through their veins. The point is that precious few cultures have succeeded in trying to quash the young male urge for aggression. With more males reaching their teen years, it is unlikely the U.S. crime rate will escape unscathed.

Of course, those same hormones that turn ten-year-old Cub Scouts into twelve-year-old thrill-seeking shoplifters, also help the football team's wide receiver catch the long pass in the end zone, and give the young soldier the courage to climb the cliffs at Pointe DuHoc against a hail of Nazi bullets. When I taught a seminar on economics and philosophy to Harvard sophomores, a favorite article explained how (according to Talmudic thought) free markets had harnessed the evil human drive (*yetzer hara*) and channeled it toward productive competition and entrepreneurship. Likewise, the Talmud teaches that lust, which comes from an evil drive, helps us procreate. We owe a lot (ourselves, in particular) to primal urges and to other manifestations of *yetzer hara*. An absolute goody two-shoes is unlikely to make children or much of a living. The Talmud tells a story of a land that captures the evil spirit. Later they discover that there is not one fertilized egg in the land.

For most young men (most of the 40 percent who get arrested), crime is a transitional event. In a provocatively titled article, "Homeboys, Dope Fiends, Legits, and New Jacks," a criminologist suggested that some youngsters will dip into illegal work (including drug dealing) in order to pay their bills, while looking for more legitimate work. More important to society, though, are the hard-core breed who will, on average, commit twelve crimes during the year preceding their imprisonment. The Wolfgang study in Philadelphia found that if a young male had racked up three arrests, you could bet with a 70 percent level of confidence that he would get arrested again. Six percent of the arrestees committed five or more crimes by the age of eighteen, accounting for two-thirds of all the violent crimes committed by the sample of young males. Locking up all the male teenagers in the country therefore misses a key point: Namely, a small number end up doing most of the murdering, pillaging, and plundering.

It would be tempting to take the data on the historical male propensity to fight and steal, and resign ourselves to the cliché "boys will be boys." This would be a dangerous mistake, for each successive generation seems to get arrested for graver and graver crimes. Over the past forty years, the truly violent teens have committed more frequent and more heinous acts. In the Philadelphia study, for example, boys who grew up in the 1960s were far more likely to rob, burgle, or murder than their older counterparts who grew up in the 1950s. In other words, in the 1950s group, many more young men got in trouble with the police once but then gave up their abbreviated "life of crime." Consider the difference between the Crips/Bloods who stalk east Los Angeles and the Sharks/Jets who pranced through *West Side Story*. The Los Angeles gangs today carry Uzis, trade in heroin, and murder hundreds each year. The hotheads in Leonard Bernstein's musical pulled a switchblade at a high school dance. The rise of heinous and violent crime in the past thirty years explains why public support for the death penalty rose from under 50 percent in the early 1960s to 80 percent in the 1990s.

References to New York, Philadelphia, and Los Angeles might suggest that crime mostly infects the biggest and oldest cities. In fact, smaller Southern cities are among the most dangerous. The South suffers from a higher violent crime rate than other regions. After New York and Miami, the third most violent metropolitan area in 1993 was a city most Americans have never heard of, Alexandria, Louisiana. Little Rock, Tallahassee, and Jacksonville also finished in the top ten. Of the twenty most violent cities in the United States, the South claimed sixteen. Why is the South plagued? One can search for philosophical and mystical answers in William Faulkner's Southern Gothic tragedies. The real answers may be more simple. Warm weather keeps people out of doors and in trouble. Crime peaks when tempers flare in July and August. In addition, Southern towns and cities have grown in population in the past twenty years, stretching their infrastructure capacity while also straining their capacity to establish and maintain a community ethos.

WHY DO KIDS BECOME CRIMINALS? BREAKING DOWN THE COMPOSITE SKETCH

To understand criminality (and to eventually figure out how to fit it into our investment decisions), we must examine the attributes of the environment (schools, labor market, families) as well as individual traits (personality, IQ). Happily we do not have to choose one side and entwine ourselves in a "nature versus nurture" debate. Nor do we have to make a stark choice between Thomas Hobbes's view (that man is corrupt before he is socialized) and Jean-Jacques Rousseau's argument (that man is a rather pleasant chap before society corrupts him). A sensible compromise would admit that some people are predisposed toward crime and often find themselves in an environment that feeds their predisposition.

Biology and Personality

"The prince of darkness is a gentleman." In other words, you can dress up a devil in nice clothes and fool innocent victims. Is this true? Or can we somehow sniff out the evil souls among us as pigs hunt truffles? Caesar thought Cassius had that "lean and hungry" look. On the other hand, he did not see Brutus's knife coming. Cesare Lombroso was a Italian scientist in the nineteenth century who claimed that he could detect criminal tendencies by measuring skulls, lips, legs, and other anatomical parts. Following Darwin's evolutionary linkage of monkeys and men, Lombroso claimed that criminals tended to be more beastlike, with sloping foreheads that made them throwbacks from the nasty, brutish era of cavemen. The idea that ugly meant guilty has certainly been reinforced by centuries of children's fables. Some medieval laws even stated that if two persons fell under suspicion of crime the uglier or more deformed was to be regarded as more probably guilty.

In the early twentieth century, criminologists shredded Lombroso's research method and findings, along with other biometric studies of the time. Ugly was presumed to be as innocent as handsome. That did not stop other intrepid anthropologists from revisiting the issue. In the 1930s, a Harvard anthropologist named Earnest A. Hooton resurrected Lombroso and conducted his own study, measuring the physical characteristics of almost fourteen hundred criminals. He, too, found in criminals such traits as sloping foreheads, thin lips, and high nasal bridges. Hooton theorized that inferior bodies biased men toward crime, though different infirmities directed them to different crimes. Short, skinny men were prone to rob, but tall, heavy men were prone to murder. Hooton knew that he would be offending most of his professional colleagues and was prepared for accusations of racism and xenophobia. In his book *Crime and the Man* he stated that an anthropologist studying crime is an "ugly-duckling and is likely to be greeted by the lords of the criminological dung-hill with cries of Quack! quack! quack!" In provocatively titled books like *Apes, Men and Morons* and *Why Men Behave Like Apes and Vice Versa* Hooton urged society to totally isolate criminals: "Let us cease trying to make the world safe for morons, and endeavor rather to save it from them." Like Lombroso's work, Hooton's research was attacked for its methodology (he did not—and could not—measure the traits of criminals who did not get caught, for example), and for his inference that physical inferiority *caused* deviance. Despite the failures of Lombroso and Hooton, subsequent anthropologists have revisited biological theories of deviance. In the

1940s William Sheldon developed "somatotyping," in which he characterized body types. Sure enough, criminals tended to fall into the same category, more muscular and less linear than the average male, often with broad chests and large bones. Sheldon noted, though, that politicians often had these same features. While reading Sheldon's research, I surmised that the ultimate criminal type was symbolized by Babe Ruth: big, burly and not particularly good looking. In fact, Ruth was a juvenile delinquent, raised in a reformatory, who lacked personal discipline even as an adult. Without baseball, Ruth might very well have shown up as a statistic in Sheldon's data.

While most criminologists have tended to dismiss biological theories as quackery, it turns out that our instinctual (or learned?) prejudices about physique might give us some valuable clues. James Q. Wilson describes a U.S. study that asked 175 University of Nebraska students to look at criminal photographs and then guess which crimes the individuals committed. Remarkably, the students performed better than chance would suggest. A German study later lent some support to the Nebraska research. Again, researchers cannot show any causation—for example, that big bones cause people to hit their neighbors—but these loose associations suggest that certain people may be predisposed to crime, and are especially susceptible to corrupting influences.

Like body typing, IQ testing is treacherously controversial. Nonetheless, few researchers dispute that criminals tend to have somewhat lower IQs than the general populace (with the exception of those found guilty of securities fraud). Does this mean that lower IQ causes crime? Not directly, but perhaps a lower IQ contributes to poor school performance and frustration with legitimate job opportunities. Yet if IQs have stayed fairly steady in the past thirty years, why would crime rates have climbed so sharply until the past few years?

Time Horizons

More important than IQ scores are the personalities of criminals. Criminal personalities tend to live in the present, acting more impulsively and being less fearful of consequences. They perceive time with a short horizon: The death penalty does not sound so threatening when you are a young gang member who lives for today, and pulling the trigger is the quickest means to an end. As one prisoner put it, "You never think about doing thirty . . . when you don't expect to live to thirty." Young hoodlums cannot imagine staying in school and investing the time to learn legitimate job skills when easy cash comes to those who take.

Impulsive, disruptive tendencies show up rather early. By the time a youngster faces a high school guidance counselor, it is probably too late to change his character (though we should try). In a classic study, researchers found that a delinquent's record as a third grader usually pointed to his downward slide. Even at a young age delinquents tended to care less about their classmates, their teachers, and their futures. Other studies have even shown that cranky, difficult infants frequently grow up to be troublesome teenagers. *Lesson Number 3 for protecting yourself against crime: Check your neighborhood elementary schools, not just the high schools, for excessive truancy and disobedience.*

QUEENS, NEW YORK

When Pearl Richards got the phone call asking her to come to a parent-teacher conference, her hands started shaking and she dropped the telephone. While it dangled at the end of its twisted cord, she tried to control herself. She knew it wouldn't be easy to raise Tim in the neighborhood they called "Beirut." But she couldn't afford any better. She made his sandwiches and brought him to school each day, so that he wouldn't get ripped off by the hoods on the block. But Tim was eleven years old now. She couldn't smother him forever.

Shocked. How else could Pearl feel when she saw Tim's father sitting on a sofa in the principal's office. She hadn't seen the skinny creep for five years. Now he pretends he cares about his son.

"Ms. Richards," began the principal, Mr. Hampton, a fifty-year-old man with a round face and a closely cropped beard, "did you know that Timothy was cutting class to see his father?"

"What!" she screamed, at which the principal jumped out of his seat

to close the door. Her husband slouched, his body looking like it was being absorbed into the stripes of the sofa.

"Yes, one of our security guards has been following Timothy for a month now. Turns out Tim sneaks through the locker room exit and hunts out your husband, I mean, his father, almost every afternoon. Sometimes he finds him in Gus's Bar. Sometimes in front of the Off Track Betting stand on Queens Boulevard."

Pearl's nostrils flared so wide that Hampton braced himself for flames.

"He's a good boy, Ms. Richards," the principal added.

"He used to be! Now you've turned him into a truant!" She screamed at the father. "My sweet boy you've turned into a layabout—so he can be a nothing, an invisible loser!"

"He's still a good boy—" Hampton repeated.

"Hanging out at bars and convenience stores?" she interrupted. "That's good? Say, what kind of school is this? What kind of standards—"

"Ms. Richards. I'll tell you what Tim does when he finds his father." He picked up a sheet of paper, slipped a pair of glasses onto the bridge of his nose, and began to read.

Pearl leaned forward, her fingers fidgeting.

"Upon finding his father each afternoon, Tim Richards hands the man a package and then runs back to school. The package is usually a brown bag, sometimes plastic. Inside of that bag, we have discovered, is a sandwich."

HOW SOCIETY PUSHES THE PREDISPOSED TOWARD CRIME

While some criminals may be preprogrammed for trouble, surely families and schools must play some role in either pushing them into danger or rescuing them from misanthropy. Aristotle thought that although man was naturally inclined toward virtue, families should try to inculcate virtue through good habits so that doing good felt natural and comfortable. A family that does not teach right from wrong, or does not teach a child to think about consequences is a breeding ground for future felons. "Spare the rod, spoil the child" may overstate the case, yet researchers have found that juvenile delinquents are twice as likely to come from homes where mothers and fathers spare not just the rod, but even a verbal slap on the wrist.

Since permissive and indifferent parents can be found throughout the world it comes as no surprise that international studies come up with similar conclusions. What is the typical profile for a delinquent's family? Cold, uncaring parents breeding many children. The delinquent is usually a middle child lost in the noise and rancor. If a coarse family life encourages kids to pursue their more violent urges, broken homes compound the problem. Children with missing fathers tend to be more impulsive and less trusting. One intriguing experiment asked children whether they would prefer a 2-cent candy bar today or a 10-cent candy bar next week. Those without fathers grabbed at the 2-cent opportunity. Since personal growth and economic growth both depend on believing (and investing) in a tomorrow, a broken or uncaring family damns the child and the overall economy.

When families fail to instill a conscience or a concern for the future, the schools feel the pain. Preschool and mentoring programs have shown some success in rescuing children from downward behavioral spirals, but most boys fail, if they have spent their first four years being abused, neglected, or free from discipline. Forcing troubled, delinquent high schoolers to stay in school does little good, and usually hurts their borderline peers. A massive study of two thousand black and white high school boys actually discovered that dropping out did not make these adolescents more delinquent. Staying in school is not a solution for those who yearn to burst out.

Like bad schools, gangs often get blamed for turning kids into violent offenders. In truth, though, gangs attract (rather than create) delinquents, giving them an outlet for their existing aggression. Before joining gangs, the lonely teens have already assaulted their parents and teachers. In the 1950s, social service departments would assign social workers to gangs, a practice mocked by Bernstein and Sondheim in their song "Officer Krupke." Even with the relatively benign gangs of the 1950s, the social workers had little luck channeling their youthful energy toward more civil enterprises.

BLAME TELEVISION?

I must confess that television influenced me as a teenager. I wanted to dance after watching Fred Astaire, and I wanted to hit my brother after watching Muhammad Ali, who danced almost as well as Astaire (though Joe Frazier was no match for Cyd Charisse). In fact, police records do show that the homicide rate rises after famous prizefights. Aggressive television shows featuring cops and robbers do make kids more impulsive. And contrary to the caricature of the "coach potato," aggressive people tend to spend more hours in front of the television than the average watcher. Could the rise in crime be blamed on the rise of television in the 1960s and 1970s? While the thousands of corpses that get dragged across television screens might put calluses on our consciences, I am dubious that the impact is great, even if it is pernicious. Experiments show a very short-term influence. A child might be more willing to hit a clown if he has just watched a film showing children hitting clowns. A friend of mine worked as a manager of a McDonald's while in college. One day she dressed as the evil Hamburglar character featured in McDonald's advertisements. A "gang" of eight-year-olds jumped on her, knocked her over, and started slapping her, while parents looked on with amusement. She was never attacked when dressed in her normal work clothes. Clown suits and cartoon costumes dehumanize the wearers.

Stanley Milgram's famous experiments on authority, where subjects were willing to inflict electric shocks (actually simulated) on others at the request of white-coated laboratory officials, were extended to examine the influence of media. Sure enough, the subjects inflicted even more painful shocks after watching scenes from violent movies. Again, though, the impact was short-term. We should remember that the overwhelming number of television shows and movies depict the villain getting caught, punished, or killed. Take a walk down the "adventure" and "mystery" aisles of your local video store. The climatic scene almost always features a face-off between the hero and villain, between good and evil. Good, thankfully, triumphs. Even in Arnold Schwarzenegger's *The*

Terminator series, the villain returns in the sequel as a good guy. In television programs, acts do have consequences.

The prizefight phenomenon has been replicated by famous suicides. According to one researcher the Marilyn Monroe suicide inspired hundreds more. I suppose the media could have censored itself and kept the 1962 suicide quiet, but that same logic might have kept a muzzle on the networks during the Vietnam War. The "open society" (using Karl Popper's term, following John Stuart Mill) will constantly face trade-offs between freedom and security. One could take the argument to extremes. In Joe Orton's absurd and amusing play *Loot*, the constable refuses to publicly release the details of a murder by an armless, legless villain, for fear that it will launch a rash of copycat crimes.

DOES A POOR ECONOMY CAUSE CRIME?

If you knew nothing about the history of crime and of the economy, you would quickly conclude that the plunging crime rate of the past few years comes from the plunging jobless rate, which fell to 4.3 percent during 1998. The criminals must be going "legit," and trading in their bags of cocaine for briefcases. This quick inference—though it has *some* merit—does not hold up so well once you roll out the history books. The 1960s economy was strong, with a low unemployment rate, yet this was the beginning of crime's thirty-year rampage. In the Great Depression, violent crime plunged, even though up to 25 percent of the workforce struggled without jobs. Despite New York's murder total tumbling by more than half between 1993 and 1996, the jobless rate remained over 9 percent. The 1990s have been far kinder to Wall Street hotshots riding in limousines than to the kids they pass while speeding through the projects. In 1998, the teen jobless rate had fallen to about 14 percent (from about 18 percent in 1993), but that is roughly where it stood before the 1990 recession, and above its rate in the 1960s and early 1970s.

Believe it or not, a strong economy can sometimes lead to *more* crime. How? More wealth generates more envy and creates more things to steal. A comprehensive study covering 1933–1982 showed that the ups and downs of the economy did not affect the homicide rate much, but that auto thefts actually rose during booming economies. It is apparently hard for thieves to resist the shiny new Porsches parked in front of ritzy boom-time restaurants (though home burglary rates tended to fall). Of course, many geographic areas, particularly the most depressed urban zones, are virtually cut off from the national economy. William Julius Wilson, in his *When Work Disappears*, focused on the flight of whites, middle-class blacks, and of jobs from the cities, which left behind ghetto neighborhoods that were a bubbling stew of crime, welfare, family breakdown, and low levels of social organization, regardless of national trends.

Potential criminals are always making choices. Unfortunately, crime sometimes *does* pay—or at least criminals perceive it does. A survey of Boston youth showed that while in 1980 about 40 percent thought they could make more on the street than in legitimate jobs, by 1989 over 60 percent found the street more lucrative. This, despite 1989 being the peak of the booming "Massachusetts Miracle." Harvard labor economist Richard Freeman calculated that the youth could make about $10 per hour in street scams and drug dealing, rather than flip hamburgers for $5 or $6 per hour. A Rand study discovered that Washington, D.C., drug dealers took home even more, about $30 per hour, though they had to dodge bullets now and then.

TIME HORIZONS AND THE BUCHHOLZ HYPOTHESIS

Criminals often figure that crime pays because they care little about the future. They are willing to dodge bullets, flee police, and pocket a quick payoff, rather than make an investment in the future (school, job training). Criminologists and economists who have studied crime have not focused enough on time horizons, I think. In an economic model I published about ten years ago, I concluded that when time horizons shrink the value of acting honestly diminishes, leading to economic collapse. With due respect to one's Sunday school teacher, honesty is not always the best policy, if your goal is to get rich with the least amount of effort. Two forces normally dissuade even amoral egotists from cheating or stealing, especially in business. First, the fear of punishment. Second, the fear that a bad reputation will repel others from dealing with you *in the future*. But what if you do not care about the future? Crime goes up. (The same dynamic explains why tourists passing through tend to tip waiters less than regular restaurant patrons.) Sometimes society shrinks the time horizon, making crime look more inviting to more people. How? When governments are about to collapse, for example, South Vietnam in 1975 or Indonesia in 1998.

Another way for society to shrink time horizons is to let interest rates rise. Higher interest rates force us to discount the future more. That is, a dollar next year is worth less today, if interest rates go up. The Buchholz hypothesis, then, is that higher interest rates induce people to commit more crime because it reduces the value of their future. During the Great Depression, nominal interest rates dropped, which could solve the mystery of why crime rates actually descended amid economic misery. From the 1960s through the 1970s, interest rates began a steady climb, accompanied by higher crime rates. Violent crime peaked around 1980, as did interest rates, only to climb again in the late 1980s. The past few years have seen a rapid drop in interest rates that has tracked the plunge in violent crime, with both the crime rate and U.S. Treasury bond yields plunging to thirty-year lows.

Surely, interest rates are not the only factor. Demographics, police work, and punishment rates play a huge role. But when society tells potential felons that tomorrow counts for less, we should not be shocked when they take advantage of us today.

FOUR MORE FORCES THAT PUSHED DOWN THE CRIME RATE IN THE 1990S

Besides lower interest rates, the 1990s benefited from the following anticrime factors:

1. Windows '82 Communities throughout the country embraced the Wilson broken windows theory, creating a "zero-tolerance" attitude. Police forces, who had routinely turned the other cheek, pounced on gang members for such minor crimes as littering, loitering, and public urination. The police discovered that those committing nuisance crimes were often wanted for dangerous felonies. By making criminals "feel the heat," they gave decent neighbors the freedom to walk at night in their own neighborhoods. New York City Police Chief William Bratton (and successor Howard Safir) developed an anticrime strategy that demanded accountability from precinct commanders. Their "Compstat" system ("compare statistics") plots on a color-coded map where crimes are taking place. Precinct commanders must then explain what tactics they are taking to protect the neighborhood. The police chiefs pushed out half the commanders, who did not successfully attack the "hot spots" in their precinct. The Keystone cops parody has been replaced by an almost Robocop efficiency. The zero-tolerance campaign mirrors the effort by U.S. corporations to upgrade their quality testing for goods and services. The so-called "six-sigma" quality goal of such titans as Motorola and General Electric help explain the incredible comeback of U.S. firms competing against Japanese entities. The reputation of American products in the 1970s and 1980s for shoddiness has been replaced; and the reputation of our police forces has seen a similar revolution. In many cities, better policing has been accompanied by putting more cops on the street, which has reinforced the Windows '82 "operating system."

INDIANAPOLIS, INDIANA

Franklin Harrison hated his job as a prison guard. He was neither sadistic enough to enjoy inflicting pain, nor masochistic enough to enjoy his own misery. It took a special person to handle it, and goddammit, he wasn't special enough. But he would stay two more years so his pension would vest.

Harrison looked at his pale beefy hands and the fingers that plucked touchdown passes from the sky when he played high school football. He'd always thought of himself as a physical person. But now he hated touching. Wouldn't you get disgusted from running your fingers across the unwashed bodies of murderers, rapists, and street thugs? Too many sweaty bodies crammed into dank cells. Every judge in Indiana wanted the nickname "hang 'em high," but instead of hanging from a noose most of the felons just hung around the prisons until they grew too feeble to handle the regimen. With tough laws like "three strikes you're out," the prisons were bursting. Harrison scanned the rows of iron rooms, eighty cells on each floor, five floors high. He walked down the hallway, to the jeers of broken men. He had learned to block out their taunts. When he reached the steel-girded window at the end of the hallway, he stared across a parking lot and a green meadow at a new construction site. A school? A hospital? No. Indiana had its priorities. It was a new prison. Harrison took out a pad and jotted down a reminder to ask for a transfer to the new facility.

2. Lock 'Em Up Since the mid–1980s, America got tougher on criminals, throwing more of them in prison than ever before. While the imprisonment rate stayed steady from the 1920s to the 1970s, it has more than quadrupled in the past two decades. For every fifty workers in the United States, there is one felon sitting in prison. As a result of mandatory sentencing and "three strikes you're out" policies, the average felon serves a longer term than previously. And since the average felon commits about dozen crimes in the year before arrest, a year of extra prison times spares the community multiple crimes. We seem to have evolved our national ethos to demand justice and retribution from criminals (à la Kant), even if we cannot be sure that punishment deters.

3. The Best Defense Twenty years ago in the suburbs, "the club" referred to the Elks or 4-H. Now it means a tough, locked steel bar to scare away auto thieves. Twenty years ago, a "gated community" was a euphemism for a prison. Now it is a selling point for suburban real estate developments. In California recently, I saw a large billboard advertising a new tract as the "Lowest Price Gated Community in Los Angeles—starting at $100,000." Home burglar alarm systems have also spread throughout the country, offered by independent firms, telephone companies, and cable television systems. These "target hardening" defenses do not just appeal to the cynical or paranoid. In my neighborhood I noticed a VW van covered with "progressive" bumper stickers: "Vegetarians are sprouting up" and "Sow Justice—Harvest Peace." Sure enough, this justice-minded vegetarian had "the club" defiantly locked across the steering wheel. There may be a kind of arms race between criminals and innocents, where felons learn how to detach alarm systems, for example. Nonetheless, the arms race favors the good people, because criminals tend to be less organized and more stupid than victims. With the help of smart researchers at sophisticated corporations, criminals have trouble keeping up with the latest antitheft devices (theft by computer hackers may be more challenging). Poorer, crowded urban areas may find it harder to erect solid defenses. *Lesson Number 3 to protect against crime: Do not grow lax—maintain your crimefighting habits and tools, especially alarms and locks.*

4. The Crack in Crack Crack cocaine hit America's cities in the mid–1980s but has tailed off in recent years. Crack use took off when users realized they could get a smokeable, powerful high for just $5, compared to perhaps $100 for cocaine powder. Since the crack high wears off quickly addicts quickly came back for more— often in a frenzied mood. Jittery users met agitated dealers, creating an explosive scene at corner "drug supermarkets." The crack epidemic peaked in coastal cities about 1990 when youths began to scorn "crackheads." Young brothers who had seen older brothers murdered or addled by crack started abusing the frazzled users. Unfortunately, noncoastal cities like Indianapolis are still in the midst of a crack plague though the favorable coastal trend should be spreading.

WHY CRIME WILL REBOUND

The good news on crime will not end in a sudden orgy of murder, rape, and robbery. If the U.S. economy stays healthy, with low interest rates and better job prospects, if American families remain vigilant with anticrime devices, and if police deploy their resources smartly, we could enjoy a several more years of declining crime.

Nonetheless, we are not, as they say, scot-free. Though demography is not destiny, it does place a stumbling block on the road ahead. As I stated earlier in this chapter, the crime rate for young teens has not followed the swan dive the rate for adults did. In the mid-1980s, the arrest rate among ten- to seventeen-year-olds for violent crime was about the same as the rate for adults. Now the rate for youngsters is about 40 percent higher. In 1980 the murder rate for youngsters was about half the rate for adults. Unfortunately, the kids have caught up, and the rate is virtually even. "Entry level" crimes like picking pockets and shoplifting have resisted the overall downward trend in crime rates. This signals trouble ahead. The teenage population will grow by about 1 percent per year over the next decade. There will be about 20 percent more fourteen- to seventeen-year-olds in 2005 than in 1997, and 26 percent more black fourteen- to seventeen-year-olds. Many of these baby boomerangers will come from broken homes and bankrupt schools, and will be devoid of social conscience and concern for their futures. Crime scholar John DiIulio has coined the term "superpredators" to describe the vicious gangs that could form in scenes reminiscent of *Clockwork Orange*.

Most discussions of contemporary gangs portray them as angry, violent youths recklessly twirling knives and shooting guns when they feel "dissed" by an outsider. This is no doubt more menacing than the 1950s cliché depicting gangs as bored teenagers singing in three-part harmony under the streetlamp of a city corner. To make the contemporary image even more frightening (and more accurate), we must realize that gangs have become economic organizations, often profitably trading in drugs and illegal weapons. By becoming business units that spin off profits for kingpins, they develop a durability that extends beyond adolescence. It used to be that gang members quit after the pimples left their faces; now gang members will try to hang on into their twenties. Gang members who survive the physical risks and become leaders can clear between $30 and $70 per hour (though entry-level street dealers may earn less than the minimum wage). A gang in the Midwest actually opened up its "accounting books" to two scholars at the University of Chicago, allowing them to develop an economic model. The books revealed gross profit margins of 80 percent for sales of crack. In addition, gang behavior appeared more rational and businesslike than popular portrayals. For example, not only do gangs try to protect their physical turf, they also try to protect market share. After a gang war, which would scare off nervous buyers, the gang would slash prices below marginal cost in order to maintain market share. In many ways, local gangs operate like franchisees, paying kingpins a franchise fee (called a "tribute") in exchange for a drug-dealing territory. The point here is that by evolving into more businesslike operations, gangs have a better chance of surviving and expanding.

In the past few years, Las Vegas has been invaded by Los Angeles gangs, causing the gambling capital to buck the recent national trend toward lower crime rates. Gun-waving Crips attacked the cashier cage at the Flamingo, swiping $150,000 in cash. In September 1996, gangsters shot up rap star Tupac Shakur while he was speeding down the Strip on his way to a club with ties to the Bloods. "Gangs are involved with virtually every crime there is here," stated Sergeant Don Sutton of the city police department. "When we bust the door down in a crack house, it's always the California guys that end up supplying the place." To infiltrate the city, Los Angeles gang members shed their homeboy baggy pants, drop their identifying colors, and even change their name and social security number. They look more legit, but act more deadly. Remember, the prince of darkness is a gentleman.

A skeptic might ask why these more youthful gangs will survive, just as the Mafia looks like it is fading away. The answer has several prongs. First, we cannot forget that newer gangs—black, Chinese, Russian—have won street battles against the Mafia, so they may be the fittest in the evolutionary struggle. Second, the Mafia was generally controlled by middle-aged and older precinct managers, people who often learned that legitimate opportunities usually offered more money and certainly more safety. As a recent book put it, the Mafia declined because of a "lack of qualified personnel." As older "Mafia generations passed into jail cells or cemeteries, the succeeding generation that evolved in its place produced not stronger and smarter . . . but much dumber ones." In contrast, members of more youthful ethnic and racial groups may not see the honest alternatives so clearly. Third, the FBI and local crime units spent half a century tracking and infiltrating the Mafia, before the Mafia started looking feeble. Their efforts to understand and undermine more recent gangs are perhaps just underway.

In addition to gangs in the United States, the crime rate is also more susceptible to international terrorism. Plastic bombs, miniature missiles, and other more stealthy devices keep the FBI on edge, especially when militant nationalistic groups rage against U.S. foreign policy. A few years ago a small propeller plane landed on the South Lawn of the White House. Thankfully, it was an innocent adventure. Nonetheless, the incident proved that the most hardened targets are more porous than we thought. In 1995, members of Japan's "Supreme Truth" sect uncorked the nerve gas sarin in the Tokyo subways, killing a dozen people and injuring thousands. With billions of dollars at his disposal, the sect's mystic, herbalist leader had gone on a shopping spree in Russia's arms bazaar, purchasing "a helicopter equipped to spray deadly chemicals and training from special forces in the assembly and use of rifles and rocket-launchers." Most frightening, the police discovered enough sarin to murder millions of people. Founder Shoko Asahara's pledge to "eradicate major cities" did not sound so farfetched after all. The collapse of the Soviet Union allowed Communist bosses and their thugs to shuttle plutonium and other precious materials out of the country by plane, train, and truck. Russia's former national security chief, Alexander Lebed, has stated that up to one hundred miniature nuclear weapons ("suitcase bombs") were missing from the supply rooms of Soviet special forces. Lebed's claim sounded alarms throughout Moscow and Washington. We may never know whether Lebed was right until the first suitcase explodes. President Clinton appointed a special adviser to develop a plan to combat such terrorist threats as germ warfare and cyber-warfare, where terrorists would knock out the computer systems that guide everything from the stock market to the Strategic Air Command.

While these terrorist nightmares are usually not discussed in the same breath as the urban crime rate, a link is growing between the two. Urban gangs in the United States, for example, will receive guidance, guns, and funding from foreign entities. If the Chinese military could infiltrate fund-raising efforts of the Democrat Party, surely Chinese dope smugglers can provide financial credit and other help to U.S. gang leaders. Terrorism on our soil will lead to more police work, and to more purchases of anticrime devices by households.

There are, of course, other reasons to worry about the domestic crime rate. Some criminologists fret that the stricter federal and state welfare laws will send poor teens into the streets, angry at a system that forces their ill-prepared mothers into the workforce. So far, the results of welfare reform have been good, with many recipients getting and keeping real jobs. Will this positive trend be reversed when the next economic downturn arrives? Other criminologists wonder whether the good news on crime will continue when the next drug craze hits. Methamphetamines have begun to replace crack cocaine in many neighborhoods. Will they, like crack, light up the night with gunfire?

INVESTMENTS AND THE CRIME RATE

We are a poorer country because of crime. Robbers, burglars, and thieves directly take somewhere between $500 and $1,000 per crime, and many times that when they steal an automobile. If we add in "pain and suffering," the risk of death and other "softer" but bloodier variables that accompany violent crimes like rape, we find that crime does steal a statistically significant slice out of the economy. The largest estimate ($450 billion) comes from a paper written for the Department of Justice, though that includes such difficult to measure factors as emotional impact, depressed neighborhood property values, bankrupt businesses, etc.

The falling crime rate of the past few years has injured the stocks of those firms involved in the crime prevention industry. If this trend reverses itself in coming years, there may be opportunities to buy shares in firms whose stock prices have suffered.

CRIME PREVENTION TRAINING AND TECHNOLOGY

No part of the U.S. economy is untouched by technological revolutions—even an old, genteel game like tennis discovered lasers to pinpoint serving faults and to gauge the speed of serves. Meanwhile, players propel the ball at over 100 miles per hour using racquets constructed from new, advanced materials. Investors should look for firms that are helping to develop technological tools to fight crime. Right now, crime prevention and the penal industry are tedious and labor intensive. The ankle bracelets worn by parolees that transmit radio waves to parole officers have provided some efficiencies. Decades ago, the radio transmitter in police cars allowed law enforcement officers a huge productivity gain. Where will the next productivity leap come from?

The burglar alarm industry is a ferociously competitive field, with many technologies vying for leadership. Simple telephone lines, fiber optics, wireless transmitters, coaxial cable, and satellite transmissions wend their way into millions of houses throughout the country. Many of the vendors are still "mom and pop" operations, though nationwide firms like ADT and Brinks Security have bought up and consolidated others. (When I served in the White House, my mailbox was inundated with thousands of protests from owners of small, local alarm companies, who wanted to forbid telephone companies from entering their line of business.) Technological progress in the past ten years has pushed down the price of video surveillance, including infrared nighttime vision. In 1993, 18 percent of American homes had burglar alarms, but that number has been steadily rising. In fact, the spread of such security services has helped drive down the overall crime rate. In some areas, one thin wire into the home can provide cable television, telephone, Internet access, and burglar alarm services—of course, that wire must be hidden from the view of an intruder with garden shears. Investments in this industry will pay off even bigger when the crime rate surges again. From the professional investor's point of view, the monthly revenues to alarm service firms are about as steady and stable as the revenue streams to other utilities. Far from being a speculative gamble, such investments will appear rather conventional.

Computer technologies are forcing armies, navies and police forces to rewrite their training manuals. Consider: Air force pilots have been using flight simulators for years. Compared to actual flying, the computers obviously save on fuel costs. More important, though, they save lives and aircraft by ensuring that pilots have confronted catastrophic training conditions before they finger the actual controls of a F117A. Soldiers on the ground have also entered simulators, saving millions of dollars on live ammunition and the environmental costs of cleaning up lead artillery shells. Police forces around the world are now deploying these same training technologies, which depend on software developed by such firms as <u>Firearms Training Systems</u>. During the last year Greek police departments and the Australian army signed contracts with the Georgia-based firm (though the stock market has driven the company's share price into the ground). The software can be specifically designed for the users. For a navy or the Coast Guard, the simulators will convey the sensation of rocking seas, so that the sharpshooter can learn how to compensate for the rocking and rolling. For police forces, simulators can put marksmen in the blinding light of a setting sun, or the dangerous darkness of a moonless night.

LOW-TECH BASICS: PRIVATE PRISONS

The prison industry is similar to the hotel industry, as many disgruntled hotel guests might attest. They both have beds, high fixed costs, and various levels of service (maximum security versus minimum security; luxury resort versus motel). Entrepreneurs entered the prison industry in the 1980s, after fighting philosophical battles with groups such as the American Civil Liberties Union. It turned out to be good timing, for the U.S. imprisonment rate has been rising steadily as judges have sent a greater proportion of felons to prison, and have ordered them to serve longer sentences. The state and federal prisons will soon be holding 2 million inmates. So far, private firms house only about 2.5 percent of those people. The total number of prisoners, as well as the market share of firms such as Corrections Corporation of America (owned by Prison Realty Corporation) and Wackenhut Corrections, will grow in the years ahead. While some private prisons have seen their record stained by such events as prisoner escapes and health code violations, many state governments have found private facilities cheaper, safer, and more successful at implementing adult education programs. (Like the Marriott company, private prison firms have, in some cases, built, owned, and operated facilities while in other cases they have merely managed facilities owned by state governments.) The private industry benefits from the aging infrastructure of the state and federal facilities, which are often operating far above capacity, creating an incendiary, dangerous climate for inmates and guards. In addition, one-third of the public facilities are probably already beyond their reasonable life expectancy of fifty years.

A resurgent crime rate would help the private prison firms, though their financial success probably does not depend upon it. The biggest risk to their stock prices may be political whims. In July 1998, six prisoners escaped from Corrections Corporation's medium-security facility in Youngstown, Ohio. Public outrage led the governor to threaten closing down the prison, which pummeled the stock price. The prison upgraded security, but the incident shows how vulnerable the stock prices can be. At the same time, the incident puts enormous pressure on the private prison industry to deliver efficient, safe service to its customers (the public) and to its residents.

CONCLUSION

In the past decade, the United States has cracked down on criminals, abandoning the more lenient attitudes of the 1960s and 1970s. Rather than face an executioner, a convicted murderer sentenced to death in the 1970s would usually face "life on death row." In 1997, 74 prisoners, compared with just one in 1977, actually felt the singe and brutal jolt of an electric chair or the prick of a lethal needle. Public opinion slowly but decisively turned against felons, and more Americans now resemble the Southern governor, who when asked for his position on the death penalty, responded, "Right next to the switch."

While deterrence remains controversial among academic criminologists, Princeton's John DiIulio has pointed out, even those criminologists who dispute deterrence theory pump their brakes when a police car appears (even when they are driving to criminology conferences). Whether or not as a result of longer sentences and more severe punishments, the crime rate has tumbled since the early 1990s. Cities like New York have especially benefited. No longer is any corner of Manhattan just a block from the scene of a crime. No longer does it seem that the most common form of transportation is the stretcher. We are healthier, wealthier, and a little wiser as a result. But we are not yet relaxed, and should not be.

The next ten years will challenge police departments with a more desperate and more alienated class of offender than ever before. Locking the doors and turning on floodlamps may not be enough. A Brooklyn social worker recently testified before Congress, holding in one hand a marijuana cigarette and in the other a 40-ounce bottle of malt liquor, the two items providing a typical breakfast for many broken-hearted teens. While both are technically depressants, they often fuel violence. He cited a local saying, "There's a fight in every forty, there's a fool in every forty, and many times there's a funeral in every forty." How can we be confident of a continually falling crime rate when it is "easier to find a 9mm [gun] on many of our blocks than a book"? Social workers, politicians, policemen, and entrepreneurs will focus their talents and time on these issues. The economy and the financial markets are no more immune from a deadly social epidemic than is the individual citizen, who must double lock and dead bolt his door each evening.

9

NO SWEAT
How to Survive and Thrive Amid Global Warming

SEASIDE HEIGHTS, NEW JERSEY

Anthony Maroni grabbed his staple gun and shot the last inch of the pink, green, and yellow "Grand Opening" banner. His mother, Rose, wanted red, white, and blue, but Tony liked the colors of spumoni. And that's what his new restaurant would bring to this boardwalk on the Jersey Shore. Tony flipped open a Budweiser and gazed at the beach, decorated with bikinis and blankets. The rolling waves pummeled the sand, as high tide shrunk the beach. No matter. The loud, churning surf energized the crowd, beckoning young men to show off by diving in. And soon they'd get hungry for lunch at Tony's Napoli.

He sniffed the scent of coconut suntan oil as it wafted across the steaming beach and into his spanking-new restaurant. For a moment, Tony thought his eyes were playing tricks on him. He squinted and reached for his shades. A man in a dark gray suit was trudging across the sand toward Tony, briefcase in hand. What kind of goombah wears a suit in Seaside Heights? Would he stroll onto the floor of the New York Stock Exchange in a swimsuit? But as the strange man grew closer, Tony thought he looked both familiar and threatening. Tom Murphy.

"Nice sign, Mr. Maroni," the man said, while refusing to wipe his sweaty forehead. He took a deep breath, obviously exhausted from the walk. "I've got some bad news to deliver, though."

Then deliver it to someone else, you stuffed shirt jerk, Tony thought.

"We're canceling your property insurance."

"Turn around and drown yourself, Murphy!" Tony felt steam as his own sweat evaporated in anger. "I just built this place—you promised I'd get coverage. I borrowed money at 10 percent. You can't do this to me!"

"I understand your anger, Mr. Maroni."

"You don't understand anything, you corporate stooge. You guys were the last company left that was willing to underwrite Seaside. Now what?"

Murphy unfurled a map from his briefcase and pointed. "Mr. Maroni, you chose to build a restaurant sandwiched between a surging Atlantic Ocean and a rising Barnegat Bay. We can't underwrite a restaurant stuck in an aquatic vise. I'm sorry."

"What are you talking about? Look out there! A million bodies are sunning themselves in that same vise!"

"Yes, Mr. Maroni. But there's a difference. Look at that thermometer," he said, pointing to the Solarcane sign which flashed 102 degrees. "When that temperatures rises and when the waters begin to sweep up across the sand, those teenagers can flee in their cars back to the mainland. Your restaurant doesn't fit in the trunk of a car, does it now?"

MEKONG DELTA, VIETNAM

Thu Nguyen's muscles ached from heaving sandbags in front of his bamboo house. The sweeping rains stung at his bare back like needles. He looked down to see that his boots had blistered open. The enemy was relentlessly marching forward. He looked at his cracked, bleeding hands, which hadn't hurt so much since he crawled away from the Viet Cong in 1973. He blamed that ancient misery on the Communists. Who could he blame today? The gods? Angry ancestors?

His rice paddies, which the state just privatized, were overrun with a brown, muddy goo. Even more disgusting, the bodies of villagers washed among the grasses. He heard that a neighbor was actually using drowned bodies as sandbags. The image nauseated Thu, but he had no time for sickness. Furious winds howled through the few trees that remained rooted during the monsoon. Most had blown away in last month's disastrous storm.

The winds suddenly, impossibly, grew more fierce. A fence post—at least fifty pounds—whizzed by within inches of his right ear. A change in strategy. Instead of lugging sandbags to protect his ramshackle house, Thu clung to the sandbags to avoid being swept away. He fumbled with a piece of rope and wrapped it around a bag marked "U.S. Army, Saigon 1972." He took the ends and tied it around his waist. He wiped the mud from his eyes. Hugging the sandbag, Thu had only one comforting image—a recent postcard from his wife and daughter postmarked Atlanta, Georgia.

Newsflash

GM stock plunged today as one of the largest shareholders, the California State Pension Fund, threatened to dump all of its shares on the market. The fund demands that GM cut production of its popular, gas-guzzling Chevy Blazer and instead spin out a new version of its slow-selling electric car, the Impact. This comes one day after the UN released a controversial study condemning the U.S. government's carbon emissions policy and predicting a rash of floods that could wipe out 500,000 Bangladeshis in the next ten years. Also today, Barbra Streisand banned gasoline-powered automobiles from the set of her new film, Funny Yentl.

Pounding rains, sweeping floods, choking smoke, scorching sunshine that withers the corn. Now here is a chapter that requires Cecil B. DeMille's direction and Orson Welles's stentorian baritone. DeMille, after all, directed *The Ten Commandments* and narrated the plague scenes. Welles brought us the horrifying *War of the Worlds* radio play. This chapter contemplates the possible end of the world. In comparison, previous chapters on mutual funds and European Monetary Union might seem rather pale.

Since neither DeMille nor Welles survives, you will have to trust me to tell the startling story of how the earth may be warming up and preparing to overwhelm us with plagues not seen since biblical times. I will spell out the rather shaky scientific consensus, as well as the surprising views of critics who argue that global warming might actually help many sectors. Just as the earth has two poles, so does the debate on global climate change. Professional Chicken Littles would of course snuff out every last candle to avoid the worst-case scenarios. Professional naysayers refuse even to examine the serious scientific studies. I approach the topic with deep skepticism, for I have seen too many scientific flip-flops in the past decade. Was there a Big Bang? Were birds once dinosaurs? Is cholesterol good or bad? We do not know—though every few months newspaper headlines seem to declare a "new" definitive answer. I am reminded of a Woody Allen movie, where a character asks his father why God permitted Nazis to exist. "How should I know? I don't even know how a toaster works," the father replies. Nor do I, though I suspect that toasters add to global warming.

Remember, we do not need a definitive answer before we draw up an investment strategy. We simply need to believe that the odds of an event *exceed* those consensus odds incorporated in financial markets. A simple gambling example might help. Say that Las Vegas bookies are giving two-to-one odds that Pete Sampras will win another Wimbledon title. Now, you discover that Sampras has decided that he will play left-handed, instead of in his usual right-handed championship style. Surely, this diminishes Sampras's chances of winning. Perhaps you think his odds are now even. What should you do? Bet against him—even though you think he still has a fifty-fifty shot at winning. Why? Because the Las Vegas market incorrectly sees his chances as two-to-one. If he loses, you'll make more money.

Now let's look at global warming. You may think that the odds are just 40 percent that the world's temperatures will rise, bringing floods, famine, and vermin. Fine. Nonetheless, if the market prices for flood-sensitive goods and properties are completely *ignoring* the possibility, there is room to profit by betting on global warming. This kind of risk/reward investment logic tells me that investors must take global warming seriously, even if we ultimately doubt its impact.

We do not live in a world of either 100 percent or 0 percent probabilities. Do you pack an umbrella *only* when the chance of rain hits 100 percent and the water is pouring down? Do you venture outside *only* on perfectly cloudless days, with absolutely no chance of rain? You probably peek out the window or at the weather forecast before stepping onto your front porch in the morning. Likewise, you should peek at a long-term view of the climate before designing your long-term investment portfolio. Investors in insurance companies, agricultural goods, real estate, and emerging markets should start paying attention to the thermometer, just as they pay attention to the Dow Jones average.

In this chapter we will assess the risks of global warming, the scientific debate, as well as the economic debate over its impact. Are you feeling warm today? If so, you might want to follow *Rule Number 1: Lock in long-term property and flood insurance, if you live in coastal or low-lying regions.* Our fictional Anthony Maroni might have stayed in business if he had shifted the risk of global warming to insurance companies before the tides started sweeping over the boardwalk. Investors whose portfolios are exposed to agriculture, either by owning farm-related stocks, or actual farm land, should read this chapter carefully, for a warmer climate would drive down the value of some crops, while making others more scarce and therefore more dear.

THE BENCHMARK "CONSENSUS"

Before diving into the fascinating history and science of climate change, you should know what the consensus of experts are predicting. The depressing view is rather Humpty-Dumpty like. All the king's horses and all the king's men—in fact, 2,500 scientists gathered under the auspices of the UN's Intergovernmental Panel on Climate Change (IPCC)—have concluded that the climate will change more in the next few decades that at any time since the cave men. And unless we junk our gasoline-powered automobiles and oil heat, we cannot prevent the change. Between 1990 and 2100, the IPCC forecasts that temperatures will probably climb about 4.5 degrees Fahrenheit (they also give a range of 1.8 to 6.3 degrees Fahrenheit). Big deal, you might say. I have sweated in 110 degrees Los Angeles heat by day, only to grab bed covers when the night time thermometer dropped to 40 degrees. That is a seventy-degree swing within hours, not a few degrees over a century! The weatherman on this evening's news will probably misjudge tomorrow's temperature by about 4.5 degrees.

The following factoid might put 4.5 degrees in perspective: During the ice age that ended about twelve thousand years ago, temperatures averaged just 5 to 9 degrees cooler than they are today. Five degrees may be the only thing that stands between you and a mastodon. During that ice age, Germany was paved not with an autobahn, but with a glacier. New York City's only potholes were chips in 100 meters of ice.

At any given time, the earth's "natural" balance between sunshine/clouds, oceans/land, animal/vegetable/mineral rests on temperature changes. The temperature is a kind of lever that can shift the balance in any direction. The situation reminds me of a leveraged buyout, where the success of a company is extremely vulnerable to the level of interest rates. If interest rates rise, the borrowing company has a terribly high burden to carry in trying to pay back lenders. So, too, our current earthly balance depends much on the climate of the globe.

With warmer temperatures, the IPCC certainly does not fear hairy mastodons or the saber-toothed tigers that roamed the Midwest during the ice age. Instead, they see more furious storms and 7 percent more rain, which would help push up sea levels by one to two feet. Landlubbers would find themselves with waterfront property; many cities would get washed over like Atlantis. Saving the Netherlands would require more than a child with a Dutch-boy haircut poking his finger in a dike. A raging North Sea would probably swallow up that country. And Copenhagen's Tivoli Gardens would be turned into another Sea World theme park. The news gets worse. A more tropical climate would bring more mosquitoes. While those of us who grew up on the Jersey Shore scoffed at the mosquito by calling it "our state bird," we usually ignored the health risks. But one study projects that global warming will spark outbursts of malaria well beyond the tropics.

In 1993, CBS television brought the nightmare into American homes with its miniseries *The Fire Next Door*. In the show, which takes place in 2007, a boy travels through the American south, amid fires, super-storms, droughts, and clichés. The images went far beyond the IPCC and created a weird blend of the searing *The Grapes of Wrath* and the tacky *Towering Inferno*. CBS obviously bet that it could get American viewers interested in global warming. The response from Americans remains underwhelming, however.

What is warming the earth? The consensus (which is *not* a unanimous survey of scientific opinion) points to greenhouse gases, particularly carbon dioxide (CO_2) from burning fossil fuels. A hundred years ago, a Swedish chemist named Svante Arrhenius warned that coal burning would push temperatures higher. Greenhouse gases allow sunlight and other radiation to warm the earth, but then act like an insulating blanket that traps the heat near the planet's surface. Back in the 1820s, a French mathematician, Jean-Baptiste Joseph Fourier, depicted the earth as a "glass vessel," where air lets the sunshine in, but holds on to some of the warmth. Arrhenius's thesis fit in nicely with that model. Today, CO_2 concentrations in the atmosphere are about 30 percent higher than before the Industrial Revolution, which may explain the 1 degree rise in average temperatures over the past century. The consensus assumes that CO_2 emissions will likely *double* during the next century. Back in 1896, Arrhenius thought that doubling would take three thousand years; hence we can now list him as an optimist. Of course, the Swede did not foresee Henry Ford or his countrymen Assar Gabrielesson and Gustaf Larson, who together created Volvo.

We should not pin all of the blame on automobiles and oil heaters, though. In fact, most of the carbon dioxide escapes from "natural" sources. When plants decay, volcanoes erupt, rice paddies breathe, and cows belch they release CO_2 and methane, sending about 200 billion tons of CO_2 into the atmosphere. In comparison, our cars, trucks, and appliances give off perhaps 7 or 8 billion tons. But environmentalists believe that they have a much greater chance of persuading human beings to curtail gas-guzzling joyrides than convincing cows to hold in their gas. Hence, proposed government solutions to global warming point the finger at man-made sources of CO_2.

Most of the CO_2 released by natural and man-made sources

actually gets caught before doing damage to the atmosphere. Trees, plants, plankton, algae, and desert soils suck up more than 95 percent of the CO_2. It's just those pesky extra percentage points that create the greenhouse effect, according to the majority of earth and atmospheric scientists.

The important numbers to remember in the consensus case are these: average temperatures jump 4.5 degrees by the year 2100; CO_2 emissions double; and sea levels surge 1 to 2 feet higher. Now that we know what scientists see ahead of us, we can look backward at the earth's fascinating past for more clues.

BACK IN TIME: EDEN I AND II

Ira Gershwin was right to point out that the Rockies may crumble, for virtually nothing about the earth has been constant. If cave men had beakers and test tubes, they, too, would have worried about global warming. For the earth's climate has changed many times before, bringing new disasters and new opportunities with every shift. Most people assume that since Noah beached his ark, the earth's climate has been pretty stable, give or take a few frigid winters or wicked summers. A poetic book entitled *Wind: How the Flow of Air Has Shaped Life, Myth, and the Land* tries to educate and entice its audience. Economists, in particular, have not spent enough time studying the impact of climate on economies. Let's take a quick look at the dramatic shifts in climate that the fossils, rocks, and trees have recorded for us.

The seas in which we now sail, swim, and jet-ski once boiled. Then about 2 or 3 billion years ago, a more temperate climate took over, probably 10 to 20 degrees warmer than today's. It prevailed during the age of dinosaurs, 160 million years ago. How do we know? Dinosaur fossils lie buried near traces of tropical ferns in Big Sky country, Montana. In a real Jurassic Park, ferns left coal deposits near the South Pole. Alligators once crawled across northern Canada. Alas, the dinosaurs could not respond to the rapid climate brought on by a comet the size of Manhattan, which tore across the sky before tearing up the earth 65 million years ago. (Ironically, the dinosaurs, which died in the global climate event, left bones and bodies that gave us the fossil fuels that may be fostering a new climate event.)

Skipping millions of years of ice ages and thaws, we come to an Edenlike period that finally created a nurturing, hospitable climate for mankind. Called the "climatic optimum" by earth scientists, this global springtime bloomed about ten thousand years ago. Rather than crude hunter-gatherers in the wild, the more temperate, dependable climate allowed man to become farmers and shepherds of controlled fields and flocks. The New Stone Age turned into the Bronze Age. Temperatures averaged about 4 degrees warmer than today's during the peak period of 6,000 to 9,000 B.C., and today's deserts were sometimes swampy. Saharan cave paintings depict such water dwellers as hippos and alligators. Balmier conditions encouraged seafaring expeditions, and Scandinavian merchants shipped Baltic amber south to the Mediterranean and north to Scotland. In sum, our ancestors flourished when the temperature was 4 degrees warmer than today. *They* would not mind the IPCC's projections for 2100 A.D. But, of course, they had not yet drained the Netherlands or built homes on stilts in Malibu Canyon. True, they lived in a world 4 degrees warmer than ours—but the thermometer had not leapt those 4 degrees within a single lifetime.

While the earth cooled a bit after 3,000 B.C., another climatic optimum returned between about 900 and 1250 A.D. The Vikings made the most of the thaw, as they hunted and rested in a truly green Greenland. They could even bury their dead in the ground, which has since turned impenetrably cold. The Vikings' success in a warmer climate might repeat itself in the twenty-first century. Norwegians, Swedes, and Finns may gain the most if their northern regions thaw, inviting new agriculture and fishing. In the medieval warming, forest and farming latitudes migrated north. Wineries flourished well into the English midlands, hundreds of miles above the current "wine line." Lush Canadian forests stretched much closer to the Arctic Circle. Bountiful harvests and a booming population permitted peasants to erect dramatic Gothic castles and cathedrals in tribute to the "greater glory of God" (who, incidentally, blessed them with sunshine). Query: Could there have been a Chartres or Notre Dame or Leaning Tower of Pisa without a rising thermometer? I am always skeptical of single explanations, but better weather and bigger harvests do break open new possibilities.

Nor was the medieval climate change solely a European boon. The Sung Dynasty (960–1279 A.D.) achieved new levels of success in China. "Domestic peace, new crops, and technological advances fostered a dramatic population growth in the eleventh century," which doubled from about 50 to 100 million people. By the beginning of the Ming dynasty (1368 A.D.), with the colder clime, the population shrunk back to about 60 million.

The pendulum swung back away from Eden again, starting around 1300 A.D. and keeping the world in a new "Little Ice Age" until the 1800s. The sixteenth and seventeenth centuries punished people everywhere. In Alaska the Tlingit natives were forced to give up their verdant village as glaciers rapidly spread to what is now Glacier Bay National Park. From 1693 until 1700 all but one Scottish harvest failed, sounding death knells rivaled only by the Black Plague. A few years before Milton had written *Paradise Lost*, but we did not lose paradise; paradise fled *us*. A recent cartoon in the *New Yorker* depicts two peasants in a barren field, cloaked in pelts, scythes at the ready. "The economy's never been better," says one, raising his hand toward a cloudy sky. "Here's another potato." Shakespeare's foul weather scenes no doubt resonated with his audience, huddled in the Globe theater. Lear, in a fit of shame and anger, rushes out of his castle into a storm. Though he says, "I tax not you, you elements, with unkindness," certainly the elements take their toll on him.

No surprise that the Little Ice Age destroyed Viking colonies on Greenland, and pushed the polar caps further south. Gregg Easterbrook points out that paintings from the period show "skaters on the canals of Holland, a rare joy for skaters alive today." European painters began to incorporate harsh winters into their landscapes. The bitter winter of 1564–65 inspired the Flemish painter Pieter Bruegel the Elder to create his seminal work, *Hunters in the Snow*. Other historians argue that the American Revolution owes as much to bad weather as to John Adams. The year 1776 was preceded by decades of terrible harvests. Nonetheless, British troops demanded that the colonists feed them. Colonists could not shoulder the burden in light of the oppressive climate. Emanuel Leutze's famous portrait of George Washington crossing the Delaware looks downright Nordic to those of us who grew up in the mid-Atlantic states. Again, I refuse to chalk up an earthshaking political revolution to bad weather, but it likely played some role. Mark Twain purportedly quipped that "everyone talks about the weather—but nobody does anything about it." Maybe the colonial patriots proved him wrong.

Since a warming climate would create a fertile glow in currently cold regions but blistering heat in tropical zones, *Rule Number 2: Learn the geographic exposure of your portfolio.* In short, global warming tells you to tilt your portfolio toward the north and away from the equator. Investing heavily in the Philippines, if the temperature jumps and seas swell, would be like lying on a simmering beach without sunscreen, in other words, inviting a deadly burn. Conversely, the traditionally forbidding climates found in Canada, Scandinavia, and Russia would seem more inviting.

THE TWENTIETH CENTURY WARM-UP

Weathermen in the United States have developed a summertime cliché: "Hazy, hot, and humid." Sure enough, our days are generally hazier, hotter, and more humid than those of our great-grandfathers. The 1990s is headed for the history books as the warmest decade of the century, with the ten hottest years showing up after 1980. The summer of 1998 scorched its way into the record book, with Texas thermometers seemingly stuck at 100 degrees for the entire, brutal summer. I am tempted to say that it's a good thing that twentieth-century engineers brought us air conditioning, because we need it now more than ever. On the other hand, is it possible that our air conditioning and other modern conveniences are actually the villains that produce the heat that we try to hide from?

In this section, we will see the climatic clues that lead so many scientists to bite their nails. Then we can listen to the global warming skeptics, who tell us, to the tune of a tropical, Calypso beat, "Don't worry; be happy."

In a new book called *Riddle of the Ice*, a sea captain presents his worrisome logs of a voyage to the Arctic Circle and Labrador Sea. Are the polar caps melting? he wonders, while tacking through formerly unpassable channels. Researchers at the U.S. National Oceanic and Atmospheric Administration (NOAA) also ponder these fissures, as their network of Arctic stations above North America reveal thinner layers of ice and warmer temperatures. I have sailed to Alaska a few times in the past ten years to observe and admire the glaciers and wildlife. In each case I also flew in a helicopter and landed on the luminous blue glaciers outside of Juneau and Ketchican. To the naked and untrained eye, the glaciers look like they are shrinking. Of course, visitors probably accelerate the trend, as they stomp on ancient ice and drop cups of coffee. The hundreds of cruise ships that pass through Glacier Bay take their toll as well. A passenger on a vessel a few years ago told me that the captain sailed as close as he could to the cerulean Hubbard Glacier and then blew the ship's loud, ice-shattering horn. A few moments later, a "natural/man-made" avalanche dumped tons of glacier ice into the bay, actually lifting up the fifteen-hundred-passenger ship in its wake. This aquatic joyride accelerated the natural calving by maybe a hundred years.

At the other end of the earth, five of nine Antarctic ice shelves have disintegrated, including a massive iceberg the size of Rhode Island that broke off the Larsen Ice Shelf, crashing into the South Atlantic in 1995. Around the same time, an ice shelf hundreds of feet thick cracked apart, permitting ships to navigate the Prince Gustave Channel for the first time. The United Kingdom's station at Faraday Station in Antarctica reports that the mercury has risen by almost 5 degrees Fahrenheit in some parts.

The warnings come not just from ice cubes. The IPCC has a human witness as well, for its indictment of twentieth-century greenhouse damage. In particular, the prosecution calls the "ice man," a five-thousand-year-old corpse discovered by hikers in 1992. Apparently, the ice man had tried to cross the Alps on foot during the first climatic optimum. That was the last time the Alps had such a thin cover of ice. The ice man's bones could not have cometh up through the ground until sometime after Eugene O'Neill's 1946 play, for the earth's climate would not have permitted it. If the earth really does warm by another 4.5 degrees, we run the risk of uncovering an army of ice men, especially from Siberia, where temperatures in recent years have regularly burst records. A thousand years ago, under less frosty conditions, Siberia was not *Siberia* as we know it, a desolate tundra with moose; in the sense that Hollywood was not *Hollywood* until Louis B. Mayer and Samuel Goldwyn made it worthy of italics.

Environmentalists who argue that the earth has warmed up, also like to point out that the weather has recently grown stormier and more dangerous. Eugene Linden states that in "just a five-year period, the U.S. suffered two 'hurricanes of the century' (Andrew and Hugo), a 'five-hundred-year flood' (the 1993 Midwestern floods), at least two 'floods of the century' (the 1995 floods in the Southeast and in the Red River Valley in 1997), and a 'drought of the century' (in California). Compared to the people of India, Americans got off lucky. After the massive monsoon of 1994, parts of India suffered blazing 100 degree Fahrenheit temperatures for three months. In the midst of this boiling cauldron, rodents crawled into town spreading pneumonic plague among residents who were already battling malaria.

These tales frighten us. But how confidently can we blame global warming and ultimately CO_2 emissions for recently stormy weather? Kerry Emanuel, a meteorologist at MIT, concluded that a 3 to 4 degree Celsius rise in sea temperatures could pump up a hurricane's destructive wallop by 50 percent, inciting storm winds over 200 miles per hour. Nonetheless, Emanuel acknowledges that this is an upper bound, and that such a jump is highly unlikely. Instead of CO_2, there are other scientific explanations that might involve the moon's orbit and sunspots. I can think of nonscientific answers, too. Ancient Japanese folklore would have attributed such natural calamities to the gods, believing that the emperor had lost the "mandate from heaven." In *The Tempest*, Prospero deploys magic to conjure up a storm in order to shipwreck people who need to be straightened out.

I would remind the reader here that she does not have to be utterly convinced of the scientific reasoning in order to invest in climate change. The evidence, flimsy as it sometimes appears, does suggest that you place some of your speculative investment dollars in "rainy day" or "scorching day" accounts.

While many scientists do believe that, theoretically, a warmer climate can produce more intense storms, no one knows whether the modest 1 degree Fahrenheit increase we have seen in the last hundred years should take the blame. I am wary of extrapolating from just the 1990s, which represent just a speck on the earth's timeline. Experts and agitators have erroneously extrapolated before. Few people know that in the 1930s scientists sounded the alarms for global warming. Scientists gathered, mingled and looked worried. Eminent climatologists promised the Royal Meteorological Society that the years ahead would grow warmer. Sure enough, the climate did start shifting—it got colder again in the 1940s (which ultimately saved Russia from Hitler's invasion). In the mid-1970s, while the United States suffered under OPEC's reign, environmentalists blew the trumpets announcing a new little ice age. They changed their mind a few years later. The point is that we must look at the long run, not the periodic monsoons and cyclones that smash our homes and spin our trailer parks.

THE SKEPTICS

Cicero told the Roman Senate that "no soothsayer should be able to look at another soothsayer without laughing." Skeptics may not be giggling at the IPCC, but they are throwing three alternative arguments at the UN experts: (1) It is not getting any warmer. (2) Even if it is getting a tad steamier, man-made greenhouse gases shouldn't be blamed. (3) Even if greenhouse gases are heating things up, a little warmth may make life richer and happier, not nasty, brutish, and short.

How can anyone deny the twentieth-century warm-up? Don't they hear the glaciers crashing into the sea? Can't they feel their own sweat? It turns out that not every thermometer has picked up the temperature rise that the consensus believes in. Ground-level thermometers did show such a rise and an acceleration in the 1980s. But the pavement and lights of civilization may be distorting those readings. A thermometer in downtown Manhattan will absorb heat reflected off the skyscrapers. Every noon and midnight, weather experts send seven hundred balloons soaring into the sky to measure atmospheric conditions. NASA's atmospheric data from satellites circling the globe give more ambiguous readings, as do ocean temperature readings performed by NOAA. This is confusing, of course, since it was NOAA researchers who detected warmer *surface* temperatures on the land above North America (between the 70N and 83N latitudes). Other NOAA scientists, though, measured temperatures just yards above the Arctic Ocean, for forty years, starting in 1950. They used drifting Russian ice stations and low-flying U.S. weather reconnaissance aircraft, among other tools. Their conclusion: The western Arctic Ocean is not warming, and may even be cooling during winter and autumn. How could Arctic ocean surface temperatures fall, while Arctic land temperatures rise?

To confuse matters further, skeptics point out that some shrinking glaciers have recently performed an about-face and have begun expanding again. The Bering Glacier in Alaska retreated in the late 1980s, spurring a congressional inquiry. Unbeknownst to congressional investigators, though, the Bering Glacier was preparing to reverse course and actually begin surging forward again, up to three hundred feet per day. Greenland's glaciers, too, might be turning around and heading south again. Can we reconcile expanding glaciers with warmer temperatures? Perhaps a warmer, wetter climate is inciting more precipitation in regions previously too dry and frigid for much snow.

The skeptics then shoot arrow number two: Even if the earth is warming, we should not blame man-made greenhouse gases. First of all, they point out, about half of the warming since the nineteenth century took place before World War II. Because CO_2 emissions have pushed steadily higher since the 1940s, and even accelerated with the spread of automobiles and smokestacks throughout the world, shouldn't the warming have followed a similar trend? Skeptics argue that temperatures may even have cooled a bit from the 1940s to the 1970s, an era when tens of millions of American families made the jump from a no-car family, to a one-car family, to a two-car family. Perhaps the weakest link in the IPCC's chain of reasoning is its attempts to develop computer models for clouds. Just as clouds can look wispy, capricious, ephemeral, or ominous to poets, so are they vexing to climatologists and statisticians.

Here's where critics pounce. MIT professor of meteorology Richard Lindzen points out that since 98 percent of greenhouse gases are water vapor, a warming planet might just have more cloud cover, which could protect the planet from wild temperature swings. Cloud cover tends to cool the daytime and warm the evenings. Lindzen has become a poster boy for skeptics, and a bull's-eye target for true-believers. "I don't know what line from God he has," stated Dr. Stephen Schneider of Stanford. If Lindzen and his followers are right, our grandchildren may face a future not of plagues and cyclones, but one that's merely cloudy.

Not only do clouds obscure the IPCC's forecasts, but so does the sun. How can the sun muck things up? Isn't it the one bright constant we can depend upon? Uh, no. Macbeth says, "I 'gin to be aweary of the sun." What if the sun gets weary of us? Or tries to get too familiar? Astronomers have learned that the sun is not like an oven that God set forever at 11,000 degrees Fahrenheit. The sun generates its own eleven-year cycle of dimming and brightening that correlates with the sunspots that Galileo first recorded in the 1600s. Over a single cycle, the sun's brightness might perk up by as much as 0.5 percent. In the past decades, the sun's brightness has peaked at a 0.14 percent rise, according to Harvard researcher Sallie Baliunas. The sun's personal business cycles could explain the global warm-up of the twentieth century better than CO_2 emissions. While this solar explanation may be comforting at first, it does not get us completely off the hook. For what if the sun *and* CO_2 will be pushing temperatures higher in the next century? In that case, perhaps the IPCC's 4.5 degree forecast is too low and our grandchildren will live in a climate hazier, hotter, and more humid than we could imagine.

SAVANNAH, GEORGIA

Tammy Jode worried that the Amtrak Silver Meteor would jump the tracks as it swept through the withered grapefruit groves on its way to the Savannah station. She'd seen too many action news programs shot "live from the scene of a tragic train crash."

She shoved aside her fears by concentrating instead on her grandmother's funeral. The Old Magnolia finally gave in. By God, she wanted to make it through the sixtieth anniversary of Gone With the Wind—and she did—floppy hat on head, mint julep in hands. At ninety-eight years of age, her liver-spotted hands may have trembled, but not her spirit. The Old Magnolia refused to sell her land to real estate developers, even after the last grapefruit trees yielded only shriveled, frozen fruit. "They'll come back," she declared, year after year after year. Like a diehard Dixiecrat.

Grandma never gave up on the land; only on her flimsy offspring. She particularly scorned her son-in-law, Tammy's father. "I could carve a stronger backbone out of a banana," she said. Yet Grandma praised Tammy's "moxie." (Grandma was the only person on earth to use that word between 1970 and 2000.) To reward Tammy's spirit, the Old Magolia left all of her land to the thirty-five-year-old divorcee who had never picked up a hoe or a shovel in her life. "You can learn to use a tiller," Grandma said, "but you must be born with pluck."

So, here came Tammy, flying down on the Silver Meteor to claim her inheritance—five thousand acres of scrawny, spindly grapefruit and orange groves. The barren branches looked like an orchard of coat hangers and broken umbrellas. Tammy had confidence, though. She'd been researching citrus crops and came across a startling discovery. Warmer weather patterns had pushed Georgia's "freeze" line steadily north for the past five years. If she held on to the land, the freeze line might move past her Grandma's beaten groves. True, the Old Magnolia left her with a big plot of depressed land. But with the help of warmer weather, and her own moxie, Tammy's grapefruit and orange groves might just rise again.

Finally, the skeptics shoot the arrow that most frustrates the believers: "Even if greenhouse gases press the temperature higher, we might like a warmer climate." I will discuss this in greater depth, but for now let me briefly point out a few pleasant side effects of global warming and greenhouse gases. First, plants tend to like CO_2; as they inhale the gas, it boosts the photosynthesis process and helps them grow (a so-called "fertilizer" effect). A study in *Nature* concluded that higher CO_2 levels in Hawaii and the Arctic since the early 1960s have expanded the growing season by about a week. Most obvious, though, warmer weather would cut down on winter heating bills and on transportation costs, especially for air travel. "I have a hard time following why longer growing seasons, lower energy use and fewer subzero days in North Dakota are the new apocalypse," says Pat Michaels, a ferocious skeptic from Virginia State. The IPCC, under the auspices of the UN, cares more about the millions who live in monsoon-weary Bangladesh than the thousands who suffer North Dakota's windy winters.

A REMINDER

After plowing through the confusing science that incites believers and skeptics to mud-wrestle with each other, it is worth remembering the investor's logic. Namely, the astute investor cares whether the odds of global warming are different from the odds incorporated into market prices. I am not convinced that the earth will heat up—but right now I am pretty sure that the markets for insurance, agriculture, real estate, and fisheries mostly ignore the possibility. After two brutal winters in 1995 and 1996, Americans snatched up four-wheel-drive passenger cars made by Subaru and Audi (Volkswagen), as well as sport utility vehicles put out by Ford, Chrysler, and GM. Weather-watching investors profited.

Witnessing consumers shifting their buying patterns leads us to *Rule Number 3: Reject a static view, and invest by assuming that people will adapt.* Farmers *will* switch to crops that thrive in a warmer climate, for example. Water purification firms *will* develop cheaper kits for water-logged developing countries. Textile firms *will* market clothing materials that "breathe" and protect even better than innovative products such as Gore-Tex and Thinsulate. The investor must look ahead to see which firms will jump first on these opportunities. If the skeptics who think that a long-term global warming trend will *help* the world are correct, we can devise shrewd investments based on their optimistic scenario. In sum, no matter whose spin on global warming proves right, you can profit from the phenomenon.

DON'T JUST STAND THERE . . .

Twain's quip about no one doing anything about the weather does not apply to the national governments who have pledged to cut greenhouse gas emissions. About 150 countries have been trying to hammer out a deal, starting with the Framework Convention on Climate Change in Rio in 1992 and followed by the Kyoto Protocol in 1997. Getting diverse countries to agree to a treaty is nearly impossible. Not only does each country have different priorities and sacred cows (which, remember, release methane), but a climate change treaty would be *multigenerational*, that is, binding on our grandchildren and great-grandchildren, who are obviously not sitting at the bargaining table.

The U.S. government has been trying to rope developing nations into cutting back their noxious fumes. But they argue that since the industrialized countries generated most of the man-made CO_2 to begin with, they should bear the brunt of the cuts. Emissaries from Asia and Africa are fond of quoting statistics showing that Americans emit over 5 tons of CO_2 per capita, compared with 2.4 tons for a Japanese and .2 tons for an Indian. It is not because we breathe heavier, but because our economy produces so much more. In fact, the United States is more energy-efficient than ever; we use 30 percent less fuel to produce $1 of GDP than we did in the 1970s. In reply to the critique of developing nations, President Clinton proposes a system that would cap worldwide emissions levels, but allow countries to trade pollution permits. Let's say that James's Battery Plant located in Detroit wants to expand its manufacturing output, which would give off more greenhouse gases. Under a trading scheme, James could buy the right to release X tons of CO_2 from Nicole's firm in Timbuktu. Thus, James could pump out more batteries without increasing the total CO_2 in the atmosphere. Nicole, meanwhile, would get a nice sum of money in exchange for reducing her pollutants.

The United States has already established a successful domestic market for trading sulfur permits. Unfortunately, most other countries have less confidence in such systems. And since European countries already tax gasoline far more heavily than we do, the United States is sometimes tagged with the nickname "Uncle Smoke." The Scandinavians have most aggressively deployed carbon taxes, as well as gasoline taxes. According to Yale professor William Nordhaus, the United States would have to *double* energy prices in order to contain emissions at 1990 levels. That sounds just fine to Europeans, who already pay at least twice as much for fuel as we do. But Americans love their trucks, cars, and roadway freedom. In 1993, the Clinton presidency almost collapsed under a proposal to boost gasoline taxes by a nickel.

We cannot expect bickering governments to fix the global warming problem (assuming there is a problem). Happily, we can report technological progress outside of governmental decrees. The price of solar power has been falling so quickly in recent years that it will successfully compete with fossil fuels during the next century. More immediate, though, the collapse of the USSR also brought about the closing of dirty, money-losing factories that belched the most wicked brew into the atmosphere. In Soviet cities like St. Petersburg and Odessa, I have personally heard the widespread wheezing and coughing of a downtrodden people. The people's car of East Germany, called the Trabant, gave off thirty times the gunk and smoke of the VWs on the other side of Checkpoint Charlie.

Of course, even though new cars may be 98 percent cleaner than their predecessors from the 1970s, the sheer number of autos in the world has almost doubled in the past twenty years, to about 500 million. In Chile, twice as many cars clog up the roads as *ten* years ago, creating such poisonous air that more than one thousand children in Santiago go to the emergency room daily for respiratory problems during the winter. While the new cars are cleaner and equipped with catalytic converters, the old belching jalopies stay on the streets until they conk out forever. Commodity speculators may want to bet on palladium and platinum prices, key components in catalytic converters, which may someday be required on every gasoline-burning car in the world.

A modest, low-tech, partial solution to the CO_2 time bomb may come by simply planting trees, which absorb the gas. Every acre of forest sucks up about 3,500 tons of CO_2. At the outset of his presidency, President Bush proudly launched an initiative to plant 1 billion trees in the United States, even enlisting Queen Elizabeth, who shoveled dirt on a young plant along the South Lawn of the White House. I recall the queen's protocol officers informing their White House counterparts that, according to royal tradition, the queen would be willing to shovel "two scoops and no more."

While tree planting no doubt helps fight off CO_2, we would need an impossible number to offset the automobiles coming on line across the globe. The average automobile coughs up about 3,500 tons, about equal to an acre of forest. Somewhere a bureaucrat may be drawing up plans to require every car buyer to also buy an acre of new forest.

WHO WINS AND WHO LOSES FROM GLOBAL WARMING? A REGIONAL VIEW

The easiest way to figure out the winners and losers is to unfold a map. Countries located significantly north of the equator should not suffer much. In fact, North America (especially Canada), China, Russia, and most of Europe may prosper with longer growing seasons and friendlier winters. Because global warming would lead to higher sea levels (1 to 2 feet higher, according to the IPCC), waters may wash over low-lying areas, and zones that are already hot can expect blistering heat. Parts of Africa, southeast Asia, and Latin America may turn swampy and nearly uninhabitable. The Asian Development Bank especially worries about Bangladesh, India, Malaysia, and the Philippines. In Indonesia, large parts of Jakarta might be submerged, while the Mekong Delta could flood the rice paddies that sustain Vietnamese peasants.

These regional splits could spur a political backlash, especially since poorer countries would seem to suffer most. No wonder developing countries feel begrudged at environmental summits: They blame wealthy countries for creating the problem, and they fear that the wealthy countries will not suffer equal damage. While the gasping residents of Calcutta drown in a fetid climate, they will see photographs of Chicagoans sunbathing in November. Northerly regions may have to combat a new round of world terrorism: In contrast to today's terrorism, incited by clashes over *who occupies* disputed territory (Palestinians vs. Israelis, Basques vs. Spaniards), the new terrorism would be sparked by clashes over *who should be blamed* for the destruction and loss of land. Who will take environmental refugees? These battles will no doubt hit global markets, especially if "emerging markets" literally and figuratively turn into "submerging" markets.

MAKING MONEY BY INVESTING IN GLOBAL WARMING—A SECTOR APPROACH

Insurance Firms

Just as our fictitious Anthony Maroni learned, insurance companies will grow weary of natural calamities. Insurers generally depend on computers that crunch past data on losses and injuries in order to calculate the probability of future payouts. But old actuarial data will mislead, not help, insurers if the world's climate lurches in a new direction. By using old data for their calculations, they systematically underestimate environmental risks. Already stung by the turbulent weather of the 1990s, Travelers and Prudential insurance have stopped offering insurance for those parts of Florida that have been beaten up by raging storms, notably Hurricane Andrew in 1992. Between 1990 and 1995 insurance companies paid out $57 billion in claims worldwide, compared to $17 billion in the 1980s. A study by Travelers forecast that if temperatures climbed roughly 1 degree Fahrenheit, the hurricane season would be prolonged, generating a 30 percent rise in catastrophic damage. No wonder over two hundred top insurance executives gathered in Tokyo in December 1997, alongside the Kyoto protocol negotiators.

Since U.S. insurance companies are at the mercy of state regulators, you can expect governors and legislatures to stomp on the necks of insurance executives until they agree to continue writing policies. Will these companies be able to wiggle away from the boots of politicians? Or will they find themselves more heavily regulated? We will see a race to the exit doors for property insurers, especially in coastal regions of the United States. As for international insurers, those in Asia and Latin America may pay a terrible price—either because they lose money paying out claims, or because the national governments force them to stay in a money-losing line of business.

To an investor, those insurance companies that get through the exit doors first will look like relative winners. In contrast, those that write policies in low-lying areas or in the various hurricane and monsoon belts of the world will look bloodied. When storms and seas rip apart low-lying regions, certain businesses will prosper, namely, those that rebuild devastated areas, such as California-based Granite Construction. In addition, global engineering firms like the Bechtel Group (a closely held company), the Anglo-Norwegian Kvaerner, PLC, and the Swiss-based ABB Group (though it is strongest in electrical power) might win contracts to figure out how to protect regions from damage, whether through new irrigation systems, dams, or dikes. But those engineering firms face risks, too. Even as they win new contracting jobs as a result of global climate change, many of their old clients could be wiped out in the process.

Agricultural Firms

Dusty plains, an old steer skull, a few stalks of scorched corn, and some tumbleweed rustling by on a breeze. That is the *Grapes of Wrath* image conjured up by many global warming scenarios. The pessimists see either a perpetual Oklahoma dustbowl or a constant raging typhoon. As I have suggested, global warming will deliver a different message everywhere. Many parts of the United States might enjoy the change, even though it may pummel some of our foreign allies.

To thrive under global climate change warming, people and firms must figure out how to adapt. A personal example might help. After the blizzards of 1995 and 1996, I bought an Audi equipped with four-wheel drive. My heavy, slippery, rear-wheel drive cars could hardly spin their way out of the driveway. This was a short-term response to bad weather. If I thought we would forever endure blizzards in Washington, D.C., I would take more drastic action, like moving to California (but not Malibu).

Farmers who moved from southern Italy to New York in the 1920s learned to plant something other than olives after the first snowfall. Someone once identified insanity as doing the same things over and over again but expecting different results. Yet the initial studies on global warming and agriculture took this simplistic view and assumed that farmers would continue planting the same seeds, even if the climate took a radical turn. Under such a basic model, economists and agronomists simply asked how much damage a 4.5 degree temperature jump would do to a crop of, say, corn. Then they would take that number as the likely damage from global warming, adding up to billions of dollars in the United States alone. Robert Mendelsohn, an economist at Yale's School of Forestry and Environmental Studies, developed a smarter approach. Mendelsohn figured that since land had many uses, owners might decide to take advantage of climate change by doing something different with their property. It's not a difficult concept to grasp; you might remember when the same plot of farmland turned first into a drive-in movie lot and then into a suburban housing tract. As the temperature rises, a farmer might shift from growing wheat to growing corn to grazing livestock. Finally, with even higher temperatures, he could build retirement homes. Mendelsohn calls this flexible approach a Ricardian analysis, after the great English economist. In layman's terms, Mendelsohn accepts the IPCC's forecast, but figures that farmers will make the best of it. The United States produces plenty of warm weather crops, including cotton, fruits, vegetables, rice, and grapes. California and the citrus belt (including our fictitious Tammy Jode) would win in this reshuffling of the deck, and so global warming should raise U.S. output by almost $40 billion. The fertilizer effect of CO_2 could boost output even higher. Within the United States, the Rocky Mountains and Appalachia would turn more arid, but these regions are far less important to the agriculture industry today.

While citrus and cotton growers in the South and Californian farmers look like winners, their competitors in Mexico/Central America (fruits) and Egypt/India (cotton) suffer in a climate even warmer than today's. China and the former USSR would gain as marginal lands became more fertile as a result of more rain and higher temperatures. Forests in those northern regions would especially benefit from a combination of warmer weather and CO_2 enrichment. Forests in Canada and Scandinavia may already be heading further north, toward their old boundaries from prior to the Little Ice Age.

Placing financial bets on these agricultural shifts will be treacherous for the layperson. For one thing, we must remember that a bumper crop means lower prices for investors, while a drought could mean higher investment returns. If global climate change wipes out Colombia's coffee crop, commodity speculators who have bought coffee contracts will win (because the price rises); meanwhile, investors in Starbucks will lose, since Starbucks would have to pay much more for its beans.

Instead of trying to target specific crops, a prudent investor might simply ask, Which firms will perform well in a volatile, changing market? First, global agricultural firms like Archer Daniels Midland and Cargill (privately held) have the money and expertise to show farmers around the world how to change their crop mix to adapt to changes. Second, biotech firms that are developing new, more hardy crops will benefit. The "Green Revolution" began in the 1950s when Norman Borlaug, a plant geneticist, discovered how to grow a wheat grain that married the heavy head of a dwarf strain with the durable stalk of another variety. Investors should search out those firms that look most likely to lead the way in the next green revolution, which will take advantage of climate change. Investors should also follow the biotech firms whose researchers will have to battle new strains of malaria and typhoid, tropical diseases that could proliferate in the poorer, less sanitary nations of Africa and Southeast Asia.

Financial Firms

Third, financial firms that create and sell "weather derivatives" will profit. Almost every company doing business is exposed to the climate. Fewer families show up to Disney World if the Orlando weather is foul. Beer companies in Japan live in fear of cool summers. Down-filled ski jackets sit on the shelves during mild winters. Many companies will try to protect themselves from financial losses by buying financial instruments that pay off under certain weather conditions. Thus, if the Colorado ski season turns hot, the hotels' sales losses could be partially offset by a pay-off from a financial contract. Firms like Enron Corp. in Houston have helped create this new financial market in the past year or so. Merrill Lynch is also jumping into this business, which could quickly grow into a $70 to $100 billion market. You do not have to be a direct investor in these risky derivatives in order to profit—instead, you could buy shares in the companies that broker the deals. Better to ride on the back of the middleman and walk away mostly unscathed.

Other kinds of firms will spring up to pounce on the new opportunities. In a book entitled *The Baked Apple?* researchers explain that New York City's asphalt and concrete pushes up summertime temperatures by 3 to 5 degrees Fahrenheit. Anyone who has ever lost a shoe in Manhattan's melting, oozing blacktop would agree. New York City might eventually replace its dark roofs and pavements with light surfaces that would reflect, rather than absorb, sunlight. A company that sells advanced materials such as 3M might tackle this market.

OUR OWN FRANKENSTEIN?

If the gods struck down Prometheus for passing along fire to man, what wrath do they have in store for us? We, who will (according to the UN) knowingly change the whole world's climate? Even if the IPCC's scientific models prove faulty, the gods might decide to unleash floods and droughts just to punish us for our hubris. In ancient times, people tried to twist the weather to their liking by more primitive rites: dances, animal sacrifices, human sacrifices, and prayer. Today, half a billion people just rev up their engines and drive around, emitting greenhouse gases. The earth's atmosphere is like the thin skin of an apple compared to the whole fruit. It apparently bruises easily. Does it heal?

The science of climate change remains almost as foggy as a London morning. Thus, we must place question marks over expert assertions. Prudent investors should closely watch the debate and remember that almost any change will bring winners and losers: Spotting them ahead of the market is the challenge.

Though climate change might be most exciting to scientists, poets and writers might also find inspiration (as long as they have air conditioning). It has happened before. In the summer of 1816, the world was cooled by the floating ash from an erupted Indonesian volcano called Tambora. Some friends gathered inside a villa in Geneva, since it was too stormy to lounge outside. They made up stories while lightning and thunder rumbled along Lake Geneva. A lady named Mary spooked them all, including Lord Byron. She told them the story of a scientist who took natural, godly matters into his own hands. The doctor's name was Frankenstein.

Conclusion:

—

INTO THE BREACH

In the Louvre hangs a stunning painting by Giovanni Pannini, called "Views of Modern Rome." Pannini painted it in 1759. That was modern. Pannini depicted an opulent gallery with fifty or so architectural paintings jammed together, hanging on the walls, and leaning against one another on the floor. There, to the right, is Trevi Fountain, to the left, the Spanish Steps—all in exquisite detail. Your eye doesn't let you linger on the total work, but instead draws you to another deliciously rendered feature, a fluted column or a flying buttress. You feel like a tourist craning his neck as the sights stream by. So it is with the swirling world economy. We flip through the newspaper or through a hundred television channels unable to construct a single, constant theme, other than change itself.

Each day that I worked on this book, another story flitted across my screen. Just days after I thought I put the finishing touches on the chapter on global warming, the *Washington Post* announced, "Iceberg the Size of Delaware Breaks Off." My immediate reaction was dread. Then I figured that Delaware was a small state and that I wouldn't have to revise the chapter unless the iceberg turned out to be the size of Kentucky. The Rubik's cube character of China continues to twirl, as each month the government makes another attempt to hold on to power, while breaking the ties that bind the army and the Communist Party to businesses. Almost every day, another riveting story about baby boomers and biotechnology hits the wires, offering new opportunities for organ growth and cell rejuvenation.

Despite the crises and confusing revolutions in front of us, I remain essentially optimistic. As human beings, we do tend to learn from experience. The Great Depression has taught the

Federal Reserve Board not to permit the money supply to implode. World War II has taught us to beware of tyrants with tanks and treacherous ambitions. The marketplace has brought us better and better goods, at lower prices. Despite occasional bouts with inflation, almost all goods are more affordable than in the "good old days," however you define that nostalgic era. When Herbert Hoover touted a "chicken in every pot" the average worker had to sweat for two hours to pay for a chicken. Now it takes about fifteen minutes, and they are available as cutlets, nuggets, drumsticks, and even "fingers." Great-grandmothers today still tend to hurry off the telephone because they remember when it took an hour of work to pay for a ten-minute long-distance call. Now it costs about six minutes of work, and you might even receive frequent flyer miles for the effort. Surely, life means more than material things. Still, a warm pot of chicken soup and a telephone call from a friend can set the stage for a joyful life. In any event, defining progress is not the point of this book. Bertrand Russell pointed out that a "process which led from the amoeba to Man appeared to the philosophers to be obviously a progress—though whether the amoeba would agree with this opinion is not known."

The wonderful technological developments we have discussed do not come like sunshine, without effort. They require brains and investments. If our education system fails to teach our children reading, writing, and 'rithmetic, it will be hard to keep an optimistic outlook. We could very well produce generations of people too ignorant to handle the twenty-first century. Behold the horse. A hundred years ago, horses were gainfully employed on farms and in cities to pull carriages, haul ice blocks, and deliver fish. There aren't many jobs for horses today in New York City. Even if they offer to work at a low wage, they find few opportunities outside Central Park or underneath a mounted policeman's posterior. What would the economy do with brawny, but not brainy, children? Our present education system does not attract enough talent, nor teach enough skills. When I was a boy I used to think that teachers went home each night and read books; now I wonder whether many would know how.

However we handle the twenty-first century's crises and challenges, we can neither escape change, nor should we blame change for our woes. As investors, a shifting world opens up new opportunities. We are not potted plastic plants; we are creative, vital beings. The most successful investors, indeed, the most successful individuals will be those who do not hide in the closet, clinging to a nostalgic yesteryear that never was. I yield to Orson Welles in *The Third Man*: "In Italy, for thirty years under the Borgias, they had warfare, terror, murder, and bloodshed, but they produced Michelangelo, Leonardo da Vinci, and the Renaissance. In Switzerland, they had brotherly love; they had five hundred years of democracy and peace—and what did that produce? The cuckoo clock."

Investors of the world: Go unto the clanging breach, not into your cozy closets!

Source Notes

Chapter 1: Going Gray: How America's Aging Can Bankrupt the Government and Shake Your Portfolio

3 *The turn of the seasons does not mean*: Paul Kennedy's *The Rise and Fall of Great Powers: Economic Change and Military Conflict from 1500 to 2000* (New York: Vintage, 1989).

4 *As Thomas Stanley and William Danko pointed out*: Thomas J. Stanley and William D. Danko, *The Millionaire Next Door* (Atlanta: Longstreet Press, 1996).

7 *Our fastest growing group*: U.S. Bureau of the Census, *The State of the Nation: 1997* (Washington, D.C.: Government Printing Office, 1997). Unless otherwise noted, all U.S. population statistics come from the U.S. Bureau of the Census.

8 *Phillipe Aries's classic*: Phillipe Aries, *Centuries of Children: A Social History of Family Life* (New York: Random House, 1965).

11 *Since the goal is to "die young . . ."*: Michael D. Hurd, review of *Economics of Population Aging* by James H. Schulz, et al., in *Journal of Economic Literature* (September 1992), 1530.

12 *Still, even after adjusting for inflation*: David M. Cutler, Mark McClellan, and Joseph P. Newhouse, "What Has Increased Medical-Spending Bought?" *American Economic Review* 88 (May 1998), 132.

12 *By 1950, the figure fell to*: Dora L. Costa, *The Evolution of Retirement: An American Economic History, 1880–1990* (Chicago: University of Chicago Press, 1998), 7–10.

12 *While in the early 1960s*: Jonathan Gruber and David Wise, "Social Security and Retirement: An International Comparison," *American Economic Review* 88 (May 1998), 159–60.

12 *A staggering 79 percent thought*: Polling by *Washington Post* reported in Susan Cohen, "Generation Next," *Washington Post Magazine* (June 1, 1997), 8.

13 *In the 1940s and 1950s, Old Age Assistance*: Leora Friedberg, "The Effect of Old Age Assistance on Retirement," *NBER Working Paper*, no. 6548 (May 1, 1998).

13 *This operates like a steep tax*: R. Glenn Hubbard, Jonathan Skinner, and Stephen P. Zeldes, "Expanding the Life-Cycle Model: Precautionary Saving and Public Policy," *American Economic Review* 84 (May 1994), 177–79.

13 *And when asked, which will live longer*: Less than one-third of twenty-five- to twenty-nine-year-olds told a Gallup poll that they could depend on Social Security, according to a Gallup poll. See Laura M. Litvan, "Generation X's Social Security," *Investor's Business Daily* (March 25, 1997), 1. Also see Meredith Bagby, *Rational Exuberance* (New York: Dutton, 1998), 60, 81.

13 *In fact, they are more satisfied*: Cohen, 28.

14 *In direct contrast, today's young workers*: Kevin M. Murphy and Finis Welch, "Perspectives on the Social Security Crisis and Proposed Solutions," *American Economic Review* 88 (May 1998), 142.

14 *If he is lucky enough to earn twice the average*: Ibid., 144. These figures assume a roughly 2 percent rise in the payroll tax. If nothing is done, then the Social Security system will simply go bankrupt and not be able to pay out benefits. An "average" income today would be in the $30,000 to $35,000 range.

15 *The prime problem is that*: For a quick overview of the U.S. health-care predicament, see my *From Here to Economy: A Shortcut to Economic Literacy* (New York: Dutton, 1995), 96–103.

16 *Nor did intensive-care patients*: Elasticity of 6.2 percent found in Matthew J. Eichner, "The Demand for Medical Care: What People Pay Does Matter," *American Economic Review* 88 (May 1998), 120; Rand study discussed in Joseph P. Newhouse, *Free for All: Lessons from the RAND Health Insurance Experiment* (Cambridge: Harvard University Press, 1993); Miami versus Minneapolis spending found in Jonathan Skinner and John E. Wennberg, "How Much Is Enough? Efficiency and Medical Spending in the Last Six Months of Life," *NBER Working Paper*, no. 6513 (April 1, 1998).

16 *Prudent spending and clean living*: Victor R. Fuchs, *The Health Economy* (Cambridge: Harvard University Press, 1986), 197–98.

18 *Even a five year wait for Medicare*: Jagadeesh Gokhale and Laurence J. Kotlikoff, "Medicare from the Perspective of Generational Accounting," *NBER Working Paper*, no. 6596 (June 1, 1998); Laurence J. Kotlikoff, *Generational Accounting: Knowing Who Pays and When for What We Spend* (New York: Free Press, 1992).

19 *Second, we should not foolishly believe*: This is a point Nobel Laureate Paul Samuelson made in 1958, when many baby boomers were still toddlers. Paul A. Samuelson, "An Exact Consumption-Loan Model of Interest With or Without the Social Contrivance of Money," *Journal of Political Economy* 66 (December 1958), 467–82.

21 *Adam Smith surmised in his* Theory of Moral Sentiments: Adam Smith, *The Theory of Moral Sentiments* (1759), part VI, section II, chapter 1, (London: Oxford University Press, 1976), 219–20.

21 *Evolutionary biologists have tried to validate*: Robert Trivers, *Social Evolution* (Menlo Park, Calif.: Benjamin/Cummings, 1985), provides a nice introduction.

24 *While it's a cliché*: Constantijn W. A. Panis and Lee A. Lillard, "Socioeconomic Differentials in the Returns to Social Security," (Santa Monica, CA: RAND, 1996).

25 *Our future public pension payments*: Sheetal K. Chand, et al., "Aging Populations and the Fiscal Consequences of Public Pension Schemes with Particular Reference to the Major Industrialized Countries, *IMF Occasional Paper* (1996).

26 *Meanwhile, the United Kingdom has grown*: Caroline Daniel, "Taxing Reforms for British Retirees," *Washington Post* (August 9, 1998), C3.

28 *Other researchers urge more patience*: Barry B. Bannister, "Catch a Wave, Miss a Wave: A Different View on Stock Market Demographics," *Demographics*, published by SBC Warbug Inc. (March 14, 1997), 3–4; Sylvester J. Schieber and John Shoven, "The Consequences of Population Aging on Private Pension Fund Saving and Asset Markets," in Michael D. Hurd and Naohiro Yashiro, *The Economic Effects of Aging in the United States and Japan* (Chicago: University of Chicago Press, 1997), 111-30.

30 *About half of the wealth of American families*: William G. Gale and John Karl Scholz, "Intergenerational Transfers and the Accumulation of Wealth," *Journal of Economic Perspectives* 8 (fall 1994), 156.

31 *Grandparents already spend more*: Cheryl Russell, "The Ungraying of America," *American Demographics* (July 1997).

35 *"Best raisin bran I ate in my life,"*: Vanessa O'Connell, "Campbell Watched Innovative IQ Menus Fall into Scraps Despite Healthy Benefits," *Wall Street Journal* (October 6, 1998), 1.

35 *Around that time two prominent economists*: N. Gregory Mankiw and David N. Weil, "The Baby Boom, the Baby Bust and the Housing Market," *Regional Science and Urban Economics* 19 (1989), 235–58.

Chapter 2: The Leaning Tower of Technobabble: How to Invest in the Internet and Bioscience Revolutions

40 *"How infinite in faculty! . . ."*: Shakespeare, *Hamlet*, II, ii.

41 *Since the 1960s, NASA spends $200 billion*: The stealth technology that absorbs radar waves (rather than deflecting them) allows popcorn bags to absorb microwaves, rather than deflect them.

42 *While Huxley's supporters might claim*: For a counter view, see Bryon Appleyard, *Brave New Worlds* (New York: Viking, 1998).

42 *The proper shape of an automobile*: John Kenneth Galbraith, *The New Industrial State* (Boston: Houghton Mifflin, 1967), 30.

43 *As transaction costs in the open market*: Larry Downes and Chunka Mui, *Unleashing the Killer App* (Boston: Harvard Business School Press, 1998), 42. Coase's original paper appeared as "The Nature of the Firm," *Economica* 4 (November 1937), 386–405.

44 *But Americans in 1917 suffered*: Paul Krugman, *The Accidental Theorist* (New York: W.W. Norton, 1998), 103.

45 *Nathan Mayer Rothschild, the richest man*: David D. Landes, *The Wealth and Poverty of Nations* (New York: W.W. Norton, 1998), xvii-xviii. Shakespeare quote from *Richard III*, V, iv.

46 *So, too, for cloning, DNA research*: George Gilder, "Happy Birthday Wired," *Wired* (January 1998).

47 *"Look into the mind of the average high school . . ."*: Abraham H. Maslow, *The Psychology of Science* (New York: Harper & Row, 1966), 138. Maslow cites a study by M. Mead and R. Metreaux, "Image of the Scientist Among High School Students," *Science*, CXXVI (1957), 384–90. Bill Gates's widely reported fortune of $60 billion might change some minds today.

47 *None of us, though, has any illusion*: Gerald W. Friedland and Meyer Friedman, *Medicine's 10 Greatest Discoveries* (New Haven: Yale University Press, 1998), 231.

47 *The physicist Leo Szilard reported that*: IQ study is in Lindsey R. Harmon, "The High School Backgrounds of Science Doctorates," *Science* 133 (March 10, 1961), 679–88. Szilard anecdote is in Lewis Wolpert and Richard Alison, *A Passion for Science* (New York: Oxford University Press, 1988), 107.

48 *"Many bottles of the finest champagnes . . ."*: James Glanz, "Putting Their Money Where Their Minds Are," *New York Times* (August 25, 1998).

49 *Yale surgeon Sherwin B. Nuland*: Sherwin B. Nuland, "The Issue of Life," *Life* (fall 1998), 10.

50 *Back in 1961 a biologist named Leonard Hayflick*: See Leonard Hayflick, *How and Why We Age* (New York: Ballantine Books, 1994). His original paper on the limits of cell division appeared in 1961 in the journal, *Experimental Cell Research*.

51 *According to one report, drug innovation*: Frank R. Lichtenberg, "Pharmaceutical Innovation, Mortality Reduction and Economic Growth," *NBER Working Paper*, no. 6569 (May 1, 1998).

52 *"How sad it is! . . ."* : Oscar Wilde, *The Picture of Dorian Gray* (New York: Oxford, 1974), 25–26.

52 *"We've opened a door, but . . ."*: "Cultured Neural Stem Cells Reduce Symptoms in Model of Parkinson's Disease," *National Institute of Health Release* (July 20, 1998). Such research does raise ethical questions since the cells come from human embryos. "Right to life" groups, for example, oppose the concept, and federal law prohibits researchers for using federal funds. Researchers argue that the embryos come from spontaneously aborted fetuses and that the ultimate benefits of stem cell research should assuage concerns.

53 *In the fifth century A.D., Hindu doctors*: Peter D. Olch and Henry N. Harkins, "A History of Surgery," in Carl A. Moyer and Jonathan E. Rhoads, et al., *Surgery: Principles and Practice*, 3rd ed. (Philadelphia: J.B. Lippincott, 1965), 1717; Albert S. Lynos and R. Joseph Petrucelli, *Medicine: An Illustrated History* (New York: Abradale Press, 1987), 114–15.

54 *A drug called Herceptin*: See Robert Bazell, *Her 2* (New York: Random House, 1998).

55 *Within a few years of deploying penicillin*: Stuart Levy, *The Antibiotic Paradox* (New York: Plenum, 1992), 10. For a dramatic general discussion, see Sheryl Gay Stolberg, "Superbugs," *New York Times* magazine (August 2, 1998), 42–47.

56 *Though it sounds far-fetched and silly*: "Question for: Kevin Warwick," *New York Times* magazine (October 4, 1988), 27.

57 *Two years later, their market share*: "J&J Bets on Medical Devices," *Bloomberg Website Feature* (November 12, 1998).

58 *Because we often identify ourselves by*: Daniel J. Boorstin, *The Americans: The Democratic Experience* (New York: Vintage, 1973), 89.

61 *Economists call it "segmenting the market"*: See Carl Shapiro and Hal Varian, *Information Rules: A Strategic Guide to the Network Economy* (Boston: Harvard Business School Press, 1998).

63 *You may be a 40-year-old white male*: Chip Bayers, "The Promise of One to One (Love Story)," *Wired* (May 1998); www.wired.com/archive/6.05.

64 *"Attention is the hard currency of cyberspace"*: Thomas Mandel and Gerard Van der Leun, *Rules of the Net* (New York: Hyperion, 1996).

65 *Marketing firms employ "cool-hunters"*: See Winslow Farrell, *How Hits Happen* (New York: Harper, 1998), 40.

66 *PointCast fell from the highest flyer of 1997*: Ken Auletta, "The Last Sure Thing," *The New Yorker* (November 9, 1998), 40–47.

67 *Nine years later the same recording*: See Gwendolyn Freed, "Mozart for Morning Commute," *Wall Street Journal* (October 2, 1998).

67 *In 1998 the Boston Consulting Group*: Rebecca Quick, "Internet Retailing May Drum Up $13 Billion in Revenue This Year," *Wall Street Journal* (November 18, 1998).

67 *The corollary of Andy Warhol's fifteen minutes of fame*: Quoted in Michael R. Bloomberg, "Fantasy Valuations," *Bloomberg* magazine (July/August 1998), 17.

68 *In a simple example, University of California, Berkeley professor*: J. Bradford De Long, "The New Economy That Isn't All That New," *Wilson Quarterly* (autumn 1998).

68 *For those who want to jump into the investment*: "Foreword," by Nicholas Negroponte in Downes and Chunka Mui, xi.

Chapter 3: Kaboom! The Time Bomb That Will Shatter Mutual Funds

71 *While bank deposits have grown*: See John J. Moon, et al., "Asset Management in the 21st Century: New Rules, New Game," Goldman Sachs & Co. (1998).

72 *Thus, when it sunk, investors*: Milton Friedman and Anna J. Schwartz, *A Monetary History of the United States, 1867–1960*, present this case thoroughly (Princeton: Princeton University Press, 1963), 299–350.

75 *The wizard gave up*: Quotation from a senior equity analyst at Putnam, Lovell & Thornton, quoted in "Mutual Fund Marriages Continue," CNNfn (posted June 25, 1996 on CNNfn.com/news); Michael Peltz, "Rating the Funds Families," *Worth* (April 1998), 82; Glassman quotation from "A Move Away From Value," *Washington Post* (December 9, 1998), C1.

76 *In 1996, for example, funds*: Lynn Brenner, "Consumers Rule!," *Bloomberg Personal* (December 1997), 67.

77 *Nobel Laureate William Sharpe has shown*: William F. Sharpe, "Asset Allocation: Management Style and Performance Measurement," *Journal of Portfolio Management* (winter 1992), 7–19.

78 *Those with strong first quarters*: Keith Brown, W. V. Harlow, and Laura T. Starks, "Of Tournaments and Temptations: An Analysis of Managerial Incentives in the Mutual Fund Industry," *Journal of Finance* 51 (March 1996), 85–111.

80 *"We had a big old vault . . ."*: Jerry Knight, "A Bank Without Walls Branches Into New Territory," *Washington Post Business* (August 3, 1998), 7.

81 *Hedge fund manager James Cramer*: James J. Cramer, "The Feeling Is No Longer Mutual," *Gentleman's Quarterly* (January 1998), 63.

82 *Studies have demonstrated that*: Stephen J. Brown and William N. Goetzmann, "Performance Persistence," *Journal of Finance* 50 (June 1995), 679-98; and J. A. Christopherson, W. E. Ferson, and D. A. Glassman, "Conditioning Manager Alphas on Economic Information: Another Look at the Persistence of Performance," *Review of Financial Studies* 11 (spring 1998), 111–42.

82 *I was not alone in that advice*: Sandra Block, "No-Frills Index Funds Lure Investors," *USA Today* (April 21, 1998).

83 *When the clerk suggests an "economy"*: James R. Hagy, "Face to Face with John Bogle," *Mutual Funds Magazine* (February 1996).

83 *While people used to see mutual funds*: Brenner, 64.

84 *As the fund expanded, small cap stocks*: Steven T. Goldberg, "A Spectacularly Unstylish Fund," *Kiplinger* (July 1998).

84 *In a speech he jokingly called "Don't Buy My Fund,"*: Bogle quoted in Catherine Hickey and Valerie Putchaven, "M* Conference Report: Bogle Jr.: Don't Buy My Funds," morningstar.net (June 25, 1998).

86 *Unfortunately, momentum investing*: See Harrison Hong, Terence Lim, and Jeremy Stein, "Bad News Travels Slowly: Size, Analyst Coverage and the Profitability of. . . ," *NBER Working Paper*, no. 6553 (May 1, 1998).

86 *In the pageant, "the competitors have to pick out . . ."*: John Maynard Keynes, *The Collected Writings of John Maynard Keynes*, vol. VII (London: Macmillan/St. Martin's Press, for the Royal Economic Society, 1973), 156.

88 *What if Buffett decided*: Note that you can buy shares in Berkshire Hathaway, which is essentially Buffett's mutual fund.

88 *a gifted investor demands*: John Maynard Keynes, "Alfred Marshall," in *Essays in Biography*, in the *Collected Writings of John Maynard Keynes*, vol. X (London and New York: Macmillan/St. Martin's Press for the Royal Economic Society, 1972), 173. While Keynes was lauding his teacher Alfred Marshall, he was clearly describing himself!

88 *A study of twenty-three years of roundtable*: Hemang Desai and Prem C. Jain, "An Analysis of the Recommendations of the 'Superstar' Money Managers at Barron's Annual Roundtable," *Journal of Finance* 50, 4 (September 1995), 1257-73.

89 *Brain power alone does not yield*: Judith Chevalier and Glenn Ellison, "Are Some Mutual Fund Managers Better Than Others? Cross-Sectional Patterns in Behavior and Performance," *Journal of Finance*, 54 (June 1999).

89 *Jealous colleagues would happily turn in*: Robertson jokes that his company, Tiger Management, would not today hire a young Julian Robertson.

92 *You are not diversified if you invest*: William F. Sharpe, "Asset Allocation: Management Style and Performance Measurement," *Journal of Portfolio Management* (Winter 1992), 7–19.

Chapter 4: Red, White, and Black, Yellow, and Brown: A Darker America Demands a Darker Portfolio

98 *In thirty years, white babies will*: U.S. Bureau of the Census, *Population Projections of the United States by Age, Sex, Race, and Hispanic Origin: 1995–2050* (Washington, D.C.: U.S. Government Printing Office, 1996).

99 *They provide about 2 million jobs*: U.S. Department of Commerce, Minority Business Development Agency, "MBDA Business Communities" (Washington, D.C.: 1998).

99 *Chinese entrepreneurs created*: Ibid.

100 *Families are tossing into their shopping carts*: "No Meals, Forks or Spoons," *Forecast* (October 1996).

101 *In 1970, only 36% were*: While the white illegitimacy rate has also climbed, at 24 percent, it remains far below the level for blacks.

101 *Kids from single-parent homes*: Sara McLanahan, "Family Structure and Dependency: Early Transitions to Female Headship," *Demography* (February 1988), 1–16.

102 *The Swedish economist Gunnar Myrdal*: Gunnar Myrdal, *An American Dilemma: The*

Negro Problem and American Democracy (1944; reprint New Brunswick, NJ: Transaction Pub., 1995).

103 *A Rand study showed that the average*: Constantijn W. A. Panis and Lee A. Lillard, "Socioeconomic Differentials in the Returns to Social Security," (Santa Monica, CA: RAND, 1996).

106 *Together, Caribbean, Central and South Americans*: U.S. Bureau of the Census, *Statistical Abstract of the United States: 1996,* 116th ed. (Washington, D.C.: Government Printing Office, 1996), Table No. 8.

106 *A recent study showed that 85 percent*: RAND Corporation, *Changing Economy: The California Experience* (1997).

107 *By 1990, immigrants from*: George J. Borjas, "The Economics of Immigration," *Journal of Economic Literature* (December 1994), 1674.

108 *At the deep end, 24 percent*: Rachel M. Friedberg and Jennifer Hunt, "The Impact of Immigrants on Host Country Wages, Employment and Growth," *Journal of Economic Perspectives* (spring 1995), 26–27.

108 *The price of oil has mostly*: Even great economists have occasionally panicked about energy costs, as did William Stanley Jevons in his 1865 book, *The Coal Question.*

109 *Along twenty-sixth Street in Chicago*: "An American Success Story," *Investors Business Daily* (July 21, 1998), A6.

110 *Still, studies show that immigrants*: David Card, "Immigrant Inflows, Native Outflows, and the Local Labor Market Impacts," *NBER Working Paper,* no. 5927 (February 1997); George Borjas, Richard Freeman, and Lawrence Katz, "On the Labor Market Impacts of Immigration and Trade," in Borjas, *Immigration and the Work Force* (Chicago: University of Chicago Press, 1992), 213–44; National Research Council, *The New Americans: Economic, Demographic and Fiscal Effects of Immigration* (Washington, D.C.: National Academy Press, 1997), 221-28.

110 *According to a CBS/New York Times poll*: Reported in Ben J. Wattenberg's uplifting book, *The First Universal Nation* (New York: The Free Press, 1991), 74.

111 *Moreover, the cost of educating*: National Academy of Sciences, *The New Americans: The New Americans,* 280.

111 *Since a bigger population raises*: See Michael Kremer's intriguing article, "Population Growth and Technological Change: One Million B.C. to 1900," *Quarterly Journal of Economics* (August 1993), 681–716.

113 *They fitted their boats*: For more such fascinating stories, see Thomas Sowell's *Conquests and Cultures* (New York: Basic Books, 1998).

116 *Hispanics spend over fifteen hours*: Marcia Mogelonsky, "Watching in Tongues," *American Demographics* (April 1998).

117 *Those rosy eye-glassed Americans*: Maria Zata, "The Big Picture," *Hispanic Business* (May 1998).

117 *When realtors noticed*: David Halberstam, *The Fifties* (New York: Villard Books, 1993), 134.

118 *Between 1995 and 2010*: Fannie Mae Foundation, "Immigration and Housing in the United States: Trends and Prospects" (Washington, D.C.: Fannie Mae, 1997).

118 *In addition, low long-term*: The National Association of Realtors publishes a "Housing Affordability Index" that indicates whether a median-income family can afford a median-priced home, using conventional financing and a 20 percent down payment. "Immigration and Housing in the United States."

119 *Minorities, especially blacks, often shun*: Reynolds Farley, "Racial Differences in the Search for Housing: Do Whites and Blacks Use the Same Technique to Find Housing?" *Housing Policy Debate* 7, 1 (1996), 367–85.

119 *"Instead of helping you . . ."*: William Branigin, "Immigrants Question Idea of Assimilation," *The Washington Post* (May 25, 1998), A13. For an outrageous, sometimes disgusting, but telling riff on black tensions, see comedian Chris Rock's *Rock This!* (New York: Hyperion, 1997). This book would be rated R or X, if it were a movie. For a calmer and more sober view of Chinese tensions, see Eric Liu's *The Accidental Asian* (New York: Random House, 1998).

120 *Already, the combined pocketbooks*: "Black Buying Power by Place of Residence 1990–1997" and "Hispanic Buying Power by Place of Residence," Selig Center, University of Georgia, 1997.

Chapter 5: Rising Sun, Rising Stocks: How Japan's New Buying Spree Will Deliver New Investment Opportunities

126 *By 1991 they began a*: "Prefectural Land Prices Survey" (Tokyo: National Land Agency, October 27, 1997).

126 *Tucked in his pocket*: Sandra Sugawara, "From Debt to Desperation in Japan," *Washington Post* (August 21, 1998), G3.

127 *But nature is for me*: Quoted by Kawabata Yasunari in his 1968 Nobel Prize Lecture, trans. Edward Seidensticker (Nobel Foundation, 1968).

129 *The size of the workforce*: Robert Alan Feldman, "Japan: Investor Focus Shifts to Structural Reform," Morgan Stanley (April 21, 1998).

130 *A government survey showed*: *Annual Report on the Labor Force Survey* (Tokyo: Statistics Bureau, Management and Coordination Agency, April 1997).

132 *Racketeering charges stuck*: Bill Spindle and Norihiko Shirouzu, "Mitsubishi Racketeering Probe Widens," *Wall Street Journal* (October 27, 1997), A19.

132 *In 1993, investigators found*: The term "shadow shogun" is the title of a scathing history of the era. Jacob M. Schlesinger, *Shadow Shoguns: The Rise and Fall of Japan's Postwar Political Machine* (New York: Simon & Schuster, 1997). Schlesinger depicts a drunken scene in 1991 when Kanemaru barks at Prime Minister Kiichi Miyazawa: "Miyazawa! You're next. Miyazawa! Sing!" And the Prime Minister dutifully follows orders.

132 *The hype hurts, however*: See Warwick J. McKibbin, "The Macroeconomic Experience of Japan Since 1990: An Empirical Investigation," *Brookings Discussion Papers in International Economics* (July 1998).

140 *The People's University*: Cited in Nicholas D. Kristof, "The Problem of Memory," *Foreign Affairs* 77 (November/December 1998), 43.

140 *Japan's economic debacle*: "Internationalization of the Yen," Council on Foreign Exchanges and Other Transactions, Ministry of Finance (November 12, 1998).

141 *Though Japanese leaders*: "Opinion Survey on Foreign Affairs," Prime Minister's Office (January 1998).

142 *Furthermore, "crude rubber, tin, and bauxite . . ."*: "Statement by Suzuki Teiichi, President of the Planning Board," in David John Lu, *Sources of Japanese History*, vol. II (New York: McGraw Hill, 1974), 149.

145 *She treats the governors*: Lady Murasaki Shikibu, *The Tale of the Genji*, trans. Edward Seidensticker (New York: Knopf, 1976).

145 *Japan added farm jobs*: "Annual Report on National Accounts," Economic Research Institute, Economic Planning Agency (May 30, 1997).

Chapter 6: Europe Über Alles: How European Unity Splinters

150 *In a confidential 1990 memorandum*: David Marsh, *The Most Powerful Bank: Inside Germany's Bundesbank* (New York: Times Books, 1992), 197.

150 *Margaret Thatcher's recalls*: Margaret Thatcher, *The Downing Street Years* (New York: HarperCollins, 1993), 759.

151 *To Kohl, EMU was a pre-emptive*: Marsh, 211.

151 *Newspapers of the left*: Marsh, 211. *Bild-Zeitung* (December 11, 1991).

152 *The German Finance Ministry*: "EMU Delay Appeal Rejected," *BBC News Online* (February 9, 1998).

152 *After World War I, Germany suffered*: Rudiger Dornbusch, "Lessons from the German Inflation Experience of the 1920s," in *Exchange Rates and Inflation* (Cambridge: MIT Press, 1988), 417.

152 *John Maynard Keynes blamed much of*: John Maynard Keynes, *The Collected Writings of John Maynard Keynes*, vol. II (London: Macmillan/Royal Economic Society, 1971), 94.

153 *"There can be no hard currency . . ."*: Marsh, 3.

157 *A handful of factors tend to determine*: See Robert A. Mundell, "A Theory of Optimum Currency Area," *American Economic Review* 50 (September 1961), 657–65; Ronald McKinnon, "Optimum Currency Areas," *American Economic Review* 53 (September 1963), 717–24.

157 *Margaret Thatcher facetiously points out*: Personal conversation with Thatcher, October 13, 1996.

158 *A remarkable one-third*: U.S. Bureau of the Census, *Statistical Abstract of the United States: 1996*, 116th ed. (Washington, D.C.: Government Printing Office), no. 33.

158 *In contrast, Europeans feel*: See Barry Eichengreen, "Is Europe an Optimum Currency Area?" *NBER Working Paper*, no. 3579 (Cambridge, Mass.: National Bureau of Economic Research, January 1991).

158 *Martin Feldstein calculates*: Martin Feldstein, "The Political Economy of the European Economic and Monetary Union: Political Sources of an Economic Liability," *Journal of Economic Perspectives* 11 (fall 1997), 36.

158 *South Carolina defaulted on $22 million*: David Hale, "Investment Implications of European Monetary Union," unpublished paper (April 1997), 3.

159 *The value of France's promises*: Sheetal K. Chand, et al., "Aging Populations and the Fiscal Consequences of Public Pension Schemes with Particular Reference to the Major Industrial Countries," *IMF Occasional Paper* (1996).

160 *Max Weber, the great student of bureaucracy*: Max Weber, *From Max Weber: Essays in Sociology*, trans. and eds. H. H. Gerth and C. Wright Mills (New York: Oxford University Press), 226.

161 *Germany cannot resist her allure*: Friedrich Nietzsche, *Beyond Good and Evil*, translation by Walter Kaufman (New York: Vintage, 1966), 130–31.

162 *And, given the generosity*: Paul Krugman, *The Accidental Theorist* (New York: W.W. Norton & Co., 1998), 38, 35.

164 *She went on to remind us that*: Personal conversation with Thatcher, October 13, 1996.

166 *If EMU proceeds smoothly*: See Richard Portes and Helene Rey, "The Emergence of the Euro as an International Currency," *NBER Working Paper*, no. 6424 (February 1, 1998).

166 *Germans, for example, have placed*: Patrick Artus, "Is the Euro Bound to Become an International Currency?" *CDC Marches Research Paper*, no. 97.08 (May 12, 1997), 13.

168 *Meanwhile, the Union Bank of Switzerland*: Quoted in "A Structured Debate," *Latin America Trade Finance* (a supplement of *Latin Finance* magazine) (September 1998), 18.

168 *Europe's pursuit of Latin America*: Jennifer Rich, "What Happens Next," *LatinFinance* (September 1998), 29–30; Ernest S. McCrary, "Low Blows," *Global Finance* (October 1998), 159.

169 *In contrast, Germany is diluting*: One mathematical simulation concluded that German rates may rise 0.3 percent, but Club Med rates would fall 2.8 percent. Fritz Breuss, "The Economic Consequences of a Large EMU—Results of Macroeconomic Model Simulations," *European Integration Online Papers* 1, 10 (May 1997), 8.

170 *From 1980 to 1997, Merrill Lynch's*: Martin Fridson and Christopher Garman, "Lessons from the U.S.," *The Euro* (September–October 1998), 39.

Chapter 7: Hold That Tiger: How to Play the China Card Past the Year 2000

176 *This viewpoint harkens*: See Todd G. Buchholz, "The Angry Oracle Called Karl Marx," in *New Ideas from Dead Economists* (New York: Penguin, 1999).

177 *A survey showed that*: Namju Cho, "Growing Number of Layoffs Is Spawning an Increase in Crime Rate and Suicides," *Wall Street Journal* (May 5, 1998), A19.

179 *As he put it, "I have two choices . . ."*: Daniel Yergin and Joseph Stanislaw, *The Commanding Heights* (New York: Simon & Schuster, 1998), 196.

179 *By 1995 Deng and his followers*: Alvin Rabushka, "The Great Tax Cut of China," *Wall Street Journal* (August 7, 1997).

180 *For example, the movie* The Jazz Singer: Perhaps the Jolson version best captures the paradox of technology, since it was among the first of the "talkies."

181 *During a heralded 1992 tour*: Daniel Burstein and Arne De Keijzer, *Big Dragon* (New York: Simon & Schuster, 1998), 49.

181 *Deng concluded that*: David S. G. Goodman, *Deng Xiaoping and the Chinese Revolution* (London: Routledge, 1994), 109–10.

181 *This is the kind of thinking*: Even in the United States we have struggled from time to time with this tension between political and economic freedom. Conservative commentator William F. Buckley, Jr., used to joke that liberal politicians would permit nude lap dancing, so long as the dancers got paid a minimum wage. Conservatives would presumably ban the dancing but would not care how much the dancers were being paid.

181 *After all, South Korea, and much of*: Henry S. Rowen, "The Short March: China's Road to Democracy," in *The National Interest* (Fall 1996), 61.

184 *"Westerner . . . you find it beautiful."*: David Henry Hwang, *M Butterfly* (1987).

185 *The government has backed computer game*: "China's Transformation: The Greatest Leap Yet," *Washington Post* (October 10, 1997), C4.

185 *Despite an American advertising slogan*: Matt Forney, "Patriot Games," *Far Eastern Economic Review* (October 3, 1996), 22–28.

187 *By snatching up those Mattel dolls*: Geoff Lewis and Marshall Keeling, "Indonesia's Barbie Dolarised Economy," *Monograph* (New York: Dresdner Kleinwort Benson, March 10, 1988), 2–4.

189 *In the 1992 presidential campaign*: A misnomer, most favored nation (MFN) status does not give a country extra trading privileges; it merely prevents the United States from levying extra fees, tariffs, and regulations. For example, in 1998, only Cuba, Iraq, and Iran were denied MFN.

193 *A 1997 CIA report revealed*: Harry S. Rowen, "The Short March: China's Road to Democracy," in *The National Interest* (fall 1996).

193 *A 1997 CIA report revealed*: James Kitfield, "China's Long March," *National Journal* (April 25, 1998), 926–28.

195 *According to press reports*: "Regional Briefing," *Far Eastern Economic Review* (April 9, 1998). Chinese spokesmen denied the story.

196 *In March 1998, Zhu announced*: "Zhu's Big Plans," *China Focus* (New York: Dresdner Kleinwort Benson, April 1998), 2–3.

196 *In fact, he even wanted local towns*: "USSR," *The Economist* (July 13, 1991), p. 110.

196 *By producing better products*: "Zhu's Big Plans," 3.

198 *Imagine, a system that piles*: Donaldson, Lufkin, and Jenrette, *Portfolio Manager's Weekly* (August 13, 1997), 59.

200 *Its sales will soon hit $1 billion*: "Business in Asia," *Economist* (March 9, 1996).

201 *They then pulled out a picture of Amway's*: John Pomfret, "China Bans Direct Marketing to Attack Scams," *Washington Post* (April 28, 1998), C12.

201 *L'Oreal has opened up a second plant*: *China Statistical Yearbook* (Westport, CT: Praeger, 1997).

203 *A recent book entitled* China Can Say No: Zhang Xiaobo and Song Qiang, "China Can Say No to America," *New Perspectives Quarterly* (fall 1996), 55–56.

204 *Only when the fog*: William H. Overholt, *The Rise of China* (New York: W.W. Norton, 1993), 26–27.

Chapter 8: Lock 'Em Up: The War on Crime Goes into Retreat

206 *In 1982, the political scientist*: James Q. Wilson and George Kelling, "Broken Windows: The Police and Neighborhood Safety," *Atlantic Monthly* (March 1982), 29–38.

208 *We will have 20 percent*: Dan Carney, "Experts and Lawmakers Disagree . . . On Stemming Juvenile Crime," *National Journal* (April 12, 1997), 846.

208 *Crime already costs the economy*: Ted R. Miller, Mark A. Cohen, and Brian Wiersema, "Victim Costs and Consequences" (Washington, D.C.: U.S. Department of Justice, 1996).

208 *We cannot rush right into stock*: Karl Menninger, *The Crime of Punishment* (New York: Viking, 1968). After reading Menninger's tract I felt as Freud did about Jung, "he's crazy." For a hard-nosed antidote to Menninger, see Ernest van den Haag's *Punishing Criminals* (New York: Free Press, 1975). Incidentally, van den Haag is a trained psycho-analyst.

210 *In contrast, the murder rate by teenagers*: Federal Bureau of Investigation, *Crime in the United States, 1997 Uniform Crime Reports* (Washington, D.C.: U.S. Department of Justice, 1998).

211 *While DNA researchers have not located*: Sarnoff A. Mednick, William F. Gabrielli, Jr., and Barry Hutchings, "Genetic Influences in Criminal Convictions: Evidence from an Adoption Cohort," *Science* 224 (1984), 891–94.

211 *While burglary and assault peak early*: Rowe and C. R. Tittle, "Life Cycle Changes and Criminal Propensity," *The Sociological Quarterly* 18 (1977), 228.

211 *Of course, many critics in the black community*: Richard B. Freeman, "Why Do So Many Young American Men Commit Crimes and What Might We Do About It?," *Journal of Economic Perspectives* 10 (winter 1996), 26.

212 *Martin Wolfgang's pathbreaking report*: Martin Wolfgang, "Crime in a Birth Cohort," *Proceedings of the American Philosophical Society* 117: 404–11; David Farrington, "Longitudinal Research on Crime and Delinquency," in N. Morris and M. Tonry, eds., *Crime and Justice*, vol. 1 (Chicago: University of Chicago Press, 1979).

212 *Now and then a "drunken buggy-driving incident . . ."*: David Remnick, "Bad Seeds," *The New Yorker* (July 30, 1998), 29–30.

212 *An absolute goody two-shoes*: Seymour Siegel, "A Jewish View of Economic Justice," *This World* (1982); H. Bialik and Y. Ravnitsky, *The Book of Legends*, (New York: Schocken, 1992), 542.

213 *In a provocatively titled article*: J. Hageborn, "Homeboys, Dope Fiends, Legits, and New Jacks," *Criminology* 32 (May 1994), 197–219.

213 *More important to society, though*: Anne Morrison Piehl and John J. DiIulio, "Does Prison Pay? Revisited," *Brookings Review* (winter 1995), 21–25.

213 *Six percent of the arrestees*: Marvin E. Wolfgang, et al., *Delinquency in a Birth Cohort* (Chicago: University of Chicago, 1987).

213 *In the Philadelphia study, for example*: Ibid.

213 *The rise of heinous and violent crime:* Cheryl Russell, "True Crime," *American Demographics* (April 1995).

214 *Of the twenty most violent cities*: Ibid.

215 *Following Darwin's evolutionary linkage*: James Q. Wilson and Richard J. Herrnstein, *Crime and Human Nature* (New York: Simon & Schuster, 1985), 71–74.

215 *In his book* Crime and the Man: Earnest A. Hooton, *Crime and the Man* (Cambridge: Harvard University Press, 1939), 3.

215 *In provocatively titled books like* Apes, Men and Morons: Earnest A. Hooton, *Why Men Behave Like Apes and Vice Versa* (Princeton: Princeton University Press, 1940), 230.

215 *Like Lombroso's work, Hooton's research*: See S. J. Pfohl, *Images of Deviance and Social Control: A Philosophical History*, 2nd ed. (New York: McGraw Hill, 1994), 104.

215 *Sure enough, criminals tended to*: William H. Sheldon, *The Varieties of Temperament* (New York: Harper, 1942).

216 *A German study later lent some support*: Wilson and Herrnstein, 80.

216 *As one prisoner put it, "You never think . . ."*: Quoted in John J. DiIulio, Jr., "Help Wanted: Economists, Crime and Public Policy," *Journal of Economic Perspectives* 10 (winter 1996), 17.

217 *tended to care less*: John J. Conger and Wilbur C. Miller, *Personality, Social Class, and Delinquency* (New York: John Wiley & Sons, 1966), 61–81.

217 *"Spare the rod, spoil the child" may*: See W. McCord and J. McCord, *Origins of Crime* (New York: Columbia University Press), 79–82.

219 *Cold, uncaring parents breeding*: See Michelle Lea Cherne Anderson, "The High Juvenile Crime Rate," *Criminal Law Bulletin* 30, 1 (1994), 54–75.

219 *Those without fathers grabbed*: Walter Mischel, Yuichi Shoda, and Monica L. Rodriquez, "Delay of Gratification in Children," *Science* 244 (1989), 933–38; Walter Mischel, "Father-Absence and Delay of Gratification," *Journal of Abnormal and Social Psychology*, 63 (1961), 116–24.

219 *A massive study of two thousand*: Jerald G. Bachman, S. Green, and I. D. Wirtanen, "Dropping Out—Problem or Symptom?" *Youth in Transition*, vol. 3 (Ann Arbor: University of Michigan Insitute for Social Research, 1971).

220 *In fact, police records do show*: David P. Phillips, "Suicide, Motor Vehicle Fatalities, and the Mass Media," *American Journal of Sociology* 84 (1979), 1150; Phillips, "The Impact

of Mass Media Violence on U.S. Homicides," *American Sociological Review* 48 (1983), 560–68.

220 *Sure enough, the subjects inflicted*: Richard H. Walters, Edward L. Thomas, and C. William Acker, "Enhancement of Punitive Behavior By Audio-Visual Displays," *Science* 136 (June 1962), 872–73; Stanley Milgram, *Obedience to Authority* (New York: HarperCollins, 1983).

222 *A comprehensive study covering 1933–1982*: Philip J. Cook and Gary A. Zarkin, "Crime and the Business Cycle," *Journal of Legal Studies* 14 (1985), 115–28.

222 *William Julius Wilson, in his* When Work Disappears: William Julius Wilson, *When Work Disappears: The World of the New Urban Poor* (New York: Knopf, 1996).

222 *A Rand study discovered that Washington, D.C.*: Freeman, p. 31. Nobel Laureate Gary Becker gets the credit for first developing a serious economic model about crime and economic choices in his "Crime and Punishment: An Economic Approach," *Journal of Political Economy* 76 (March/April 1968), 169–217.

223 *In an economic model I published*: Todd G. Buchholz, "Revolution, Reputation Effects, and Time Horizons," *Cato Journal* 8 (spring/summer 1988), 185–97.

224 *The so-called "six-sigma" quality goal*: "Six sigma" is a statistical term developed by Motorola and implemented by other companies to set goals for outstanding quality control. Under six sigma, manufacturing processes may have 3.4 defects per million. General Electric trains individuals in quality control and awards them "black belts."

225 *We seem to have evolved our national ethos*: For a discussion of deterrence versus retribution, see my "Punishing Humans," *Thought* 59 (September 1984).

226 *Unfortunately, non-coastal cities like Indianapolis*: Andrew Lang Golub and Bruce D. Johnson, "Crack's Decline: Some Surprises Across U.S. Cities," *Research in Brief* (National Institute of Justice, July 1997), 1, 3.

227 *Crime scholar John DiIulio has coined*: William J. Bennett, John J. DiIulio, and John P. Walters, *Body Count* (New York: Simon & Schuster, 1996).

228 *A gang in the Midwest actually opened*: Steven D. Levitt and Sudhir Alladi Venkatesh, "An Economic Analysis of a Drug-Selling Gang's Finances," *National Bureau of Economic Research Working Paper*, no. 6592 (June 1, 1998).

228 *"When we bust the door down . . ."*: David Cogan, "The Gang's All There," *Los Angeles* (August 1998), 30.

229 *As older "Mafia generations passed . . ."*: Ernest Volkman, *Gangbusters: The Destruction of American's Last Mafia Dynasty* (New York: Faber & Faber, 1998), 309.

229 *With billions of dollars at his disposal*: Carney, "The New Terrorism: Coming soon to a city near you," *Economist*, (August 15, 1998), 17–18.

230 *The largest estimate ($450 billion) comes*: Miler, Cohen, and Wiersema, "Victims Costs and Consequences."

Chapter 9: No Sweat: How to Survive and Thrive Amid Global Warming

239 *And unless we junk our gasoline-powered*: John T. Houghton et al., eds., *Climate Change 1995: The Science of Climate Change, Contribution of Working Group I to the Second Assessment Report of the Intergovernmental Panel on Climate Change* (New York: Cambridge University Press, 1996).

241 *And Copenhagen's Tivoli Gardens*: Robert T. Watson, Marufu C. Zinyowera, and Richard H. Moss, eds., *Climate Change 1995: The Impacts, Adaptation, and Mitigation of Climate Change—Scientific-Technical Analysis, Contribution of Working Group II to the Second Assessment Report of the Intergovernmental Panel of Climate Change* (New York: Cambridge University Press, 1996).

241 *But one study projects that global warming*: Willem J. M. Martens et al., "Potential Impact of Global Climate Change on Malaria Risk," *Environmental Health Perspective* (May 1995).

241 *A hundred years ago, a Swedish chemist*: Spencer R. Weart, "The Discovery of the Risk of Global Warming," *Physics Today* (January 1997), 34–40.

243 *Economists, in particular, have not*: Jan DeBlieu, *Wind: How the Flow of Air Has Shaped Life, Myth, and the Land* (Boston: Houghton Mifflin, 1998). Thomas Gale Moore's *Climate of Fear* (Washington: Cato Institute, 1998) looks at global climate change and economic history, taking an upbeat view of warming. Thomas Schelling provided an early model for professional economists in his article "Some Economics of Global Warming," *American Economic Review* (March 1992), 1–14. William Cline also developed a model in 1992 for the Institute for International Economics, in a book *The Economics of Global Warming* (Washington, D.C.: Institute for International Economics, 1992).

244 *In sum, our ancestors flourished*: Moore states that Archaeological evidence, including inscriptions on "oracle bones" indicate that Chinese mid-winter temperatures were as much as 9 degrees hotter prior to 3,000 B.C., allowing rice to be planted a month earlier than today. H. H. Lamb, *Climate: Present, Past and Future*, vol. 2 (London: Methuen, 1977), 251.

245 *By the beginning of the Ming dynasty*: Charles Hucker, *China's Imperial Past* (Stanford: Stanford University Press, 1975), 330. Also see Kang Chao, *Man and Land in Chinese History: An Economic Analysis* (Stanford: Stanford University Press, 1986).

245 *From 1693 until 1700 almost every Scottish*: H. H. Lamb, 471.

245 *"Here's another potato"*: Frank Gotham, *The New Yorker* (July 13, 1998), 46.

245 *Though he says, "I tax not you . . ."*: William Shakespeare, *King Lear*, III, ii.

245 *No surprise that the Little Ice Age*: Gregg Easterbrook, *A Moment on the Earth* (New York: Penguin Books, 1995), 279.

245 *According to one historian, The bitter*: H. H. Lamb, 275. Lamb also argues that paintings of the era depicted more cloud cover than those that preceded or followed.

246 *Colonists could not shoulder*: David Smith and William Baron, "Growing Season Parameter Reconstruction for New England Using Frost Records 1697 to 1947," cited in Linden, 23.

247 *In a new book*: Myron Arms, *Riddle of the Ice* (New York: Anchor, 1998).

247 *Researchers at the U.S. National Oceanic*: R. S. Bradley, F. T. Keimig, and H. F. Diaz, "Recent Changes in the North American Arctic Boundary Layer in Winter," *Journal of Geophysical Research* 98 (1993), 8851–58.00 *At the other end of the earth*: See, for example, D. G. Vaughan and C. S. M. Doake, "Recent Atmospheric Warming and Retreat of Ice Shelves On the Antarctic Peninsula," *Nature* (January 25, 1996).

248 *The United Kingdom's station at Faraday*: Eugene Linden, *The Future in Plain Sight* (New York: Simon & Schuster, 1998), 86.

248 *That was the last time the Alps*: David Roberts, "The Iceman: Lone Voyager from the Copper Age," *National Geographic* (June 1993).

248 *If the earth really does warm by another 4.5°*: Keith R. Briffa, et al., "Unusual Twentieth-Century Summer Warmth in a 1,000-Year Temperature Record from Siberia," *Nature* (July 13, 1995), 156–59

248 *Eugene Linden states that*: Linden, 89.

249 *Nonetheless, Emanuel acknowledges*: Kerry Emanuel, "The Dependence of Hurricane Intensity on Climate," *Nature* (April 1987), 483–85 and private correspondence, July 8, 1998.

250 *Every noon and midnight, weather experts*: S. George Philander, *Is the Temperature Rising? The Uncertain Science of Global Warming* (Princeton: Princeton University Press, 1998), 119.

251 *Their conclusion: the western Arctic*: J. D. Kahl, D. J. Charlevoix, N. A. Zaitseva, R. C. Schnell, and M. C. Serreze, "Absence of Evidence for Greenhouse Warming Over the Arctic Ocean in the Past Forty Years," *Nature* 361 (1993), 335–37. Researchers at the Scripps Institution of Oceanography in California found large sea-surface temperature changes that suddenly appeared and disappeared along the entire West Coast over the past 80 years. Since 1977, though, they have found more and more "warm" events. John A. McGowan, Daniel R. Cayan, and Leroy M. Dorman, "Climate-Ocean Variability and Ecosystem Response in the Northeast Pacific," *Science* 281, 5374 (July 10, 1998),

251 *The Bering Glacier in Alaska*: Easterbrook, 293.

252 *"I don't know what line from God he has,"*: William K. Stevens, "Skeptic Asks, Is It Really Warmer?" *The New York Times* (June 17, 1996). The IPCC has conceded that "The

single largest uncertainty in determining the climate sensitivity to either natural or anthropogenic changes are clouds . . . weaknesses in the parameterization of cloud formation and dissipation are probably the main impediment to improvements in the simulation of cloud effects on climate. R. S. Stone found that clouds confound the models, while discovering warmer winters and springs, but cooler autumns along the Siberian-Alaskan coastline. R. S. Stone, "Variations in Western Arctic Temperatures in Response to Cloud Radiative and Synoptic-Scale Influences," *Journal of Geophysical Research* 102 (1997), 21, 769–21, 776.

252 *Macbeth says*: William Shakespeare, *Macbeth*, V, v.

252 *In the past decades*: For a layman's explanation of Baliunas's research, see Matt O'Keefe, "Solar Waxing," *Harvard Magazine* (May/June 1998). Economists tend to be wary of sunspot cycles, ever since William Stanley Jevons misused them in the nineteenth century to explain agricultural cycles.

254 *A study in* Nature *concluded*: C. D. Keeling, J. F. S. Chin, and T. P. Whorf, "Increased Activity of Northern Vegetation Inferred From Atmospheric CO_2 Measurements," *Nature* 382 (1996), 146–49.

254 *"I have a hard time following . . ."*: Easterbrook, 301.

256 *Emissaries from Asia and Africa*: Christoper Flavin and Odil Tunali, *Climate of Hope*, (Washington D.C.: Worldwatch Institute, 1996), 32.

256 *The United States has already established*: Richard Schmalensee, et al., "An Interim Evaluation of Sulfur Dioxide Emissions Trading," *Journal of Economic Perspectives* (1998).

256 *According to Yale professor William Nordhaus*: Peter Passell, "How Fast to Cut Back? Two Views?," the *New York Times* (November 28, 1997). A number of conservative economists, including Robert Hahn of the American Enterprise Institute and Martin Feldstein of Harvard, have suggested that they might approve carbon taxes—if other taxes were cut to offset the revenues. In the Bush White House, I and other economists suggested higher gasoline taxes in exchange for lower personal income taxes. As I recall, it was Dick Schmalensee, an MIT professor serving as a member of the Council of Economic Advisers, who said it wouldn't work because it was "good policy, and therefore, bad politics."

257 *The price of solar power has been falling*: Ujjayant Chakravorty, James Roumasset, and Kinping Tse, "Endogenous Substitution among Energy Resources and Global Warming," *Journal of Political Economy* 105, 6 (December 1997), 1201.

257 *In Chile, twice as many cars*: "Hot Wheels," *Washington Post* (July 11, 1998), A16; Anthony Faiola, "Santiago Children Gasp for Cleaner Air," *Washington Post* (July 12, 1998), A19.

258 *In Indonesia, large parts*: Asian Development Bank, *Climate Change in Asia: The Thematic Overview* (Manila, 1994).

259 *Between 1990 and 1995 insurance companies*: Flavin and Tunali, 6.

260 *A study by Travelers forecast*: Cited in Linden, 91.

261 *Someone once identified insanity*: Of course, by this definition quantum theory (whereby atoms may act in varied ways) is insane.

262 *Finally, with even higher temperatures*: Robert Mendelsohn, William D. Nordhaus, and Daigee Shaw, "The Impact of Global Warming on Agriculture: A Ricardian Analysis," *American Economic Review* 83, 4 (September 1994), 753–55. For more on David Ricardo, see my *New Ideas from Dead Economists* (New York: Penguin, 1999) 68–90.

263 *Merrill Lynch is also jumping*: See Sharon Walsh, "A Hot (and Cold) New Investment Opportunity," *Washington Post* (July 4, 1998), C12.

264 *In a book entitled* The Baked Apple?: Douglas Hill, ed., *The Baked Apple?: Metropolitan New York in the Greenhouse* (New York: Annals of the New York Academy of Sciences, 1996).

Conclusion: Into the Breach

263 *Bertrand Russell pointed out*: Bertrand Russell, *Mysticism and Logic* [1917], in *The Collected Papers of Bertrand Russell*, vol. 8, ed John G. Slater, (London: George Allen and Unwin, 1986), 43.

Index